The Sheraton World Cookbook

The Sheraton World Cookbook

Coordinated and edited by Vera Krijn

Food Consultant, Judith L. Strada

The Bobbs-Merrill Company, Inc.
Indianapolis/New York

Published by The Bobbs-Merrill Company, Inc.
Indianapolis, New York
ISBN: 0-672-52761-8, *Pbk.*, 0-672-52672-7
Library of Congress Catalog Card Number: 80-2736

Designed by: *J. Tschantre Graphic Services, Ltd.*
Illustrations by: *Stan Skardinski/Evelyne Johnson Associates*
Manufactured in the United States of America
Seventh Printing, Second Printing Pbk.

The Sheraton World Cookbook

Sheraton Chefs
from around the globe

request

the pleasure of your company

on a

Gourmet Tour of
the World

Time: at your convenience
Place: your home

Bon Voyage et Bon Appetit

Contents

Introduction

If you love to cook, you undoubtedly love the adventure of trying exciting new recipes. This collection of recipes from around the globe is full of adventure. Whether you are new to cooking and are looking for unusual ways to create dining experiences, or a sophisticated cook and world traveler eager to re-create the flavor of your latest journey, you will discover what you are looking for in *The Sheraton World Cookbook.*

The finest chefs from Sheraton hotels throughout the world offer creative interpretations of authentic local dishes from their regions. The diversity of cooking represented is spectacular. It ranges from the familiar to the exotic, from classic French favorites to fare that would be served at a Bedouin feast in the deserts of the Middle East.

The creators of these recipes have been widely acclaimed. Every four years the International Culinary Olympics, a competition among the great chefs of the world, takes place in Frankfurt, Germany. In 1980, forty-three Sheraton chefs captured one Grand Prix, and forty-four other gold, silver, and bronze medals for presenting their original recipes.

Sheraton's commitment to the culinary arts also was made evident with the introduction of its own European "Chef of the Year" contest. At this event, their chefs were invited to enter their best *nouvelle-cuisine* creations. The contest was judged by an international jury made up of the world's leading culinary experts, including Paul Bocuse, who has been decorated and honored by French President Giscard d'Estaing; Jean Troisgros, a leading French culinary chef and owner of a three-star French restaurant; and Alain Chapel, brilliant chef and chief ambassador of the *nouvelle-cuisine.* Bocuse pronounced the contest a "grand événement gastronomique." Bocuse's words aptly describe this volume as well.

To taste Sashimi Raratonga, Poularde à la Pattaya, Banana Bread, and Carrot Halwa is to visit Korea, Thailand, Singapore, and India. The Middle East offers such delights as Dolmas from Turkey, Couscous from Abu Dhabi, and even an exotic Rice Pudding, a favorite throughout the region. Europe and Scan-

dinavia are represented by elegant dishes like Soupe aux Escargots, Poached Salmon with Mousseline Sauce, and English Sherry Trifle. From Latin America, the selection of recipes includes Ceviche from Peru, Black Bean Soup from Brazil, Quesadillos from Mexico, and Coconut Tarts from Bolivia. North America comes forth with a bountiful sampling of American and Canadian regional cooking with recipes such as Baked Stuffed Salmon, Honey Pecan Fried Chicken, and Black Bottom Pie.

It is a special privilege to be able to share with you such a wealth of recipes created by some of the world's master chefs—dishes that will enchant your family and guests alike. More than four thousand recipes were submitted for inclusion in this book, out of which our culinary experts selected the outstanding recipes offered here. Each recipe has been kitchen-tested and expertly adapted to the appropriate measurements and quantities for you to prepare in your own kitchen.

The book is divided into world regions: North America (including Hawaii), Latin America, Europe, the Middle East, and the Far East (including India), presenting the cuisines of those areas. In addition to the local dishes, hotels in those regions also offer tastes of other world cuisines; thus, you may occasionally find recipes grouped under a region that did not initially develop them.

When you are cooking for company, you will find *The Sheraton World Cookbook* the perfect resource. Each chapter contains imaginative menu suggestions to guide you to the pleasure of serving meals in which every dish perfectly complements every other. A chapter of imaginative sandwiches features ideas from different countries. A party chapter presents entertainment themes with an international flavor—a New England clambake, a Hawaiian luau, a Mexican fiesta, an English tea party, and a New York City brunch. There is also a chapter on beverages with instructions for making a tantalizing array of drinks.

This book captures the fabulous experiences of eating abroad as you cook some of the exclusive and favorite creations of Sheraton chefs and share them with your family and friends. You will enjoy discovering the world of international cuisine through this culinary journey.

The Cuisine of North America

and Hawaii

North America

Appetizers

Shrimp à la Peter Kaiser
  Hotel Triumph-Sheraton
  Toronto, Canada
Jalapeño and Shrimp Hush Puppies
  Sheraton-Dallas Hotel
  Dallas, Texas
Riverhouse Crab Cakes
  Sheraton Salisbury Inn
  Salisbury, Maryland
Calista King Crab Crêpes
  Sheraton-Anchorage Hotel
  Anchorage, Alaska
Pâté de Volaille Suprême
  Sheraton-Plaza
  Chicago, Illinois
Escargots en Croûte
  Sheraton-Columbus Hotel
  Columbus, Ohio
Capitol Cheese Truffles
  Sheraton-Washington Hotel
  Washington, D.C.
Avocado Tempura
  The Sheraton Centre
  New York, New York
Rissoles Bienville
  Sheraton-Charleston Hotel
  Charleston, South Carolina

Salads

Johann Strauss Salad
  Sheraton-Boston Hotel
  Boston, Massachusetts

Oriental Chicken Salad
  Sheraton-Town House
  Los Angeles, California
Fennel with Special Dressing
  Sheraton-Carlton Hotel
  Washington, D.C.
Fresh Broccoli Salad Royale
  Sheraton at St. Johns Place
  Jacksonville, Florida
Summer Salad
  Sheraton-Century Center Hotel
  Oklahoma City, Oklahoma
Palace Court Salad
  Sheraton-Palace Hotel
  San Francisco, California

Soups

Avgolemono Soup
  Sheraton Twin Towers Hotel
  Orlando, Florida
New England Clam Chowder
  Sheraton-Boston Hotel
  Boston, Massachusetts
Seafood Gumbo
  Sheraton-New Orleans Hotel
  New Orleans, Louisiana
Shrimp Soup
  Sheraton Inn-Portland Airport
  Portland, Oregon
Cream of Leek Soup
  Sheraton Palm Coast Resort Inn
  Palm Coast, Florida

Continued

Iced Cucumber and Beet Soup
Sheraton-Hopkins Airport Hotel
Cleveland, Ohio
Watercress Soup
Sheraton-Carlton Hotel
Washington, D.C.
Cold Peach Soup
Huntington-Sheraton Hotel
Pasadena, California

Entrees

Slow-Roasted Prime Ribs of Beef
Sheraton-Denver Airport
Denver, Colorado
Corned Beef Dinner
Sheraton Steamboat Resort
Steamboat Springs, Colorado
Buffalo Barbecue
Sheraton-Century Center Hotel
Oklahoma City, Oklahoma
Hickory-Smoked Brisket
Sheraton-Washington Hotel
Washington, D.C.
Barbecued Beef Texas Style
Sheraton-Houston Hotel
Houston, Texas
Steak Tartare
Sheraton-Villa Inn
Burnaby, British Columbia
Lamb Noisettes en Papillote
St. Regis-Sheraton Hotel
New York, New York

Festive Lamb Kebabs
Sheraton-Hopkins Airport Hotel
Cleveland, Ohio
Southern Baked Ham
Sheraton-Atlanta Hotel
Atlanta, Georgia
Apple Stuffed Pork Chops
Sheraton-Little Rock
Little Rock, Arkansas
Fillet of Pork with Pears
Sheraton-Plaza 500
Vancouver, British Columbia
Paupiettes de Veau Calvados
Sheraton West Hotel
Indianapolis, Indiana
Roast Veal Normande
The Sheraton Centre
New York, New York
Chicken Suprême and Potato Dumplings
Billings Sheraton Hotel
Billings, Montana
Plantation Chicken and Corncakes
Sheraton Convention Center Hotel
Memphis, Tennessee
Honey Pecan Fried Chicken
Sheraton Inn-Shreveporter
Shreveport, Louisiana
Stuffed Halibut Steak
Sheraton-Universal Hotel
Los Angeles, California
Rainbow Trout with Shrimp Stuffing
Sheraton-Yankee Clipper Hotels
Fort Lauderdale, Florida
Scrod with Dill Sauce
Sheraton-Boston Hotel
Boston, Massachusetts

Missouri Catfish on the Riverfront
Sheraton-St. Louis Hotel
St. Louis, Missouri
Finnan Haddie St. Regis
St. Regis-Sheraton Hotel
New York, New York
Fillet of Red Snapper Nectarine
Sheraton Plaza La Reina Hotel
Los Angeles, California
Baked Stuffed Salmon
Sheraton-Landmark Hotel
Vancouver, Canada
Homard du Ciel
Sheraton-Boston Hotel
Boston, Massachusetts
Shrimp Omelet with Hot Gingered Fruits
Sheraton West Hotel
Indianapolis, Indiana

Side Dishes

Sweet Potatoes in Orange Baskets
Sheraton-Dallas Hotel
Dallas, Texas
Jacques Carrot Soufflé
Sheraton Baton Rouge Hotel
Baton Rouge, Louisiana
Sweet Corn Fritters
Sheraton-Renton Inn
Seattle, Washington
Bavarian Village Bread
The Sheraton Centre
Toronto, Canada

Desserts

Melon Balls Comtesse Sarah
Hotel Triumph-Sheraton
Toronto, Canada
White Chocolate Mousse
Sheraton-Washington Hotel
Washington, D.C.
Black Bottom Pie
Sheraton-Dallas Hotel
Dallas, Texas
Key Lime Pie
Sheraton Royal Biscayne Hotel
Key Biscayne, Florida
Caroline's Delight
Sheraton-Center Inn
Charlotte, North Carolina
Rum Pecan Pie
Huntington-Sheraton Hotel
Pasadena, California
Shoofly Pie
Sheraton Lancaster Resort
Lancaster, Pennsylvania
New York Cheesecake
New York Sheraton Hotel
New York, New York
Strawberry Short Cake
Sheraton Harbor Island Hotel
San Diego, California
Bread Pudding with Rum Sauce
Sheraton-New Orleans Hotel
New Orleans, Louisiana

The Cuisine of North America

No other region of the world offers such a varied range of cuisine as does the North American continent.

It was inevitable: import the culinary talents of people from more than a hundred lands to a continent with an abundance of the creatures and crops of forests, plains, mountains, and streams "from sea to shining sea"; then add the demands of a growing nation. The result: a veritable atlas of dining. Thus, it should be no surprise to find recipes ranging from Pâté de Volaille Suprême to New York Cheesecake offered by our North American chefs.

The array of foods indigenous to the continent is truly bountiful. The coastal waters provide lobster, clams, oysters, cod, haddock, and halibut; the vast plains supply corn (and corn-fed cattle), wheat, soybeans, oats, and barley. We find wild turkey, pheasant, deer, partridge, apples, tomatoes, oranges, and berries— and that is only the beginning. Nowadays, many imported foods are available.

Distinct regional cuisines have developed, and you will find them represented here. Specialties of the South include Bread Pudding with Rum Sauce and Southern Baked Ham; among the western dishes are Apple Stuffed Pork Chops and Barbecued Beef Texas Style. There is New England Clam Chowder from Boston, Key Lime Pie from Florida, Vancouver's Baked Stuffed Salmon, and Palace Court Salad from San Francisco, along with many wonderful versions of foreign dishes.

It is an exciting cuisine, and whether you are an experienced cook or a novice, these recipes provide a wealth of opportunity for innovation.

Appetizers

Shrimp à la Peter Kaiser

Serves 6

Hotel Triumph-Sheraton
Toronto, Canada

Chantarelles, mushrooms that grow in the forests of France during the summer and fall, are highly prized for their pale yellow ruffled caps, which resemble upside-down petticoats. Their distinctive flavor blends with many other rich flavors in this elegant appetizer to make Shrimp à la Kaiser unforgettable!

    Chantarelles are available, preserved, in gourmet sections of grocery stores or in gourmet shops.

2 tablespoons butter
½ cup finely chopped onion
Small pinch each of fresh or dried sage, thyme, dill, and oregano
Pinch of freshly ground black pepper
¼ teaspoon crushed bay leaves
¼ teaspoon salt
¼ cup dry white wine
1 small tomato, squeezed to release juices and seeds, finely chopped
6 large domestic mushrooms (about 2 ounces total), gently boiled 5 minutes to soften, finely chopped

2 ounces finely chopped chantarelle mushrooms
Café de Paris Butter (recipe follows)
12 raw jumbo shrimp (1½ to 2 ounces each), shelled but with tails left on, if desired, deveined, butterflied (cut almost in half) lengthwise, then opened and flattened out
¼ cup fine dry white bread crumbs
3 tablespoons melted butter
Paprika to taste

Melt butter over medium-high heat in a heavy saucepan. Add the chopped onion and all herbs and spices. Sauté 2 to 3 minutes. Swirl in the white wine, add chopped tomato and domestic and chantarelle mushrooms. Boil gently 5 minutes or so, stirring frequently, until most of the pan juices have evaporated. Remove from heat and let cool.

    When room temperature, stir the mushroom mixture into the prepared Café de Paris Butter. Place butterflied shrimp on a lightly buttered baking sheet and top with generous tablespoons of stuffing. Crown with approximately 1 teaspoon bread crumbs on each shrimp, drizzle over the melted butter, and color with a small amount of paprika. (Shrimp may be refrigerated several hours at this point.)

    Bake shrimp on the top rack of a preheated 300-degree oven 15 to 20 minutes, until the shrimp is just cooked through. Serve, 2 shrimp per person, while hot.

Café de Paris Butter:

¼ pound softened butter
1 egg yolk, lightly beaten
1 small anchovy fillet
1 small clove garlic, mashed
1½ teaspoons fresh lemon juice
½ teaspoon chopped fresh parsley

½ teaspoon dry mustard
¼ teaspoon freshly ground black pepper
⅛ teaspoon fresh or dried tarragon leaves
⅛ teaspoon Worcestershire sauce
Pinch of fresh or dried marjoram

Combine all ingredients in a blender or bowl. Blend or beat with an electric mixer 2 or 3 minutes, until the mixture is soft, light, and well combined. Refrigerate Café de Paris Butter, covered, until ready to use.

Jalapeño and Shrimp Hush Puppies

Makes about 30 hush puppies

Sheraton-Dallas Hotel
Dallas, Texas

¼ cup minced onion
¼ pound raw shrimp, shelled and
  deveined, minced
1 whole jalapeño pepper (canned or
  fresh), seeded and minced
1 teaspoon chopped fresh parsley
2 teaspoons vegetable oil
2 cups white cornmeal

1 tablespoon all-purpose flour
1 teaspoon baking powder
1 teaspoon salt
1½ cups water
1 egg, lightly beaten
1 tablespoon melted bacon drip-
  pings
Sufficient oil for deep frying

Sauté onion, shrimp, jalapeño pepper, and parsley in 2 teaspoons oil for 1 or 2 minutes. Set aside.

Mix together the cornmeal, flour, baking powder, and salt. Bring 1½ cups water to a rolling boil. Take pan off the heat. Pour in the cornmeal mixture and beat together well. Cool 2 or 3 minutes, then add sautéed ingredients, egg, and bacon grease, beating well after each addition. The completed dough should be fairly dry but cohesive. Cool.

Fill a pan with 3 or 4 inches of oil. Bring up to 375 degrees on a deep-fry thermometer. Drop full teaspoons of dough into the hot oil and fry about 1 minute, until golden brown and cooked through. Drain and serve hot.

Riverhouse Crab Cakes

Serves 8

Sheraton Salisbury Inn
Salisbury, Maryland

Riverhouse Crab Cakes can be served on toast points as substantial appetizers, or more informally on small poppy-seed buns as an entrée. In either case, offer lemon wedges on the side, or your choice of sauces—perhaps mustard or tartare.

1 pound shredded crabmeat
2 cups fine dry white bread crumbs
¼ cup mayonnaise
3 eggs, lightly beaten
1 teaspoon dry mustard

½ teaspoon Worcestershire sauce
½ teaspoon salt
½ teaspoon pepper
Sufficient oil for deep frying
Garnish: Lemon wedges

Place all ingredients except 1 cup bread crumbs and the oil in a bowl and mix thoroughly. Form into 8 balls. Roll and coat well with reserved bread crumbs, patting down slightly into flat, plump cakes.

Pour several inches of oil into a heavy pan and bring up to 325 degrees on a deep-fry thermometer. Fry a few crab cakes at a time, turning once, until golden brown on both sides and hot throughout, approximately 4 or 5 minutes. Drain cakes briefly on paper towels and keep them warm while frying remaining crab cakes. Serve immediately.

Calista King Crab Crêpes

Makes 40 portions

Sheraton-Anchorage Hotel
Anchorage, Alaska

This dish is most impressive when made with six-inch-long pieces of crabmeat. To get crabmeat of this size, purchase whole Alaskan king crab legs and shell them to obtain the necessary lengths. If this is not possible, the recipe will still succeed nicely using lumps of crabmeat.

Crêpes:

1 cup milk
1 egg plus 1 egg yolk, lightly beaten
1 cup all-purpose flour
¼ teaspoon salt

Pinch of nutmeg
1 tablespoon finely chopped fresh
 chives
Butter

Continued

Whisk or stir milk and eggs into flour until smooth. Season with salt, nutmeg, and chives. Refrigerate batter several hours or overnight.

When batter has rested, place a 6-inch crêpe pan or skillet over medium-high heat. Grease pan with a small amount of butter. When hot pour in 1/10 of the crêpe batter, tipping the hot skillet to spread batter out thinly and evenly. Let crêpe cook 15 to 30 seconds, until the top dries out and the bottom browns lightly. Flip over and brown the other side lightly. Turn crêpe out to cool. Proceed in the same fashion, making 9 more crêpes.

Filling:

1/4 pound mushrooms, cleaned and
　coarsely chopped
1/4 cup finely chopped onion
1 tablespoon butter
1/2 teaspoon salt
Pinch of white pepper
1 tablespoon minced fresh parsley
1 cup Béchamel Sauce (recipe, page
　275)

1 pound whole or lump Alaskan king
　crab leg meat
1/2 cup all-purpose flour
2 eggs, lightly beaten
3/4 cup fine dry white bread crumbs
Sufficient oil for deep frying

In a large heavy saucepan over medium-high heat, briefly sauté mushrooms and onions in butter. Lower heat; add salt, pepper, parsley, and béchamel sauce. Simmer 5 minutes, until very thick. Spread 2 to 3 tablespoons filling on each crêpe. Place crabmeat off center on each crêpe and roll tightly. Refrigerate at least 2 hours, or overnight.

When ready to fry, cut crêpes into 4 equal pieces. Roll each piece in flour, then eggs, then bread crumbs, and secure with a toothpick. Deep-fry the crêpes at 375 degrees on a deep-fry thermometer, until well browned, approximately 25 seconds. Serve piping hot with the following Mustard-Dill Sauce.

Mustard-Dill Sauce:

1/2 cup prepared mustard
2 egg yolks
1/4 teaspoon salt
Pinch of white pepper
3 tablespoons sugar

3 tablespoons chopped fresh dill or 1/2
　tablespoon dried dill
2 tablespoons white wine vinegar
6 tablespoons olive oil

Whisk together mustard, egg yolks, salt, pepper, sugar, and dill until bubbles form. Gradually add the vinegar, then drizzle in the oil and continue whisking until thickened. Chill until ready to serve.

Pâté de Volaille Suprême

Makes 1 large pâté

Sheraton-Plaza
Chicago, Illinois

The use of a meat grinder or a food processor is prerequisite to making this smooth, elegant chicken pâté. Depending on the processor used, the chicken may have to be puréed in two or more batches. The pâté may be served thickly sliced for luncheons or late-night suppers (for twelve), or thinly sliced as an appetizer (serving fifteen or more). The recipe can easily be cut in half to serve fewer, but the result will be much less impressive.

½ pound chicken livers
½ teaspoon salt
5 pounds chicken breasts, skinned
  and boned
5 eggs
2½ teaspoons salt
½ teaspoon white pepper

½ teaspoon freshly grated nutmeg
¼ cup brandy
¼ cup dry sherry
¾ cup chopped walnuts
1 pound (about 16 strips) bacon
Garnishes: Radish roses, watercress,
  cornichons

Preheat oven to 375 degrees. Place chicken livers in a pan and cover with water seasoned with ½ teaspoon salt. Bring to a boil, then gently simmer 5 minutes. Drain, cool the livers, and set aside briefly.

Grind or process the skinned and boned chicken breasts until they are very fine or almost pastelike. Add the poached chicken livers and process or grind them into the breasts until they are fully incorporated and invisible.

If you are using a food processor, continue to do so, or do as you would when using a grinder and transfer puréed chicken to a large bowl. Beat in the eggs one at a time, using an electric mixer, and beating 1 to 1½ minutes between each egg addition. Add salt, pepper, and nutmeg. Beat 3 minutes longer, adding brandy and sherry toward the end of this time.

Select a terrine or bread pan with at least a 2-quart capacity and line it with about 10 strips of bacon. Pour in half of the chicken pâté mixture. Sprinkle chopped walnuts on mixture. Add the balance of the chicken mixture, mounding slightly in the center. Cover the top well with remaining bacon strips.

Set terrine in a large shallow baking pan and place in the preheated oven. Fill baking pan with several inches of hot water. Bake 1 hour or a little longer, until pâté is cooked through.

Remove terrine from the oven and cool down to room temperature. Cover and refrigerate, 6 to 8 hours or overnight, until well chilled.

To present, pâté may be unmolded and served with congealed fat surrounding it, or with fat scraped off, if desired. Garnish with watercress, radish roses, and cornichons.

Escargots en Croûte

Serves 6

Sheraton-Columbus Hotel
Columbus, Ohio

2 dozen snails
¼ cup brandy
Pinch of marjoram
Pinch of thyme
⅛ teaspoon tarragon
2 teaspoons minced garlic
½ teaspoon salt

⅛ teaspoon freshly ground black
   pepper
¾ pound puff pastry (your own
   recipe or frozen puff pastry shells)
⅓ pound goose liver pâté
2 tablespoons minced fresh parsley
Garnish: *Lemon wedges*

Place snails in a strainer and rinse. Drain well. Place in a small bowl and combine with the brandy, marjoram, thyme, tarragon, garlic, salt, and pepper. Cover and refrigerate 1 or 2 days, turning occasionally during this period.

Two or three hours before serving, begin assembling hors d'oeuvres. Roll out cold puff pastry dough until very thin (approximately ¹⁄₁₆ inch thick). When rolled out, place dough on a cookie sheet and refrigerate 1 or 2 hours, allowing pastry dough time to relax and chill. When chilled, take dough out of the refrigerator. Cut into 24 circles, each 2½ to 3 inches in diameter.

Preheat the oven to 425 degrees. Place 1 teaspoon goose liver pâté on each of the circles. Top with a drained, marinated snail. Sprinkle on a little parsley. Pull sides of the dough up and over to completely enclose the snail. Press edges together to seal shut.

Place Escargots en Croûte on a baking sheet, seam side down, and bake in preheated oven until crisp and brown, approximately 12 to 15 minutes. Serve hot, accompanied with lemon wedges.

Capitol Cheese Truffles

Makes about 30 truffles

Sheraton-Washington Hotel
Washington, D.C.

¼ pound unsalted butter, softened
¼ pound Gouda or Cheddar cheese,
   grated
2 tablespoons Port wine
¼ teaspoon seasoned salt

⅛ teaspoon white pepper
1½ cups fine dry pumpernickel bread
   crumbs
Sliced fresh fruit (such as apples or
   pears)

Cream the butter well in a food processor or blender. Add the grated cheese and purée. Pour in the Port, season with salt and pepper, and blend until well combined. Refrigerate the mixture until it is firm enough to handle.

Shape the cheese into small balls and roll in bread crumbs until thoroughly coated. Chill well before serving cheese truffles with sliced fresh fruit.

Avocado Tempura

Makes 60 hors d'oeuvres

The Sheraton Centre
New York, New York

The next time you want a deliciously different hot hors d'oeuvre, be sure to make Avocado Tempura. The crisp dark brown exterior breaks away to reveal a smooth green avocado center flecked with crunchy golden cashews. Out of politeness, most people will try to stop after they have eaten two or three, but you'd better plan on more per person.

3 green onions	*½ pound (about 2 cups) salted*
3 large ripe avocados	*cashews, chopped*
¼ cup fresh lemon juice	*⅓ pound Monterey Jack cheese,*
3 or more dashes Tabasco sauce, to	*shredded*
taste	*½ cup all-purpose flour*
1 teaspoon salt	*1½ cups fine dry white bread crumbs*
¾ teaspoon ground coriander	*Sufficient peanut oil for deep frying*

Mince both green and white portions of green onions and drop into a glass, ceramic, or stainless-steel bowl. Peel and seed avocados and add to green onions. Immediately add the lemon juice, Tabasco, salt, and coriander. Mash with a fork until mixture is well combined. Stir in the chopped nuts and shredded cheese.

Roll small balls (about 1 tablespoon each) of avocado mixture lightly in flour, then coat well with bread crumbs.

Pour several inches of oil into a heavy pan and bring to a temperature of 350 degrees on a deep-fry thermometer. Fry the avocado balls until crisp and deep golden brown, about 2 minutes. Drain and serve while still hot.

Rissoles Bienville
(Meat Pastries)

Makes about 2½ dozen pastries

Sheraton-Charleston Hotel
Charleston, South Carolina

This recipe is time-consuming as well as delicious, so why make just a few when to make many takes not much longer? The pastries can be frozen before baking, then defrosted in the refrigerator again before baking.

Continued

Rissoles Bienville (continued)

¾ pound beef sirloin, cut in ¼-inch
   dice
1 tablespoon vegetable oil
⅓ cup chopped onions
1 teaspoon minced garlic
¼ cup dry white wine
2 tablespoons tomato purée
2 tablespoons chopped red pimentos
¼ cup dark raisins, plumped in ½ cup
   water and drained

2 tablespoons Brown Sauce (recipe,
   page 276)
2 drops Tabasco sauce
1 teaspoon salt
Freshly ground black pepper, to taste
1 egg yolk
2 tablespoons milk
Approximately 2 pounds brioche
   dough

Heat oil in large skillet over high heat. Quickly brown the meat. Add onions and garlic. Cook 2 minutes, or until onions are limp. Lower the heat; add wine, tomato purée, pimentos, and raisins. Cook 5 to 7 minutes longer. Add brown sauce, Tabasco, salt, and pepper. Continue simmering until liquid is somewhat reduced and mixture begins to hold its shape. Cool.

Preheat oven to 375 degrees. Combine egg yolk and milk. Roll brioche dough out to approximately ¼-inch thickness. Cut into 3-inch rounds. Place approximately 2 teaspoons filling on one half each round. Brush edges of rounds with egg mix. Fold over empty half to enclose meat, pinching edges securely. Brush with more mix and prick tops with a fork. Bake approximately 8 to 10 minutes, or until pastries are puffed and golden brown. Serve immediately.

Salads

Johann Strauss Salad

Single Serving

*Sheraton-Boston Hotel
Boston, Massachusetts*

The Johann Strauss is a fine luncheon or dinner salad that combines spinach, chicken, and crab with fruit.

3 ounces fresh spinach, washed,
   trimmed and julienned
3 ounces white chicken meat,
   cooked and julienned
1 ounce sliced mushroom

2 ounces snow crabmeat
¼ avocado, sliced
2 ounces French dressing
½ hard-cooked egg, chopped
Garnishes: Orange slices, strawberry

Cover the bottom of a salad bowl with the spinach. Add the chicken, mushroom, snow crab, and avocado. Add French or your favorite dressing and mix ingredients well. Sprinkle with chopped egg. Garnish salad with orange slices topped with a strawberry.

Oriental Chicken Salad

Serves 6–8

Sheraton-Town House
Los Angeles, California

This chicken salad is sensational: colorful, tasty, and as easy and quick to make as you could possibly hope for. Loaded with vitamin-rich vegetables, it looks and tastes delicious. Vegetarians can substitute cubed tofu for the chicken.

Chicken Salad:

3 pounds chicken breasts, poached, skinned, boned, and cut into ¼-inch slivers
8 leaves of Boston lettuce
1 large red bell pepper, seeds and ribs removed, cut into ¼-inch slivers
1 green bell pepper, seeds and ribs removed, cut into ¼-inch slivers
½ pound Chinese pea pods, blanched, left whole if small, or cut into ¼-inch slivers

2 cups ¼-inch celery slices
2 large tomatoes, cut into thin wedges
½ pound water chestnuts, sliced ¼-inch thick
1 cup bean sprouts
2 hard-cooked egg yolks, sieved
3 tablespoons toasted sesame seeds
Fresh Ginger Root Dressing (recipe below)

For a festive presentation, mound chicken lightly in the center of a large shallow dish. Surround with colorful rows of lettuce, bell pepper, pea pods, celery, tomatoes, and water chestnuts. Garnish with bean sprouts, sieved egg yolks, and sesame seeds. Serve with Fresh Ginger Root Dressing.

Fresh Ginger Root Dressing:

¼ cup soy sauce
½ cup salad oil
¼ cup olive oil
⅓ cup white wine vinegar
3 tablespoons fresh lemon juice
½ teaspoon sesame oil

½ to ¾ teaspoon grated or finely chopped fresh ginger root, to taste
½ to 1 teaspoon salt, to taste
¼ teaspoon white pepper
¼ teaspoon sugar

Place all dressing ingredients in a bowl and whisk or stir together well. Dressing may be refrigerated for a short while before using.

Fennel with Special Dressing

Serves 6

Sheraton-Carlton Hotel
Washington, D.C.

2 bunches fennel, trimmed
1 cup olive oil
1 clove garlic, finely chopped
¼ cup vinegar
4 tablespoons Parmesan cheese,
    grated

1 tablespoon oregano
3 sprigs fresh parsley,
    finely chopped
Juice of 2½ lemons
Salt and pepper, to taste

Wash and clean the fennel; cut each stalk lengthwise into 6 sections. To make dressing, blend together all ingredients except fennel. Serve the dressing with the fennel.

Fresh Broccoli Salad Royale

Serves 6

Sheraton at St. Johns Place
Jacksonville, Florida

1½ pound of fresh broccoli, trimmed
1 tablespoon ginger powder
3 ounces fresh orange juice
3 ounces olive oil

1½ ounces white wine vinegar
3 hard-cooked eggs, chopped
Garnishes: Toasted almonds, grated
    Swiss cheese

Cook broccoli until crisp (do not overcook). Put ginger powder, orange juice, olive oil, and vinegar in a bowl. Stir slowly. Add chopped eggs.

When broccoli has cooled, place it in a salad bowl and pour the mixed dressing over it. Marinate for 8 hours in refrigerator. When ready to serve, garnish with almonds and sprinkle with grated swiss cheese. Serve chilled.

Summer Salad

Serves 6

Sheraton-Century Center Hotel
Oklahoma City, Oklahoma

This spicy salad is a hit with Oklahomans, and wherever you live, you surely will agree with them.

4 tomatoes
1 medium-sized onion, chopped fine
2 jalapeño peppers
2 avocados
Salt and white pepper, to taste

1 teaspoon rosemary
1 cup olive oil
¼ cup white vinegar
4 slices bacon
½ head iceberg lettuce

Cut tomatoes in half and slice ¼-inch thick. Peel the onion and chop fine. Slice the peppers very thin. Cut avocados in half, remove pit, and peel and slice them ½-inch thick. Mix ingredients together and add salt and white pepper, rosemary, olive oil, and vinegar. Toss lightly and let stand for at least 30 minutes in the refrigerator. Fry the bacon crisp.

Serve salad on lettuce on a chilled salad plate. Sprinkle with crumbled bacon.

Palace Court Salad

Serves 6

*Sheraton-Palace Hotel
San Francisco, California*

Ever since its creation in the 1920s, this seafood salad has been a highlight of the famous Garden Court Restaurant. Printed in various forms before, this is the restaurant's original recipe, served with its equally famous Green Goddess Dressing. Fresh ingredients are the key to success with each of these recipes.

¾ pound fresh cooked shredded
   crabmeat
½ cup finely minced celery
4 to 6 tablespoons mayonnaise
1 teaspoon fresh lemon juice
¼ teaspoon salt
6 cups finely shredded iceberg lettuce

6 slices (½ inch thick) of large
   tomatoes
6 freshly poached large artichoke
   bottoms
6 hard-cooked eggs, peeled and very
   finely chopped
Garnish: *Lemon wedges*

To make the seafood filling, mix just enough mayonnaise into the shredded crabmeat, and celery to hold it all together. Too much mayonnaise will mask the delicate crab flavor. Season with lemon juice and salt.

Arrange shredded lettuce on 6 large salad plates. For each serving, place a tomato slice in the center of the lettuce and top with an artichoke bottom. On each bottom mound ⅙ of the crab mixture, spoonful by spoonful, until a tower of crab results. Scatter chopped egg around the artichoke bases. Chill salads well before serving with Green Goddess Dressing (recipe as follows) and lemon wedges.

Continued

Green Goddess Dressing:

5 or 6 anchovy fillets, mashed
1 green onion, both green and white
   portions, minced
¼ cup minced fresh parsley

2 tablespoons minced fresh tarragon
3 tablespoons tarragon vinegar
½ cup minced fresh chives
3 cups mayonnaise

Put all ingredients in a blender or large bowl and mix together thoroughly. You will have about 3½ cups of dressing. Serve chilled.

Soups

Avgolemono Soup

Makes about 9 cups

Sheraton Twin Towers Hotel
Orlando, Florida

One of the most famous sauces in Greek cooking today is avgolemono, a tart creamy sauce of eggs and lemon juice. It is added to soups and stews, and is served with many meat and vegetable dishes as well. Here the sauce is served in the classically simple soup.

4- to 5-pound stewing chicken
8 cups water
1 carrot, peeled and coarsely
   chopped
1 stalk celery, coarsely chopped
1 onion, peeled and quartered

8 peppercorns
Salt and white pepper, to taste
½ cup long-grain white rice
4 eggs
¼ cup fresh lemon juice

Rinse chicken thoroughly inside and out. Place chicken in a large pot and pour 8 cups water over it. Add chopped carrot, celery, onion, and peppercorns. Bring to a boil, reduce heat, cover, and simmer chicken over low heat 2 to 3 hours, in which time chicken will render its flavorful juices. Skim the surface. Add salt and pepper to taste toward the end of the stewing process.

    After stewing, remove chicken from the pot. (Save it for other uses or discard.) Strain and discard vegetables and chicken debris. Skim off fat floating on the surface of the soup base, or refrigerate soup base until fat congeals on top and can be removed easily.

    When ready to serve, reheat the soup base to a gentle boil, add the rice, and cook, uncovered, until rice is tender, about 20 minutes. When rice is tender, remove soup from heat to stop the boiling. You are now ready to proceed with the avgolemono sauce.

Whisk or beat the eggs well. Gradually beat in lemon juice. Slowly drizzle 1 cup hot soup base into the eggs and lemon, stirring constantly. Take care not to curdle the eggs by adding the hot liquid too quickly.

Put soup pot back on the stove over low heat. Slowly pour hot avgolemono sauce into soup base, whisking vigorously the whole time. Stir 10 minutes or longer, until soup thickens nicely. Never allow soup to boil once the avgolemono sauce is added or it will curdle and your soup will not have the smooth texture desired.

New England Clam Chowder

Makes about 2½ quarts

Sheraton-Boston Hotel
Boston, Massachusetts

This is a fine standard chowder; the tarragon adds an interesting note. Those who prefer a pristine white chowder should be sure to remove the soft black portion of each clam. Although edible, it tends to discolor the soup.

¼ pound butter
½ cup chopped onions
½ cup chopped celery
⅓ cup chopped leek, white portion only
2 trimmed green onions, both green and white portions, chopped
⅔ cup all-purpose flour
2 cups Fish Stock (recipe, page 280)
2 cups clam juice
4 cups light cream or half and half

¼ cup dry white wine
1 pound clams, coarsely chopped
2 small potatoes, boiled, peeled, and diced
1 teaspoon fresh tarragon or ½ teaspoon dried tarragon
Salt and freshly ground black pepper, to taste
Garnish: Chopped fresh parsley or fresh dill

Melt butter in a large pot over medium-high heat. Stirring constantly, sauté chopped onion, celery, leek, and green onion 3 to 4 minutes until vegetables soften. Add the flour and cook, stirring, 5 minutes longer, watching to see that the roux does not brown.

Lower the heat. Stirring constantly, slowly pour in the fish stock, then the clam juice. Simmer the soup base 25 to 30 minutes. After simmering, stir in the cream and white wine, then add the chopped clams, diced potatoes, and tarragon.

Gently simmer the soup, without allowing it to boil, an additional 8 to 10 minutes. Season with salt and freshly ground black pepper. Serve garnished with chopped fresh parsley or fresh dill.

Seafood Gumbo

Makes about 7 quarts

Sheraton-New Orleans Hotel
New Orleans, Louisiana

On a cool day, when the thought of standing by the stove preparing a classic southern dish appeals to you, make this Seafood Gumbo. The nut brown roux that forms the initial flavor base demands a lot of attention, but it gets the gumbo off to an authentic start.

For a different flavor, you can make this gumbo with chicken, substituting it for the shellfish in the recipe.

¾ cup vegetable oil
¾ cup all-purpose flour
2½ cups chopped onions
1 tablespoon minced garlic
3 cups chopped tomatoes
¾ cup chopped green bell peppers
½ cup chopped green onions
3 tablespoons chopped fresh parsley
1½ pounds blue crab, shells cracked;
    or 1½ pounds dungeness crab,
    shells cracked
2 pounds uncooked medium-sized
    shrimp, shelled and deveined
1½ pounds smoked sausage, skinned
    and sliced ¼ inch thick

1¼ pounds fresh okra, sliced ½ inch
    thick
2½ quarts water
4 bay leaves, crushed
2 teaspoons thyme leaves
5 teaspoons salt
1 teaspoon black pepper
1 to 2 teaspoons cayenne pepper, to
    taste
8 whole cloves
¼ teaspoon mace
5 teaspoons fresh lemon juice
2 cups shucked oysters
3 to 6 cups boiled long-grain white
    rice

Pour oil into a heavy bottomed 8-quart pan and place over low to medium heat. When oil is warm, slowly add flour and stir until smooth. Stirring constantly, cook roux 30 to 45 minutes, until medium brown in color. Watch the heat carefully so as not to scorch the roux or it will have to be discarded and started over again.

When the roux is properly browned, add the onions and garlic. Stir and sauté 2 to 3 minutes. Mix in chopped tomatoes, bell pepper, green onion, and parsley. Stir and sauté 10 to 15 minutes longer, until vegetables have softened. Then add the crab, ½ the shrimp, all the sausage and okra. Stirring constantly, slowly pour in 2½ quarts water. Bring to a boil over medium-high heat. Lower heat, add all the spices and lemon juice and simmer the gumbo, uncovered, 45 minutes to 1 hour.

About 15 minutes before serving, add the remaining shrimp and all the oysters. (Now is the time to add a little water if a thinner gumbo is desired.) Simmer gently.

Let the gumbo sit 3 or 4 minutes off the heat, then serve in shallow soup bowls, ladled over ½ to 1 cup boiled white rice.

Shrimp Soup

Makes about 3½ quarts

Sheraton Inn-Portland Airport
Portland, Oregon

This slightly spicy yet delicately flavored soup is pleasing to the eye as well as to the palate. Serve in small bowls as a first course or in larger portions as an entrée, accompanied by a green salad, french bread, and sweet butter.

3 tablespoons butter
1 cup chopped onion
1 clove garlic, mashed
1 cup chopped green bell pepper
½ cup chopped celery
¼ pound (about 1½ cups) mushrooms, chopped
2 large tomatoes, peeled and chopped
1 pound raw shrimp, peeled and deveined (and chopped if shrimp are medium-sized or bigger)
3 quarts Fish Stock (recipe, page 280)

¼ cup chopped fresh parsley
1 teaspoon salt
½ teaspoon crushed bay leaf
¼ teaspoon pepper
¼ teaspoon tarragon
¼ teaspoon chervil
¼ teaspoon oregano
¼ teaspoon sweet basil
¼ teaspoon thyme leaves
Pinch of dill
1 cup sauterne wine

Melt butter in a large heavy pot over medium-high heat. Stir and sauté the onions, garlic, bell pepper, and celery 4 to 5 minutes to soften and release flavors. Add the mushrooms and sauté 3 or 4 minutes longer. Finally, add the chopped tomatoes and shrimp. Pour in the fish stock; add all herbs and spices. Bring to a boil, then reduce heat to low and simmer 1½ hours, uncovered.

Just before serving, pour in the sauterne and simmer briefly. Correct seasonings to taste, and serve hot.

Cream of Leek Soup

Serves 4–6

Sheraton Palm Coast Resort Inn
Palm Coast, Florida

1 bunch fresh leeks
8 ounces butter
4 ounces all-purpose flour
2¼ cup Chicken Stock (recipe, page 279)

Salt and pepper, to taste
2 dashes of Accent
Dash of nutmeg
1 pint heavy cream
Garnish: Chopped fresh parsley

Continued

Clean leeks thoroughly of all sand, then cut into thin slices and set aside. Melt butter in a saucepan, stir in the flour, and add the chicken stock gradually. Stirring constantly, cook on low heat until smooth (about 2 minutes). Add the leeks and spices, and simmer for about 20 minutes or until leeks are tender, stirring frequently. Before serving, mix in heavy cream. Garnish with chopped parsley.

Iced Cucumber and Beet Soup

Serves 6–8

Sheraton-Hopkins Airport Hotel
Cleveland, Ohio

2 cups peeled and chopped cucumber
1 cup cooked beets julienned
1 clove minced garlic
4 cups sour cream

1 cup milk
½ cup chopped fresh chives
½ cup chopped fresh parsley

Place cucumbers, beets, and garlic in a stainless-steel bowl and add the sour cream, mixing all ingredients gently. Add milk slowly until well blended. Blend in parsley and chives. Serve in chilled soup cups, and garnish with one ice cube per serving.

Watercress Soup

Serves 6

Sheraton-Carlton Hotel
Washington, D.C.

2 bunches watercress
4 tablespoons butter
¾ cup all-purpose flour
8 ounces milk
5 cups water

1 teaspoon sugar
Salt and pepper, to taste
½ medium-sized onion, finely
  chopped

Trim and wash watercress very thoroughly and set aside. Melt butter over low heat; add flour slowly and blend 3 to 5 minutes. Scald milk and slowly stir into flour mixture. Add water, watercress and remaining ingredients. Cook, slowly, 15 to 20 minutes. Strain, chill, and serve.

Cold Peach Soup

Makes 4 cups

Huntington-Sheraton Hotel
Pasadena, California

Cold Peach Soup is perfect for a summer luncheon or supper.

2¼ *pounds ripe peaches, skinned,*
pitted and sliced, or 2 lb. canned
water-packed peaches
½ *cup orange juice*
1 *teaspoon finely grated orange rind*

½ *cup Marsala or other sweet wine*
¼ *cup sugar*
3 *tablespoons cornstarch*
⅛ *teaspoon ground cloves*
Garnish: *Fresh mint sprigs*

Place all ingredients except mint leaves in blender or food processor. Purée thoroughly. Pour fruit mixture into a heavy medium-sized saucepan. Bring soup to a slow boil. Lower heat. Simmer and stir soup 8 to 10 minutes, until soup clears and thickens slightly. Chill. Serve in ice cold glasses or bowls garnished with mint leaves.

Entrees

Slow-Roasted Prime Ribs of Beef

Serves 10–12

Sheraton-Denver Airport
Denver, Colorado

Nothing could be more tempting to eat than a big prime rib roast. Standing tall, in all its glory, waiting for the cut of a knife to separate it into tender portions of meat, it is enough to humble almost any other cut of beef.

7- *to 8-pound rib roast, well*
trimmed and tied
1 *large clove garlic, mashed*
¼ *teaspoon salt*
¼ *teaspoon freshly ground black*
pepper
Pinch of oregano

Pinch of rosemary
1 *onion, peeled and coarsely*
chopped
2 *carrots, peeled and coarsely*
chopped
2 *stalks celery, coarsely chopped*
Dash of Worcestershire sauce

Take roast out of the refrigerator and let stand at room temperature for about 2 hours to take off the chill. Preheat oven to 350 degrees.

Mash together the garlic, salt, pepper, oregano, and rosemary; rub seasonings into the roast. Place meat fat side up on a rack in a shallow roasting pan.

Place meat in the oven and roast approximately 45 minutes, until lightly browned. Open the oven and scatter the chopped vegetables in the pan around the roast. Close the oven, then

Continued

reduce temperature to 225 degrees. Bake approximately 2½ hours for rare (140 degrees on a meat thermometer), or longer for more well done.

When the meat is done to your satisfaction, take roast out of the oven and place it on a carving board to rest for about 10 minutes before carving.

Meanwhile, if enough juice has been rendered by the meat, prepare a natural gravy. Remove excess fat from the pan and place pan over low heat. Stir in a suitable amount of water (1 to 2 cups), scraping to deglaze the bottom of the pan. Season with salt and pepper and a dash of Worcestershire sauce. Reduce gravy slightly, strain, and check seasonings. Serve warm, with the roast beef.

Corned Beef Dinner

Serves 6

Sheraton Steamboat Resort
Steamboat Springs, Colorado

Corned beef is much too good a dish to save for St. Patrick's Day alone. Serve it whenever brisk weather makes you want a hearty, flavorful, easy-to-prepare meal.

3 pounds corned beef brisket
1 large onion, quartered
1 bay leaf
1 teaspoon celery seed
1 clove garlic, crushed
¼ teaspoon peppercorns
6 medium-sized carrots, peeled
    and cut into 2-inch pieces
6 medium-sized potatoes, peeled
    and quartered

6 medium-sized onions, peeled
    and quartered
1 small turnip, peeled and
    quartered
1 small cabbage, cored and cut
    into wedges
Accompaniments: *Hot mustard,*
    horseradish

Rinse the corned beef. Refrigerate overnight submerged in cold water.

When you are ready to cook, pour off the water and discard it. Place the brisket in a large pot and cover with boiling water. Add the quartered large onion, bay leaf, celery seed, garlic, and peppercorns. Bring to a boil, then lower heat, cover, and simmer the corned brisket for approximately 3 hours, or until fork tender.

About 40 minutes before the meat has finished cooking, add the carrots, potatoes, onions, and turnip to the pot. Cover again, bring water to a new boil, then lower heat to simmer once more. After these vegetables have simmered about 25 minutes, add the cabbage to the broth and simmer, covered, 10 to 15 minutes longer, until done.

Serve sliced corned beef with vegetables around it. Accompany with a serving bowl of broth and a lot of hot mustard and horseradish.

Buffalo Barbecue

Serves 4-6

*Sheraton-Century Center Hotel
Oklahoma City, Oklahoma*

Buffalo steaks are not something you see frequently at the meat counter, but when available, they are well worth preparing for those who like a strong, rangy flavor to their meat.

3 pounds buffalo rib eye steak, approximately 2 inches thick; or 3 pounds of beef rib eye steak, 2 inches thick
4 tablespoons softened butter
1½ teaspoons salt
1½ teaspoons freshly ground black pepper

2 tablespoons dry mustard
2 teaspoons paprika
2 tablespoons olive oil
1 teaspoon Worcestershire sauce
Garnish: *Chopped fresh parsley*

Wipe steak dry. Make a paste of softened butter, salt, pepper, mustard, and paprika. Rub both sides of the steak with 3 tablespoons of the seasoned butter. Let the buttered steak sit an hour or so, refrigerated, to absorb flavors.

When ready to charcoal-broil, combine the olive oil and Worcestershire sauce. Place buffalo steak on barbecue and grill 8 to 10 minutes on one side. Turn and baste meat lightly with olive oil mixture, then grill 8 to 10 minutes on the other side. Turn and baste again. Continue grilling the meat, turning occasionally, until done to your satisfaction.

Serve steak smeared with remaining butter and sprinkled with parsley.

Hickory-Smoked Brisket

Serves 10–12

*Sheraton-Washington Hotel
Washington, D.C.*

2 tablespoons liquid smoke
6- to 7-pound boneless brisket, well trimmed
⅔ cup vegetable oil
⅓ cup white wine vinegar

2 teaspoons hickory-smoked (charcoal-flavored) salt
1 teaspoon garlic salt
1 teaspoon freshly ground black pepper
3 cups hickory-flavored barbecue sauce

Rub liquid smoke over entire surface of brisket. Place meat in a shallow pan and pour over it thick vinaigrette made by blending the oil and vinegar. Refrigerate 4 to 5 hours, turning occasionally. Just before cooking, remove brisket from marinade and pat dry. Rub salts and pepper into both sides of beef for a fully seasoned flavor. Brush with ¼ cup barbecue sauce.

Continued

When coals are ready, toss on a layer of dampened hickory chips and position grill 5 inches above the coals. (It is preferable to use a covered grill.) Sear meat 5 to 6 minutes on each side.

Remove brisket from grill. Place it on two large layers of heavy-duty aluminum foil and coat with additional ½ cup barbecue sauce. Seal foil carefully to prevent juices from escaping.

Place sealed brisket back on grill and roast 45 minutes on each side, or until done to desired degree. Renew coals as necessary.

Remove meat carefully from the foil, saving any juices to add to remaining barbecue sauce. Serve brisket, thinly sliced against the grain, with warmed barbecue sauce and crusty french bread. Any leftover brisket is excellent served cold.

Hickory-Smoked Brisket can be barbecued over an open grill the entire time, but for even heat distribution it is best prepared, once wrapped in foil, in a closed grill. Bear in mind that the brisket will cook faster in a closed grill, thus shortening the length of time the meat stays on the grill.

Barbecued Beef Texas Style

Serves 6   *Sheraton-Houston Hotel*
                                                                                               Houston, Texas

This thick, spicy barbecue sauce is excellent over beef or poultry. Make an extra batch to freeze so that you always have some on hand. Here the sauce is served over thickly sliced, well-done roast beef, with crisp hamburger buns underneath.

Barbecue Sauce:

2 tablespoons oil
1½ cups minced onions
1 tablespoon minced garlic
4 cups prepared chili sauce
⅔ cup lemon juice
¼ cup red wine vinegar
1 tablespoon Worcestershire sauce
2 tablespoons liquid smoke

1 tablespoon prepared mustard
⅔ cup dark brown sugar, loosely
   packed
1 tablespoon paprika
2 teaspoons salt
½ teaspoon cayenne pepper
¼ teaspoon freshly ground black
   pepper

Heat oil in large heavy skillet over medium-high heat. Sauté onions and garlic 2 to 3 minutes. Pour in the chili sauce, then add all other ingredients. Lower the heat and simmer sauce at least 30 minutes to blend the flavors, stirring occasionally.

Presentation:

1½ pounds well-done roast beef,
   thickly sliced and warmed

6 hamburger buns, split and toasted
Garnish: *kosher dill pickles*

Lay roast beef (¼ pound per person) over toasted hamburger buns. Top with hot Barbecue Sauce and garnish with kosher dill pickles.

Steak Tartare

Single Serving

Sheraton-Villa Inn
Burnaby, British Columbia

4 anchovy fillets
¼ cup capers
Pinch of salt
12 olives, chopped
¼ cup chopped fresh parsley
2 small chopped gherkins
1 egg yolk
1 teaspoon prepared mustard

3 teaspoons salad oil
3 teaspoons malt vinegar
¼ teaspoon Worcestershire sauce
Dash of Tabasco sauce
Salt and pepper, to taste
¼ ounce cognac
6 ounces coarsely ground
beef tenderloin

In a large wooden bowl mash the anchovies, capers and pinch of salt with a fork, then add all other ingredients except meat. Mix well. When thoroughly combined, add meat and mix again. Be certain that the meat is well chilled; even better, place mixing bowl in an ice bed. Season well with salt and freshly ground pepper from a pepper mill.

Steak Tartare should be neatly formed into a steak shape and served with french bread and crusty rolls or garlic bread.

Lamb Noisettes en Papillote

Serves 4

St. Regis-Sheraton Hotel
New York, New York

These noisettes are small, succulent pieces of meat from the rib chops of the lamb. Have a butcher bone out the ribs, trim the meat of all fat, and cut the meat into inch-thick pieces. Each noisette will be very small—no more than two inches wide. Because of their small size, Lamb Noisettes en Papillote should be served two per person.

1½ pounds lamb noisettes (8 3-ounce
pieces)
4 tablespoons butter
½ pound chicken livers
4 to 6 ounces lean cooked (but not
smoked) ham cut into 8 slices each
approximately ⅛ inch thick

3 to 4 tablespoons cognac, brandy, or
Madeira
Salt and pepper, to taste
2 tablespoons minced fresh parsley

Continued

Begin by cutting 8 hearts out of cooking parchment paper or tin foil, each heart 10 inches wide by 12 inches high. Coat one side of each heart with oil. Do not oil if using foil. Set aside.

Preheat oven to 400 degrees. Trim noisettes of any remaining fat and pound to flatten them slightly. Melt all the butter over medium-high heat in a heavy skillet. Add lamb, sauté approximately 2 minutes on each side, just until browned. Remove the lamb. In the same butter, quickly sauté the chicken livers for 1 minute or less, until they turn pale brown and firm up slightly. Chop them coarsely and set aside.

To assemble each serving, lay out a parchment heart oiled side down. Place a ham slice trimmed to fit on one side of the heart, cover with a lamb noisette, then top with 1 tablespoon of chicken livers. Sprinkle on 1 or 2 teaspoons cognac, brandy, or Madeira, salt and pepper to taste, and minced parsley. Fold over the empty half of the heart and crease the edges into a hem. Crimp the hem shut all the way around, securing with toothpicks if necessary. Place papillotes on rack in a shallow roasting pan and bake at 400 degrees 10 to 15 minutes, until parchment browns and crisps.

Serve immediately, instructing guests to tear each papillote open from the center.

Festive Lamb Kebabs

Serves 8

Sheraton-Hopkins Airport Hotel
Cleveland, Ohio

These multicolored kebabs are at their best when barbecued, but they can also be broiled.

1½ cups dry white wine
⅔ cup fresh lemon juice
2 cups vegetable oil
4 large garlic cloves, mashed
1½ teaspoons oregano
1 teaspoon thyme leaves
1 teaspoon sweet basil
3 tablespoons Worcestershire sauce
1½ teaspoons salt
½ teaspoon freshly ground black
 pepper

4½ pounds boneless lamb, cut into
 1¼-inch cubes
1½ pounds small white onions,
 peeled
1 medium-sized (about 3½ pounds)
 pineapple
4 green bell peppers, seeded, ribs
 removed, cut into eighths
16 preserved kumquats
1½ pounds large mushrooms,
 cleaned and stemmed

Combine wine, lemon juice, oil, garlic, oregano, thyme, basil, Worcestershire sauce, salt, and pepper. Add cubed lamb and mix gently. Cover and refrigerate the lamb overnight. Turn meat several times during this period.

When ready to assemble the kebabs, begin by parboiling the onions 3 to 5 minutes to soften them slightly. Drain and set them aside. Skin and core the pineapple. Cut pineapple into 2-inch pieces. Set aside.

Remove lamb from marinade, saving marinade to brush on kebabs as they roast. Thread skewers decoratively with lamb, peppers, pineapple, onions, kumquats, and mushroom caps. Barbecue or broil kebabs 15 to 20 minutes, or until done to taste. Turn and baste with marinade as necessary.

Southern Baked Ham

Serves 4–6

Sheraton-Atlanta Hotel
Atlanta, Georgia

1 smoked picnic ham, about 4
   pounds
½ cup granulated sugar

½ cup dark brown sugar, loosely
   packed
½ cup prepared mustard
2 ounces honey

Blend the two sugars together and set aside. Blend mustard and honey. Baste ham with honey-mustard mix and coat heavily with the blended sugars.

Bake slowly at 325 degrees for approximately 1½ hours (18 to 20 minutes per pound), until sugar has melted to a golden brown.

Apple Stuffed Pork Chops

Serves 6

Sheraton-Little Rock
Little Rock, Arkansas

6 very thick loin pork chops, about 10
   to 12 ounces each, trimmed of
   most fat
1 cup fine dry bread crumbs
6 tablespoons peeled, cored, and
   finely chopped apple
6 tablespoons finely chopped celery
6 tablespoons dark raisins
3 eggs, lightly beaten

1¼ teaspoons salt
½ teaspoon pepper
¼ teaspoon sage
½ cup all-purpose flour
3 tablespoons butter
¼ cup or more hot water
Garnish: *Chopped fresh parsley*
Optional: *Sautéed apple rings*

Preheat oven to 350 degrees. Cut a deep pocket into the side of each pork chop; set aside.

Mix together the bread crumbs, apple, celery, and raisins. Add the eggs, ¾ teaspoon salt, ¼ teaspoon pepper, and sage. Stuff each chop with equal portions of the filling.

Combine the flour, remaining ½ teaspoon salt, and ¼ teaspoon pepper. Dredge the chops through the seasoned flour.

Continued

Melt 3 tablespoons butter in a large heavy skillet over medium-high heat. Brown the chops well, 2 to 3 minutes to a side. When browned, place in a large shallow, buttered baking dish. Cover loosely with foil and bake in preheated oven 45 minutes or longer, until cooked through.

Remove chops from pan and place on warm plates. Pour hot water into the hot pan and stir, scraping the pan bottom, to create a natural gravy. Season further if necessary. Pour gravy over the pork chops, then sprinkle on parsley. Serve with sautéed apple rings, if desired.

Fillet of Pork with Pears

Serves 6

Sheraton-Plaza 500
Vancouver, British Columbia

Small, slender pork tenderloins yield delicate fillets that are served two to three per person. Have your butcher cut the tenderloins into fillets or buy the necessary amount of whole tenderloins and cut your own.

2 cups Chicken Stock (recipe, page 279)
3 large ripe but still firm pears
2¼ pounds pork tenderloin, cut into 18 2-ounce fillets

5 to 6 tablespoons clarified butter (recipe, page 277)
Salt and pepper, to taste
2 tablespoons minced shallots
6 ounces mild blue cheese

Pour chicken stock into a pan wide enough to accommodate the pears; bring to a gentle boil. Peel pears, slice in half lengthwise, and core. Poach pear halves in simmering stock 2 to 3 minutes, covered, until just tender. Remove pears and set them aside. Boil chicken stock rapidly until reduced to 1 cup. Set stock aside.

Preheat oven to 350 degrees. Pound fillets to flatten slightly. Melt 2 to 3 tablespoons butter in a large frying pan over medium-high heat. Sauté fillets, 6 to 8 at a time, 2 minutes on each side, until lightly browned. When browned, place fillets in a large, shallow baking dish. Replenish the butter in the pan as needed to finish sautéeing the pork. Season fillets with salt and pepper.

When all meat is browned, prepare a thin sauce by sautéeing shallots over medium heat in the same frying pan, adding additional butter if necessary. Cook shallots 2 or 3 minutes, until soft. Pour into the pan the reduced chicken stock and simmer sauce 1 or 2 minutes, scraping the pan as you stir. Keep warm.

Fill poached pears with equal portions of blue cheese, then place them on top of the sautéed pork fillets. Bake at 350 degrees 15 to 20 minutes, or until cheese melts and meat is cooked through.

When meat is done, pour the shallots and chicken stock over it. Serve immediately.

Paupiettes de Veau Calvados
(Stuffed Veal in Apple Brandy Sauce)

Serves 4–8

Sheraton West Hotel
Indianapolis, Indiana

Your guests' appetites, combined with what you select to accompany these small rolls of apple-stuffed veal, will determine whether you serve one or two paupiettes per person. Be sure to remove the toothpicks or string found in each paupiette, or you may bite into more than you bargained for.

Paupiettes de Veau:

8 slices (1 pound) veal scallops
5 tablespoons butter
½ cup finely chopped onion
1 cup peeled finely diced tart apple
1 large clove garlic, mashed
½ cup fine dry white bread crumbs

¼ teaspoon thyme leaves
¼ teaspoon poultry seasoning
½ teaspoon salt
⅛ teaspoon pepper
1 tablespoon vegetable oil

Trim scallops of any remaining fat or membrane. Place each between sheets of waxed paper and pound well to flatten out and tenderize. Flattened scallops should be no more than ¼ inch thick. Set meat aside.

Sauté onions, apples, and garlic in 4 tablespoons of butter over medium-high heat until apples and onions are just tender. When tender, add bread crumbs and spices. Stir and sauté 1 minute longer to blend flavors.

Preheat oven to 325 degrees.

Place equal amounts of filling on each scallop. Roll and secure with toothpicks or kitchen string. Sauté the paupiettes in remaining tablespoon butter and 1 tablespoon oil over medium-high heat until lightly browned on all sides.

When sautéed, arrange paupiettes in a baking dish, cover loosely with tinfoil, and bake 20 minutes, or until heated and cooked through. While paupiettes are baking, prepare the Calvados Sauce (recipe below).

Calvados Sauce:

1 cup heavy cream
⅓ cup Calvados (apple brandy)

⅓ cup apple cider
Salt and white pepper, to taste

Place all ingredients in a small heavy saucepan. Bring to a gentle boil over medium-high heat. Boil, stirring occasionally, 5 minutes or longer until liquid is reduced to 1 cup. Spoon 1 or 2 tablespoons sauce over each paupiette and serve while hot.

Roast Veal Normande

Serves 6–8

*The Sheraton Center
New York, New York*

3½ pounds boneless veal roast
1 teaspoon powdered sage
1 teaspoon celery salt
½ teaspoon freshly ground black
   pepper
6 tablespoons butter
1 tablespoon oil
1½ cups chopped onions
2 carrots, peeled and chopped
2 stalks celery, chopped
1 large clove garlic, peeled and cut in
   half
1 bay leaf, crushed
½ teaspoon thyme leaves
4 large tart green cooking apples

3 tablespoons dry sherry
⅓ cup cognac or brandy
1½ cups heavy cream
1 teaspoon fresh tarragon or ½
   teaspoon dried tarragon leaves
⅔ cup loosely packed grated Swiss
   cheese
salt and pepper, to taste

Preheat oven to 350 degrees. Combine sage, celery salt, and ground pepper, and rub over entire surface of the roast. Using a large ovenproof pan, brown the veal well on all sides in 2 tablespoons butter and 1 tablespoon oil. This should take about 10 minutes over medium-high heat.

When meat is well browned, pour off any excess fat in the pan. Scatter onion, carrot, celery, garlic, bay leaf, and thyme around the veal. Place pan in middle of preheated oven and roast veal for 30 minutes. Turn meat over, cover loosely with foil, and continue roasting another 45 minutes. Finally, turn and roast meat, still loosely covered, for additional 30 minutes. Total roasting time is 1¾ hours.

Meanwhile, peel, core, and slice apples. Melt remaining 4 tablespoons butter in skillet and sauté apples 3 or 4 minutes, until tender but still slightly crisp. Sprinkle with sherry and set aside.

When veal roast is done, warm brandy over medium-high heat in a small pan. Ignite. When flames die out, pour liquor over the roast. Remove roast from the pan and transfer to a heated platter to rest while making the gravy.

Add cream and tarragon to roasting pan and place over medium-high heat. Bring liquids to a boil, stirring constantly to deglaze the pan and slightly reduce the sauce. At the last moment, add grated cheese, stirring just long enough for it to melt into the completed gravy sauce. Remove from heat and season further with salt and pepper, if desired.

Surround the roast with sautéed apples and serve with the hot gravy.

Chicken Suprême and Potato Dumplings

Serves 2–4

Billings Sheraton Hotel
Billings, Montana

Here is a sophisticated version of the traditionally informal chicken and dumplings. Tender chicken breasts take the place of the usual whole stewed chicken, and they are served in a clear, light chicken broth. An attractive way to serve this dish would be in individual shallow bowls, one or two breasts and two plump dumplings per serving.

Chicken Suprême:

2 large chicken breasts, split in half
1 medium-sized onion, peeled and
    quartered
1 stalk celery, coarsely chopped
1 whole clove
1 bay leaf

1 tablespoon fresh lemon juice
1 teaspoon salt
8 peppercorns
Potato Dumplings (recipe below)
Garnish: *Chopped fresh parsley*

Rinse chicken breasts well. Place in a saucepan and cover with cold water. Bring to a gentle simmer and poach the breasts about 2 minutes. Drain breasts well, discarding water. Rinse the chicken breasts and the pan to remove any undesired film. (All this is done to ensure a clear broth for the finished dish.)

Return the chicken to the pan, cover with fresh cold water, and add the remaining vegetables and seasonings. Poach the breasts at a simmer, never allowing them to boil, for approximately 12 to 15 minutes. Remove pan from heat and let breasts cool down in the broth. When breasts are cool, take them out of the broth and skin and bone them carefully, trying to keep suprêmes (breast meat) in one neat piece. Discard the skin and bones.

Strain the stock, then taste and correct the seasonings, if necessary.

To serve, reheat the stock at a simmer, then add the breasts and dumplings. When all elements are warm, serve the chicken breasts and dumplings in their broth, one or two breasts per person, two dumplings each. Garnish with parsley.

Potato Dumplings:

⅓ cup sifted all-purpose flour
½ teaspoon baking powder
1 teaspoon salt
¼ teaspoon white pepper
½ cup fine dry white bread crumbs,
    with crusts removed

1 tablespoon cold butter
¼ cup grated potato
1 tablespoon minced onion
1 egg, lightly beaten

Continued

Place in a bowl and stir together the flour, baking powder, salt, and pepper. Add the bread crumbs and stir well. Cut or rub in the butter until the mixture resembles coarse meal.

Grate ¼ cup raw potato into a tea towel, working quickly so that the potato does not have time to brown. Squeeze potatoes in the tea towel to remove any excess moisture.

Stir the potatoes and minced onions into the bread-crumb mixture. Add the egg; lightly mix all together. Stop mixing as soon as the dumpling dough holds together.

Form dough into 8 dumplings. Slide dumplings into gently boiling salted water. Simmer about 12 to 15 minutes, until dumplings are cooked through. Take dumplings out of the water with a slotted spoon and drain briefly.

Plantation Chicken and Corncakes

Serves 6   *Sheraton Convention Center Hotel*
                                                      Memphis, Tennessee

This is a traditional American creamed chicken dish, perfect for family get-togethers or informal gatherings. The corncakes served under the creamed chicken are just the right touch to make this dish a little more special.

Plantation Chicken:

2 tablespoons butter
¾ cup finely chopped onions
½ cup finely chopped carrot
½ cup finely chopped celery
½ cup butter
½ cup all-purpose flour
1 cup Chicken Stock (recipe, page 279)
3 cups milk

1 teaspoon salt
¼ teaspoon white pepper
Optional: pinch of cayenne pepper
3- to 4-pound chicken, poached, skinned, and boned, with meat diced or shredded
1 cup fresh or frozen green peas
1 tablespoon chopped pimento
1 to 2 tablespoons dry sherry, to taste

Melt 2 tablespoons butter in a large heavy pan. Add the chopped onion, carrot, and celery. Sauté over medium-high heat 3 to 4 minutes, stirring constantly. Remove from heat; scrape vegetables into a bowl and set them aside.

In the same pan, melt ½ cup butter over medium-high heat. Stir in the flour, preferably with a wire whisk. Cook, stirring constantly, for 4 or 5 minutes, being careful not to brown the roux. Slowly stir in the chicken stock and milk. Simmer or gently boil the chicken sauce 20 to 25 minutes, stirring occasionally. Keep a watchful eye on the pot so that the sauce does not scorch. Season with salt and white pepper and add a pinch of cayenne, if desired.

When properly simmered, add diced chicken, sautéed vegetables, green peas, chopped pimento, and sherry. Simmer 10 minutes more. If creamed chicken is too thick for your taste, thin out with small additions of milk.

Serve hot, over just-baked Plantation Corncakes.

Plantation Corncakes:

This thin, firm corncake, or cornbread, makes a perfect base for creamed dishes like Plantation Chicken. The corncake is purposely firm and slightly dry so that it does not get soggy when under creamed toppings.

1 cup yellow cornmeal
½ cup all-purpose flour
½ teaspoon salt
1 teaspoon baking powder
1 teaspoon sugar

1½ cups buttermilk
1 egg, lightly beaten
2 tablespoons melted bacon
 drippings, cooled; or 2 tablespoons
 melted butter, cooled

Preheat oven to 425 degrees. Grease a shallow baking pan, approximately 9 x 12 inches. Shortly before pouring in the batter, place the empty pan in the oven to heat through.

Sift together all dry ingredients. Beat in the buttermilk, egg, and melted bacon drippings.

Pour corncake batter into the hot pan and bake 15 to 20 minutes, until dry to the touch. Cut into six 4-inch squares, top with hot Plantation Chicken, and serve immediately.

Honey Pecan Fried Chicken

Serves 6–8

Sheraton Inn-Shreveporter
Shreveport, Louisiana

Here is a unique fried chicken recipe that is sweet, crunchy, and rich. The buttermilk-soaked chicken is fried, then served piping hot, drizzled with sweet pecan sauce.

Fried Chicken:

2 frying chickens, each about 3
 pounds, cleaned and cut into
 serving pieces
4 cups buttermilk

1 cup all-purpose flour
¾ teaspoon salt
¼ teaspoon pepper
Sufficient oil for deep frying

Place chicken pieces in a large bowl and cover with buttermilk. Let chicken soak at least 1 hour, refrigerated. When ready to cook, drain chicken for a few moments, then coat thoroughly with flour that has been seasoned with salt and pepper.

Fry the chicken in hot oil until crisp golden brown and cooked through.

Continued

Honey Pecan Sauce:

1 cup butter   ½ cup chopped pecans
½ cup honey

Bring ingredients up to a gentle boil. Arrange hot chicken on serving dishes; drizzle honey pecan sauce over it. Serve immediately.

Stuffed Halibut Steak

Serves 6   *Sheraton-Universal Hotel*
                                                    Los Angeles, California

Halibut Steak:

2½ tablespoons oil   2 large ripe tomatoes
½ pound mushrooms, cleaned and   1 large ripe avocado
   minced   3 tablespoons freshly grated
2 tablespoons dry bread crumbs   Parmesan cheese
2 tablespoons minced fresh chives   Mustard Sauce (recipe follows)
1⅔ teaspoons Mixed Salt (recipe   Garnish: *Lemon wedges*
   follows)
6 halibut steaks, each about ¾ inch
   thick, skinned and boned

Preheat oven to 400 degrees. Heat 1 tablespoon oil in saucepan over medium-high heat. Sauté mushrooms 1 or 2 minutes; stir in bread crumbs, chives, and 1 teaspoon Mixed Salt. Let cool. Cut a pocket into each steak and fill pockets with equal portions of cool mushroom mixture.

Brush the bottom of a baking dish with ½ tablespoon oil and sprinkle with ¼ teaspoon Mixed Salt. Arrange steaks in dish, brush with remaining tablespoon of oil, and sprinkle with as much remaining Mixed Salt as desired. (Steaks may be refrigerated at this point, covered, up to 2 hours.)

Place fish in the preheated oven and bake 15 minutes, or until cooked through. When fish is done, arrange alternate slices tomato and avocado on each steak. Sprinkle with grated cheese. Quickly glaze under a hot broiler just until cheese is lightly browned.

Serve immediately, accompanied by Mustard Sauce and garnished with lemon wedges.

Mixed Salt:

²/₃ teaspoon garlic powder
½ teaspoon poultry seasoning

½ teaspoon white pepper
Dash of cayenne pepper

Mix all ingredients well.

Mustard Sauce:

2 teaspoons dry mustard
2 tablespoons white wine vinegar
2 cups mayonnaise

4 tablespoons Brown Sauce (recipe,
   page 276)

Mix all ingredients well. Refrigerate if sauce is not to be used immediately. Sauce tastes best served at room temperature.

Rainbow Trout with Shrimp Stuffing

Serves 4

*Sheraton-Yankee Clipper Hotels
Fort Lauderdale, Florida*

4 rainbow trout, each about 6
   ounces, cleaned and boned
   through the belly
2 tablespoons butter
2 tablespoons finely chopped shallots
¾ cup finely sliced mushrooms
½ pound raw shrimp, peeled,
   deveined, and chopped
¼ cup dry white wine

½ cup fine dry bread crumbs
1 egg, lightly beaten
2 tablespoons finely chopped fresh
   parsley
½ teaspoon salt
¼ teaspoon white pepper
½ cup heavy cream
Garnishes: *Fresh dill, lemon slices*

Rinse boned trout well and pat dry with paper towels. Set aside.

Preheat oven to 400 degrees. Melt butter in a heavy saucepan over medium-high heat. Add the shallots and mushrooms and sauté 2 to 3 minutes. Toss in the chopped shrimp; sprinkle 2 tablespoons wine over them and cook 1 minute longer, until shrimp just barely turns pink. Scrape shrimp mixture into a bowl and let cool. Mix in bread crumbs, egg, parsley, salt, and pepper.

Fill boned trout with equal portions of the shrimp stuffing. Place trout in a shallow buttered baking dish. Sprinkle on remaining 2 tablespoons wine. Cover loosely with tin foil and bake 15 minutes. After 15 minutes, pour cream over the fish and bake 5 minutes longer, uncovered, or until trout is cooked through.

Place cooked trout on warm plates. Stir the sauce in the baking pan well. Season with additional salt and pepper, if desired. Pour a little cream sauce over each trout and serve, sprinkled with parsley. Garnish with fresh dill and lemon slices. Serve with parsley potatoes.

Scrod with Dill Sauce

Serves 4

Sheraton-Boston Hotel
Boston, Massachusetts

Scrod, young codfish, are prized for their delicate white meat. Here the scrod is served in a reduced wine sauce that will compliment other types of whitefish as well.

2 tablespoons butter	*1½ teaspoons fresh dill or 1 teaspoon*
4 tablespoons finely minced shallots	*dried dill*
1½ cups dry white wine	*Salt and white pepper, to taste*
3 cups heavy cream	*2 pounds scrod fillets*

Melt butter in a small heavy saucepan over medium-high heat. Stir in minced shallots and sauté until shallots are tender. Add 1 cup white wine.

Slowly boil the wine, uncovered, approximately 15 minutes, to reduce the wine to ½ cup. When wine is reduced, add the cream and reduce the sauce again for approximately 15 minutes, uncovered, until it reaches a scant 2 cups. The finished sauce should have a smooth, fairly thick consistency. Stir the sauce often during the reduction process to prevent scorching. Add dill, salt, and white pepper. Keep warm.

While sauce is reducing, preheat oven to 350 degrees and prepare the fish. Lay scrod fillets in a buttered baking dish. Pour over ½ cup white wine, sprinkle with salt and white pepper to taste. Cover fish loosely with tinfoil and bake approximately 15 minutes, or until fish flakes (proof that it is cooked through). Do not overbake or scrod will loose its delicate texture.

Remove baked scrod from wine and place on warm plates. Coat lightly with the dill sauce. Serve accompanied by small boiled potatoes and vegetables of your choice.

Missouri Catfish on the Riverfront

Serves 4

Sheraton-St. Louis Hotel
St. Louis, Missouri

Catfish is a whiskered favorite of many midwestern and southern fish fanciers. Here it is served in a slightly formal fashion—fried, then masked with a thin wine sauce.

2 pounds boneless catfish fillets	*¾ cup dry white wine*
1 cup all-purpose flour	*3 tablespoons fresh lemon juice*
1½ teaspoons salt	Garnishes: *Chopped fresh parsley,*
1 teaspoon white pepper	*lemon wedges*
4 tablespoons unsalted butter	

Dredge catfish fillets through flour seasoned with salt and white pepper.

Melt butter over medium-high heat in a large heavy skillet. Sauté catfish until lightly browned on both sides and cooked through. Drain briefly on paper towels, then place on serving dish. Keep warm while making sauce.

Pour wine and lemon juice into the hot frying pan. Stir and scrape bottom of the pan 1 or 2 minutes to pick up flavor. Pour the thin sauce over fried catfish, sprinkle with parsley, and serve with lemon wedges.

Finnan Haddie St. Regis

Serves 8

St. Regis-Sheraton Hotel
New York, New York

Finnan Haddie St. Regis has been called by many one of the finest haddie dishes they have ever eaten. You will find that the rich creamy sauce complements the smoke-flavored finnan haddie perfectly. The entire dish may be assembled in advance and refrigerated for a short while; but most devotées say it is best served promptly, perhaps with a simple fresh green salad, french bread—and champagne!

1½ pounds finnan haddie (smoked haddock)
3 cups St. Regis Béchamel (recipe below)
Salt and white pepper, to taste
4 small potatoes, boiled, peeled, and sliced ¼ inch thick

4 hard-cooked eggs, peeled and cut into thin wedges
4 tablespoons freshly grated Parmesan cheese
Garnish: *Parsley sprigs*

Place finnan haddie in a pan and cover with boiling water. Simmer 3 to 4 minutes to soften and tenderize the fish. Remove, drain, and cut fish into plump, bite-sized pieces. Add the haddie to the Béchamel sauce and gently heat through. Salt and pepper to taste.

Preheat oven to 350 degrees. Layer sliced potatoes and eggs in bottom of a shallow buttered baking dish, or in individual buttered ramekins. Pour over hot finnan haddie mixture. Sprinkle on grated Parmesan cheese. Bake briefly in preheated oven to heat through. When dish is hot, run under the broiler just long enough to brown the Parmesan cheese. Serve garnished with parsley sprigs.

St. Regis Béchamel:

6 tablespoons butter
6 tablespoons all-purpose flour

2 cups half and half
1 cup milk

Melt butter in a medium-sized saucepan over moderate heat. Add flour and stir with a wire whisk or wooden spoon 3 to 4 minutes to cook out the flour taste. Gradually add the half and half and the milk, stirring constantly. Simmer the sauce an additional 15 to 20 minutes, stirring occasionally.

You will have about 3¾ cups sauce, which may be refrigerated for several days or frozen.

Fillet of Red Snapper Nectarine

Serves 6

*Sheraton Plaza La Reine Hotel
Los Angeles, California*

*4 tablespoons butter
½ cup finely chopped onions
¾ cup dry white wine
½ teaspoon freshly grated lemon peel
¼ teaspoon fresh tarragon leaves or
  ⅛ teaspoon dried tarragon leaves*

*2 pounds red snapper fillets
Salt and pepper, to taste
1 pound fresh ripe nectarines, peeled,
  pitted, and cut into thin wedges
Garnish: Minced fresh parsley*

Melt 2 tablespoons butter over medium heat in a small saucepan. Add the onions and sauté 2 to 3 minutes until tender. Take pan off the heat; stir in the wine, grated lemon peel, and tarragon. Set aside.

Preheat oven to 350 degrees. Cut the red snapper fillets into serving pieces. Arrange fish in a large buttered baking dish and sprinkle on salt and pepper to taste. Tuck in nectarine slices. Pour wine sauce over the fish and nectarines. Dot with remaining 2 tablespoons butter. Sprinkle with parsley.

Bake red snapper in preheated oven until fish flakes when pierced with a fork, about 20 to 30 minutes, depending on thickness of fillets.

When done, serve red snapper and nectarines with toast points or over a bed of boiled white rice, accompanied with pan juices.

Baked Stuffed Salmon

Serves 12

*Sheraton-Landmark Hotel
Vancouver, Canada*

Have a fish merchant cut the salmon fillets necessary for this impressive dish from the center section of the fish. They should be at least 1½ inches thick if possible. If fillets are unavailable, boned salmon steaks may be substituted.

Salmon and Stuffing:

*½ cup butter
1 cup minced green onions
2 cups oysters, rinsed and minced
2 cups minced fresh parsley
⅓ cup lemon juice
3 cups diced white day-old bread,
  with crusts removed*

*3 egg yolks, lightly beaten
Salt and pepper, to taste
4½ pounds (12 6-ounce fillets) fresh
  salmon
½ cup butter, melted*

Melt ½ cup butter in a heavy skillet over high heat. Add onions and sauté until soft. Stir in oysters and cook briefly, just to heat through. Add parsley and lemon juice. Continue stirring and cooking for about 5 minutes. Fold in diced bread, stir, and cook until all pan juices are absorbed. Remove mixture from heat and cool. When cool, mix in the egg yolks. Season with salt and pepper to taste.

Preheat oven to 375 degrees. Cut a pocket ¾ of the way through the thick part of each fillet. Gently stuff oyster dressing into pocket. Place stuffed salmon in a baking dish, drizzle over melted butter, and cover loosely with tinfoil. Lower oven temperature to 300 degrees. Bake for approximately 15 minutes, or until salmon is done. Serve with the following sauce.

Sherry Sauce:

This is a thin but very rich sauce. Only 3 or 4 tablespoons are needed to coat each salmon fillet. This recipe makes about 3 cups of sauce.

1 cup Béchamel sauce (recipe, page 275)
¼ cup water
¼ cup fresh lemon juice

⅓ cup dry sherry
1 pound butter
3 tablespoons minced fresh parsley

Combine Béchamel, water, lemon juice, sherry, and butter in a small heavy saucepan over medium heat. Stir with a whisk until sauce is creamy and smooth. Add minced parsley. Serve warm.

Homard du Ciel
(Lobster from Heaven)

Serves 4

Sheraton-Boston Hotel
Boston, Massachusetts

6 live clams or 2 ounces whole clams
4 lobsters, 1 to 1½ pounds each; or lobster tails, 8 to 10 ounces each
4 tablespoons butter
3 tablespoons minced shallots
3 tablespoons minced green onions
½ cup thinly sliced mushrooms
2 ounces scallops, diced

2 ounces small shrimp, peeled and deveined
¾ cup dry white wine
3 cups heavy cream
Salt and white pepper, to taste
Optional: Small pinch of cayenne pepper
¾ cup fine dry white bread crumbs

Place live clams in ¼ inch of hot water, cover, and boil 6 to 8 minutes or until they open. Cool. Remove clams from their shells, discarding any that do not open. Chop clams coarsely.

If lobsters are live, plunge them head first into enough boiling salted water to cover them well.

Continued

Return water to a boil, reduce heat, and simmer lobsters 10 to 12 minutes. Take lobsters out of the water, cool, then split lobsters in half lengthwise.

Whether lobsters are freshly poached or purchased cooked, take lobster meat out of shells, dice, and set aside. Clean the shells out well if they are to be used for presentation.

Melt 2 tablespoons of butter in a heavy saucepan over medium heat. Sauté the shallots and green onions 2 or 3 minutes, until soft. Add sliced mushrooms and sauté 1 minute longer. Add diced lobster, scallops, shrimp, and clams. Continue sautéeing gently 2 or 3 minutes longer. remove seafood and vegetables from the pan with a slotted spoon. Pour in the white wine. Raise the heat to high and reduce the wine to 3 or 4 tablespoons, stirring frequently.

When wine is reduced, pour in the cream and reduce again, stirring constantly, until sauce measures a scant 2 cups. Lower the heat and return sautéed seafoods and vegetables to the sauce. Simmer 2 or 3 minutes, then season with salt and white pepper, to taste, and cayenne pepper, if desired.

Divide the lobster mixture evenly among 4 ramekins or 4 lobster shells. Sprinkle with bread crumbs, and dot with remaining 2 tablespoons butter. Bake in a preheated 350 degree oven until lightly browned on top. Do not allow mixture to boil or sauce may separate.

Shrimp Omelet with Hot Gingered Fruit

Serves 4

Sheraton West Hotel
Indianapolis, Indiana

Shrimp Omelet:

> 6 tablespoons butter
> ½ pound small whole shrimp,
>   precooked, peeled, and deveined
> 1 teaspoon fresh lemon juice
> 8 large eggs

> ¼ cup milk
> ⅛ teaspoon curry powder
> ½ teaspoon salt
> ¼ teaspoon pepper
> Hot Gingered Fruits (recipe follows)

Melt 2 tablespoons butter in small skillet. Toss in shrimp; sprinkle lemon juice over them. Sauté shrimp quickly until just heated through. Keep warm.

Beat eggs, milk, curry powder, salt, and pepper with a fork or wire whisk until mixture is well combined.

Melt 1 tablespoon butter in omelet pan or skillet over high heat, until butter sizzles but is not yet brown. Pour in ¼ of the egg mixture. Let eggs settle a few seconds, then gently stir once or twice with a fork until eggs reach a soft custard consistency. Spoon 2 generous tablespoons warm shrimp down the center of the omelet, fold in half, and put on a warm plate or platter.

Repeat the process for the remaining three omelets. Garnish with any remaining shrimp.

Hot Gingered Fruits:

3 cups sliced fresh fruit
4 tablespoons butter
¼ cup light brown sugar, loosely
    packed
¼ teaspoon ginger

⅛ teaspoon salt
2 tablespoons lemon juice
Optional: *Raisins, sliced almonds*

Select firm but ripe fresh fruit, such as apples, peaches, pears, pineapples, and bananas. Core, peel when necessary, and slice into attractive shapes approximately ½ inch thick.

Melt butter over medium-high heat in a large skillet. Add brown sugar, ginger, and salt, stirring until sugar melts. Pour in the lemon juice. Fold in the fresh fruits and sauté 1 to 2 minutes, stirring gently. Finished fruit should be hot and well glazed, but still slightly firm inside. Serve sprinkled with raisins and almonds on top, if desired.

Hot Gingered Fruit is best served immediately, but it can rest up to 1 hour, then be gently reheated.

Side Dishes

Sweet Potatoes in Orange Baskets

Serves 4

Sheraton-Dallas Hotel
Dallas, Texas

4 large navel oranges
2 tablespoons unsalted butter,
    softened, plus 2 teaspoons
    unsalted butter, cut into bits
4 large sweet potatoes, boiled,
    peeled, and mashed

1 egg
4 teaspoons salt
½ teaspoon white pepper
¼ teaspoon grated lemon rind
2 tablespoons finely chopped walnuts

Preheat the oven to 350 degrees. With a sharp heavy knife, cut a 1-inch-deep slice from the stem end of each orange; discard cut slice. Squeeze the oranges, saving the juice for some other purpose. With a small sharp knife, scrape and cut away the pulp and membranes from the orange shells, keeping the shells intact and as regular in shape as possible. Set the shells side by side in a baking dish just large enough to hold them.

In a large mixing bowl, beat the softened butter into the mashed sweet potatoes, then beat in the egg, salt, white pepper, and lemon rind. Taste for seasoning. Fill each orange basket with the potato mixture, swirling the tops attractively with a rubber spatula. Sprinkle the filling with the walnuts, and dot with the butter bits, dividing the bits equally among the baskets. Bake in the center of the oven for 45 minutes, until the tops are lightly browned. Serve at once, with roast ham or chicken.

Jacques Carrot Soufflé

Serves 4–6

Sheraton Baton Rouge Hotel
Baton Rouge, Louisiana

Carrot soufflé makes a wonderful side dish for turkey, chicken, ham, even beef. Try it in place of sweet potatoes next time.

1 pound carrots, peeled and cut into
   1-inch chunks
4 large eggs
¾ cup all-purpose flour
⅛ teaspoon salt
1 teaspoon baking powder

½ cup sugar
1 tablespoon softened butter
2 teaspoons vanilla
1 teaspoon freshly grated nutmeg
2 to 3 tablespoons grated orange rind

Preheat oven to 350 degrees. Butter a 1-quart soufflé dish.

Boil carrots in a little water 20 to 30 minutes until tender. Drain and place carrots in a bowl, then whip them with an electric mixer until mashed. Let cool to room temperature, then mix in eggs, one at a time, beating 1 or 2 minutes after each egg is added.

Sift together the flour, salt, and baking powder. Mix into mashed carrots along with the sugar. Add softened butter, vanilla, and nutmeg, and continue to beat carrots until well combined.

Pour soufflé into buttered dish. Sprinkle with grated rind. Bake 40 minutes, or until soufflé has puffed and firmed. Serve at once.

Sweet Corn Fritters

Makes about 2 dozen fritters

Sheraton-Renton Inn
Seattle, Washington

These sweet corn fritters are perfect served with fried chicken, fried fish, barbecued beef, or other informal meals. They are even delicious at brunches. Serve them lightly coated with syrup or sprinkled with powdered sugar; or allow your guests to choose from various syrups and dress their own.

1½ cups sifted all-purpose flour
1½ teaspoons baking powder
¼ teaspoon baking soda
Pinch of salt
4 teaspoons sugar
2 eggs

6 to 8 tablespoons milk
½ cup whole kernel corn
½ cup creamed corn
Sufficient oil for deep frying
Serve with: *Flavored syrups,*
   powdered sugar

Mix together the flour, baking powder, soda, salt, and sugar. Place eggs in a medium-sized bowl and beat with electric mixer 30 seconds or so until frothy. Add 6 tablespoons milk and all dry ingredients. Stir and add whole kernel corn and creamed corn. Fritter batter should resemble thick pancake batter. If batter is too thick, beat in 1 or 2 tablespoons more milk, until desired consistency is reached.

Fill a deep heavy pan with 3 or 4 inches of oil. When oil reaches 350 degrees on a deep-fry thermometer, begin dropping in the batter, generous tablespoonful at a time. Fry a few fritters at a time for 2 to 3 minutes, until crisp, golden brown, and cooked through. Drain briefly on paper towels. Keep warm while frying remaining fritters. Serve fritters warm, with syrups, powdered sugar, or both.

Bavarian Village Bread

Serves 10–12

The Sheraton Centre
Toronto, Canada

This stuffed bread makes an informal luncheon possible whenever unexpected company drops by. Just take one or two of these stuffed loaves out of the freezer, slice, defrost, and serve with cold beer, pickles, and fresh fruit.

1 large loaf French bread
1 pound cooked ham, minced
1 pound cooked corned beef, minced
⅓ cup chopped green bell pepper
⅓ cup chopped red pimentos

¼ cup chopped fresh parsley
¾ cup butter, softened
Salt and pepper, to taste
2 large celery sticks, trimmed to fit
into french bread

Cut French bread in half (widthwise, not lengthwise). Using a long, slender knife, hollow out ¾ of the soft interior bread in each half. Save soft bread for other uses.

Mix all remaining ingredients together except the celery. Stand each bread half on end and pack firmly with stuffing. Push a celery stick down into each half until it is completely covered.

Tightly wrap each loaf in foil and freeze until hard. When ready to serve, unwrap the loaves and slice while still frozen into 1-inch-thick pieces. Place on serving plates and let stand 10 minutes to thaw. Stuffed bread has a tendency to crumble, so it is best served with knives and forks.

Desserts

Melon Balls Comtesse Sarah

Serves 10–12

Hotel Triumph-Sheraton
Toronto, Canada

2 2-pound cantaloupes, halved and
   seeded
1 cup apricot preserves

⅔ cup chilled Port wine
Garnish: *Fresh mint leaves*

Scoop out flesh of cantaloupes with a melon-ball cutter and place in bowl.

Melt apricot preserves in a heavy saucepan over medium heat. Slowly reduce to ⅔ cup of thick glaze, stirring occasionally. When reduced, remove glaze from heat and pour over the melon balls, stirring gently. Chill at least 1 hour.

Drain juice exuded by the melon before mixing in the chilled Port wine. Serve garnished with fresh mint leaves.

White Chocolate Mousse

Serves 12

Sheraton-Washington Hotel
Washington, D.C.

¼ pound white chocolate
1 tablespoon water
2 tablespoons clear Crème de Cacao
1½ cups heavy cream

4 egg whites, at room temperature
¼ cup sugar
Garnishes: *Toasted slivered almonds,*
   grated bittersweet chocolate

Place white chocolate and water in top of double boiler. Place pan over hot but not boiling water; stir chocolate gently until melted. Take pan off heat and stir in Crème de Cacao. Let cool.

Whip heavy cream until soft but firm peaks form. In a separate stainless-steel or copper bowl, whip the egg whites until soft peaks form, then gradually add sugar, beating until peaks become fairly stiff and satinlike. Gently fold the whites into whipped cream, drizzle over and fold in the chocolate mixture.

Spoon chocolate mousse into small dessert cups, cover with plastic wrap, and freeze. To serve, let mousse sit several minutes at room temperature to soften. Garnish with grated bittersweet chocolate and toasted almonds.

Black Bottom Pie

Makes one 9-inch pie

Sheraton-Dallas Hotel
Dallas, Texas

Black bottom pie takes its name from the rich layer of chocolate custard found at its bottom, hiding underneath a golden rum custard layer in turn concealed by a cloud of whipped cream. Each colorful layer complements the other in taste, texture and appeal. Although the recipe is lengthy, it is really quite simple to make, and every minute put into it is justified by every bite taken out.

Pie:

1 cup milk
¾ cup half-and-half
4 eggs, at room temperature, separated
½ cup sugar
1 tablespoon cornstarch
1 tablespoon gelatin
¼ cup cold water
2½ ounces semisweet chocolate
½ teaspoon vanilla

1 9-inch Chocolate Pie Crust (recipe follows)
⅛ teaspoon cream of tartar
¼ cup sugar
1 to 2 tablespoons rum, to taste
1 cup heavy cream
2 tablespoons confectioners' sugar
Garnish: ½ ounce shaved or grated semisweet chocolate

Bring the milk and the half-and-half to a boil and remove from heat. Place egg yolks in a heavy pan. Beat yolks several minutes with a portable electric mixer or whisk, until light. Mix the sugar and cornstarch together, then add to the egg yolks. Beat 1 to 2 minutes longer. Continue beating while slowly pouring in the hot milk and the half-and-half.

Place pan over low heat and cook about 15 minutes, stirring constantly with a spatula or a wooden spoon, until a custard forms that is thick enough to coat a spoon. Never allow the custard to boil or it will curdle.

When custard is done, remove pan from the heat. Soften gelatin in cold water for 2 to 3 minutes, then stir it well into the hot custard. Now take 1¼ cups hot custard out of the pan and place it in a bowl. Leave the remaining custard in the pan and set aside.

Slowly melt the chocolate in a small heavy saucepan over very low heat, stirring constantly. When melted, pour the chocolate very slowly, stirring constantly, into the 1¼ cups custard in the bowl. Add the vanilla. Pour chocolate custard into prepared pie shell and refrigerate to firm up.

Place egg whites in a clean dry copper or stainless-steel bowl. Beat eggs with a whisk or at medium speed in an electric mixer, until foamy. Sprinkle on cream of tartar. Beat faster until soft peaks form. When soft, begin adding ¼ cup sugar, 1 tablespoon at a time. Beat well after each addition, until a stiff, shiny meringue results.

Continued

If the custard remaining in the pan has not reached a stage looser than, but similar in thickness to, the meringue, place it in a shallow bowl of ice water and stir constantly until the custard reaches this thick, syrupy stage. On the other hand, if the custard is too stiff, place pan back over warm water and stir until it softens appropriately. Cool again if necessary.

Stir ¼ of the meringue into the custard, along with the rum. Then, using a very light touch, gently fold in the remaining meringue.

Spread rum layer over the chocolate layer. Chill 30 minutes or more until firm. When firm, whip the cream into soft peaks. Sprinkle on and beat in the confectioners' sugar. Spoon sweetened whipped cream on the top of the pie. Garnish with shaved or grated chocolate. Refrigerate until well chilled.

Chocolate Pie Crust:

> 4 tablespoons butter, melted
> 1⅓ cups chocolate wafer crumbs
>   (about 2 dozen wafers or cookies)

Pour melted butter into the cookie crumbs. Stir until all crumbs are moist. Press into a 9-inch pie plate. Bake at 350 degrees for 5 minutes. Remove and cool to room temperature.

Key Lime Pie

Makes one 9-inch pie

Sheraton Royal Biscayne Hotel
Key Biscayne, Florida

Small key limes, grown mainly in Florida, contribute a unique flavor to this pie. If key limes are unavailable, however, other limes may be substituted. Either way, a winner.

Set out the eggs and milk so that they reach room temperature. The custard will set faster, and the whites will whip higher, if the chill is off these ingredients.

> 2 eggs, separated
> 1 cup plus 2 tablespoons sugar
> ½ cup milk
> 1 tablespoon gelatin
> ½ cup key lime juice or other lime
>   juice

> 1 teaspoon grated lime rind
> 2 cups heavy cream
> 1 9-inch baked Graham Cracker
>   Crust (recipe, page 282)
> 1 teaspoon vanilla
> Garnish: *Lime twists*

In the top of a double boiler, mix the egg yolks, ½ cup sugar, and the milk. Place over simmering hot water. Do not allow the water to touch the bottom of the pan holding the yolks. Stir constantly, using a whisk, 10 to 15 minutes, until eggs form a loose, frothy custard sauce, thick enough to coat a spoon.

Mix together the gelatin, lime juice, and lime rind. Let sit 1 to 2 minutes to soften, then add to warm custard. Cook and stir the custard about 1 minute, until the gelatin is dissolved and well blended. Remove pan from heat and cool mixture down to room temperature.

While custard is cooling, whip 1 cup heavy cream into soft but firm peaks. This will make 2 cups whipped cream. Set aside briefly.

Place egg whites in a clean dry copper or stainless-steel bowl. Beat on medium speed until foamy, then raise speed and beat until soft peaks form. Begin beating in ½ cup sugar, a tablespoon at a time, until peaks become firm and satinlike.

If, at this point, the custard has not reached a consistency that resembles very loosely whipped cream (or thin mayonnaise), hasten the process by placing custard pan in a bowl of ice water. Stir custard constantly until thickened properly. Watch carefully that you do not go beyond this consistency or custard will have to be rewarmed to soften, then cooled again.

Fold the 2 cups whipped cream into the properly thickened egg-custard mixture. Then gently fold in the stiff egg whites. Pour the mixture into prepared Graham Cracker Crust. Chill until firm. When firm, whip remaining cup of cream with 2 tablespoons sugar and the vanilla until soft peaks form.

Spread cream on top of lime filling, mounding attractively in the center. Chill well before serving garnished with twisted lime slices.

Caroline's Delight
(Walnut Meringue Ice Cream Pie)

Makes one 9-inch pie

Sheraton-Center Inn
Charlotte, North Carolina

Meringues are best baked on fairly dry days, so select a not too humid day to create this dream-come-true ice cream pie. The chewy meringue, luscious ice cream, and velvety rich caramel sauce will have dinner guests enraptured and asking for seconds.

Ice Cream Pie:

2 egg whites, at room temperature
Pinch of salt
1½ cups loosely packed light brown
  sugar
½ cup finely chopped walnuts
½ pint (1 cup) high-quality coffee ice
  cream, slightly softened

2 pints (4 cups) high-quality vanilla
  ice cream, slightly softened
Caramel Sauce (recipe follows)
Garnish: 2 tablespoons toasted
  slivered almonds

Lightly butter a 9-inch pie plate. Preheat oven to 325 degrees.

Place egg whites in a clean dry copper or stainless-steel bowl. Beat on medium speed until foamy. Sprinkle in salt, raise speed, and beat until soft peaks form. When egg whites are soft,

Continued

begin beating in the brown sugar, 1 tablespoon at a time. Beat each tablespoon in well before adding the next, all of which should take approximately 5 minutes. Finally, fold in the chopped nuts.

Scoop the meringue into the prepared pie plate. Press out with a spatula to form thick walls and a bottom. Place meringue shell in the oven, lower temperature to 300 degrees, and bake 35 to 45 minutes, until meringue puffs slightly and turns crisp on the outside. It should still be slightly soft inside.

Take meringue shell out of the oven and place it in a draft-free location to cool. When cool, place meringue in freezer to harden so that the bottom of the shell will not be crushed when the ice cream is added.

Once hard, spread the softened coffee ice cream in the bottom of the shell, then the vanilla, mounding nicely in the center. Freeze until firm. Because of the meringue, the pie is best served the same day.

To serve, take the pie out of the freezer and let it sit at room temperature several minutes, to soften the meringue slightly. Present Caroline's Delight topped with warm caramel sauce and toasted almonds, or cut pie into wedges and serve, passing sauce and toasted almonds.

Caramel Sauce:

2 tablespoons butter
1 cup dark brown sugar
¼ cup water

¼ cup evaporated milk
½ teaspoon vanilla

Place butter, sugar, and water in a small heavy saucepan. Bring to a boil over medium to medium-high heat. Boil gently 8 to 10 minutes, until mixture just reaches the firm ball stage (245 degrees on a candy thermometer).

Remove pan from heat; stir approximately 1 minute to cool down slightly. Slowly drizzle in evaporated milk and vanilla, stirring constantly. Serve either warm or cold. If the sauce is not used immediately, it may be refrigerated, then reheated.

Rum Pecan Pie

Makes one 9-inch pie

Huntington-Sheraton Hotel
Pasadena, California

⅓ cup butter, softened to room
   temperature
2 cups powdered sugar
2 egg yolks, at room temperature
¼ cup dark rum
½ teaspoon vanilla
⅛ teaspoon salt

1½ teaspoons gelatin
2 tablespoons warm water
2 cups (about 7 ounces) chopped
   pecans
1¼ cups heavy cream, whipped
1 9-inch baked Graham Cracker
   Crust (recipe, page 282)

Using an electric mixer set on medium speed, blend the butter, sugar, egg yolks, rum, vanilla, and salt. When blended, turn speed to high and whip well 8 to 10 minutes.

Meanwhile, soften gelatin in warm water for 1 or 2 minutes. Beating constantly, slowly add the softened gelatin to the egg-rum mixture. Continue beating, 1 to 2 minutes to distribute the gelatin evenly.

Stir in most of the nuts, saving some for garnish. Then fold in 2 cups whipped cream. Pour filling into the baked Graham Cracker Crust; top with remaining whipped cream and reserved nuts.

Refrigerate at least 2 hours, until well chilled.

Shoofly Pie

Makes one 9-inch pie

*Sheraton Lancaster Resort
Lancaster, Pennsylvania*

This recipe calls for unsulfured or light molasses, which makes a distinct but pleasant Shoofly Pie. If a more subtle molasses taste is desired, substitute light corn syrup for some or all of the first half-cup of molasses in the recipe.

*1 egg, lightly beaten
½ teaspoon all-purpose flour
½ teaspoon baking soda
½ cup cold water
1 cup unsulfured or light molasses
1½ cups all-purpose flour
½ cup light brown sugar, firmly
    packed*

*5 tablespoons butter
½ cup boiling water
1 9-inch unbaked Basic Pastry Shell
    (recipe, page 280)*

Preheat oven to 350 degrees. Place egg, ½ teaspoon flour, baking soda, cold water, and ½ cup molasses in a bowl and stir to blend well. Set aside.

Work together the 1½ cups flour, brown sugar, and butter, using a pastry blender, fork, or your fingers until mixture is fine, light, and crumbly in texture. Remove 1¼ cups crumbs and set aside to be used as a topping. To the remaining crumbs in the bowl, add ½ cup molasses mixed with boiling water. Stir well with a whisk or fork, then add in the cold molasses mixture. Mixture will be thin.

Pour the combined filling into the unbaked pie shell. Sprinkle evenly with reserved crumbs. Bake 45 to 60 minutes, or until center of pie has firmed up.

Serve pie warm with vanilla ice cream.

New York Cheesecake

Serves 10–12

New York Sheraton Hotel
New York, New York

Americans' love of cheesecake is more than justified by this simple yet sinfully rich version.

1 tablespoon softened butter	*½ teaspoon vanilla*
½ cup graham cracker crumbs	*2 teaspoons freshly grated lemon rind*
12 ounces cream cheese	*2 cups light cream, or 1 cup of half-and-*
¾ cup sugar	*half and 1 cup heavy cream*
5 eggs	*Garnish: Fresh strawberries, whole or*
1 tablespoon fresh lemon juice	*puréed*

Preheat oven to 325 degrees. Thoroughly butter the bottom and sides of a 9-inch-square metal cake pan or other 10-cup, square-cornered pan. (Do not use a spring-form pan or the cheese-cake may leak, spelling disaster for the cake and the cook!) Pour in the graham cracker crumbs. Tip pan in all directions to coat well with crumbs. Turn pan upside down and tap lightly to release excess crumbs. Set aside.

Using an electric mixer set on medium-high speed, whip together the cream cheese and sugar until light and fluffy, 2 to 3 minutes. Add the eggs, one at a time, beating well after each addition, scraping down the sides of the bowl occasionally. Pour in lemon juice, vanilla, and lemon rind. Mix approximately 1 minute longer. Finally, stir in the cream. Mixture will be quite loose.

Slowly pour cheesecake mixture into the crumb-lined pan. Set in a much larger, shallow baking pan and place in preheated oven. Fill large baking pan with ¾ to ½ inch of hot water. Close oven door and bake cheesecake approximately 1½ hours, until pie is firm in the center and nicely browned on top. Remove cheesecake from the oven and set it aside on a wire rack to cool. When cool, refrigerate until well chilled, several hours or overnight.

To serve, cut cheesecake into desired portions and place on dessert plates. Top with whole fresh strawberries or with a sweetened strawberry purée.

Strawberry Short Cake

Serves 10-12

Sheraton Harbor Island Hotel
San Diego, California

This is a sophisticated version of that well-loved favorite, strawberry short cake. Prepare it for formal occasions that call for a special dessert.

*Two 9-inch Strawberry Sponge
    Cakes (recipe, page 282)*
2 or more ounces kirsch, to taste
1 quart heavy cream

¼ cup sugar
4 cups sliced fresh strawberries
8 ounces sliced toasted almonds
10 to 12 whole strawberries

Slice each sponge cake in half horizontally, creating 4 layers. Brush or sprinkle each layer of sponge cake with a tablespoon or more of kirsch, to taste.

Whip the cream gently until it begins to thicken. Sprinkle the sugar on it and beat until the cream is soft but firm peaks form.

Turn over the browned top of one cake layer and place it, brown side down, on a serving plate. (Save the other brown top layer for the fourth layer of the cake.)

Spread a generous cup of sweetened whipped cream over the layer, then top with ⅓ of the sliced berries. Place a second layer of cake over the berries; smooth over it a generous cup of the cream and ⅓ of the berries. Follow the same pattern with the third layer, using the last of the sliced berries. Top with the fourth and final cake layer, brown side up. Spread most of the remaining cream on the sides and top of the cake, reserving some for cream swirls. Pat sliced toasted almonds onto the side of the cake.

Put remaining whipped cream in a pastry bag and pipe swirls onto the top. Place whole strawberries on top of or beside the swirls. Chill well before serving.

Bread Pudding with Rum Sauce

Serves 6–8

*Sheraton-New Orleans Hotel
New Orleans, Louisiana*

Bread Pudding:

3 cups milk
10 cups bread cubes
1⅔ cups raisins
½ cup pecans, minced
½ stick butter, melted
4 eggs

1 cup sugar
¼ teaspoon vanilla
¼ teaspoon allspice
¼ teaspoon nutmeg
1¼ teaspoons cinnamon
¼ teaspoon salt

In a 4-quart pot, scald milk and let cool for several minutes. Add the bread, raisins, pecans, and butter and blend well. In a separate bowl, beat the eggs and combine them with the remaining ingredients, blending until they are mixed well. Add egg mixture to the bread mixture.

Continued

Preheat oven to 350 degrees. Grease well an 8x8-inch-square cake pan. Pour pudding mixture into pan and cook for approximately 1½ hours. Test for doneness by inserting a straw in the center of the pan to see if it comes out clean; if not, bake longer. The top should be a moderate brown color when done. Serve with hot Rum Sauce.

Rum Sauce:

¾ cup sugar
½ cup water

¾ stick sweet butter
¾ cup dark rum

Cook the sugar, water, and butter 5 minutes. Gradually add the rum and cook 2 minutes longer. Serve hot over the bread pudding.

Hawaii

Soups

Hot and Sour Soup
Princess Kaiulani Hotel
Honolulu, Hawaii
Yokohama Soup
Moana Hotel
Honolulu, Hawaii

Salads

Salad Mauna Loa
Volcano House
Hawaii Volcanoes National Park, Hawaii

Side Dishes

Macadamia Nut Dressing for Turkey
Princess Kaiulani Hotel
Honolulu, Hawaii

Entrees

Mahi Mahi Florentine
Volcano House
Hawaii Volcanoes National Park, Hawaii
Seafood Curry Keaukaha
Sheraton-Waiakea Village Hotel
Hilo, Hawaii
Baked Pork King Kalakaua
Sheraton-Maui Hotel
Maui, Hawaii
Lemon Chicken Royale
Royal Hawaiian Hotel
Honolulu, Hawaii

Desserts

Molokoff Cake
Royal Hawaiian Hotel
Honolulu, Hawai
Macadamia Nut Cream Pie
Royal Hawaiian Hotel
Honolulu, Hawaii
Strawberries Sabayon
Sheraton Waikiki Hotel
Honolulu, Hawaii

Hawaii

Hawaii plays host to the full spectrum of international tastes. The truly native foods predominate at a luau, the Hawaiian feast, which is described in the party section of this book. In addition, the mixture of ethnic cultures in Hawaii has produced exotic culinary treats flavored with liqueurs and wines, oriental spices, and the piquancy of native fruits and nuts.

Soups

Hot and Sour Soup

Serves 8

Princess Kaiulani Hotel
Honolulu, Hawaii

6 cups Chicken Stock (recipe, page 279)
2 tablespoons white wine vinegar
1 tablespoon soy sauce
2 ounces shredded lean pork
12 ounces soybean curd cakes, drained and shredded
1/4 cup shredded bamboo shoots
1 teaspoon shredded fresh ginger root

1 teaspoon salt
1 teaspoon white pepper
2 tablespoons cornstarch
4 tablespoons water
1 egg, lightly beaten
Garnishes: Minced green onions, sesame oil

Bring chicken stock to a gentle boil. Add vinegar, soy sauce, pork, curd cakes, bamboo shoots, ginger root, salt, and pepper. Bring to a second, very gentle boil.

Mix cornstarch and water; stir into the soup. Heat briefly, but do *not* boil. Drizzle in the beaten egg, stirring to help it form threads as it cooks.

Serve hot, passing minced green onions and sesame oil. Instruct guests to sprinkle soup lightly with the onions, and add just a drop or two of the oil to taste.

Yokohama Soup

Serves 6

Moana Hotel
Honolulu, Hawaii

2 tablespoons butter
2 tablespoons finely chopped shallots
1 tablespoon all-purpose flour
2 cups Fish Stock (recipe, page 280)
2 cups clam juice
½ cup heavy cream

½ cup dry white wine
2 teaspoons finely chopped cooked
 spinach
Salt and pepper, to taste
Topping: *1 cup heavy cream,*
 whipped

Melt butter in a heavy saucepan over medium heat. Add shallots and sauté 1 minute. Sprinkle on flour and cook 5 minutes longer, stirring to prevent scorching. Add remaining soup ingredients. Bring to a gentle boil and season to taste.

Let soup cool down slightly before pouring into 6 one-cup ovenproof bowls. Top with whipped cream. (Cream should come up to bowl's lip.) Quickly place under broiler and glaze until whipped cream is lightly browned. Serve immediately.

Salads

Salad Mauna Loa

Serves 4

Volcano House
Hawaii Volcanoes National Park, Hawaii

3 ounces fresh spinach
2 cups coarsely shredded red
 cabbage
1 medium avocado, peeled, and sliced

2 hard-cooked eggs, cut into wedges
Cherry tomatoes
Vinaigrette dressing

Toss spinach leaves with shredded cabbage. Mound vegetables on a salad plate and surround alternately with avocado slices and egg wedges. Top with cherry tomatoes and your own vinaigrette dressing and serve.

Side Dishes

Macadamia Nut Dressing for Turkey

Makes 1 quart

Princess Kaiulani Hotel
Honolulu, Hawaii

While your cooked turkey is resting, prepare this moist, nut-flavored dressing to be served on the side.

¼ cup turkey drippings
½ cup chopped onions
¾ cup chopped celery
1 quart dry bread cubes
½ cup chopped macadamia nuts
Optional: ½ cup or more diced pineapple

1 cup turkey giblet stock, at room temperature
2 eggs, lightly beaten
½ teaspoon salt
½ teaspoon white pepper

Pour the turkey drippings into a very large frying pan. Sauté onions and celery until tender but still slightly crisp. Stir bread cubes, macadamia nuts, and pineapple, if desired, into the onions and celery. Pour over the stock and beaten eggs. Fold in thoroughly. Season with salt and pepper. Serve the dressing in a warmed casserole.

Entrees

Mahi Mahi Florentine

Serves 6

Volcano House
Hawaii Volcanoes National Park, Hawaii

Mahi Mahi, known also as dolphin, is a fish unrelated to the dolphin mammal. Mahi Mahi flourishes off the coasts of Hawaii and in the warm waters of the Pacific and Atlantic. It has a firm white flesh and is known for its slightly sweet taste. Mahi Mahi is not available everywhere, although you may be able to find frozen Mahi Mahi steaks. If not, you can substitute firm white-fleshed seafish, but the taste will not be quite the same.

Continued

Mahi Mahi Florentine:

6 skinned Mahi Mahi steaks or fillets,
   about ½ pound each
1½ teaspoons salt
¾ teaspoon white pepper
1 large onion, peeled and thinly sliced
4 tablespoons butter
½ cup dry white wine

Mahi Mahi Mornay Sauce (recipe
   below)
3 pounds fresh spinach, washed,
   stemmed, and patted fairly dry
Paprika
Garnish: *Lemon wedges*

Preheat oven to 350 degrees. Season fish with a mixture of 1 teaspoon salt and ½ teaspoon white pepper. Lay onion slices in the bottom of a large, shallow buttered baking dish. Arrange seasoned Mahi Mahi on top. Melt 2 tablespoons butter. Pour butter and wine over fish. Cover dish with tin foil and bake in preheated oven approximately 25 minutes, or until fish is cooked through.

While fish is baking, or even several hours ahead, prepare the mornay sauce (recipe below). Just before fish is taken out of the oven, make the spinach bed.

Place remaining 2 tablespoons butter in a deep pot. Add spinach, ½ teaspoon salt, and ¼ teaspoon white pepper. Cover and cook over medium heat, stirring occasionally, until spinach has wilted and is tender.

When fish is done, place wilted spinach on a warm platter, arrange Mahi Mahi on top, scatter onions over the fish, and coat with mornay sauce. Sprinkle with paprika for color and garnish with lemon wedges.

Mahi Mahi Mornay Sauce:

4 tablespoons butter
4 tablespoons all-purpose flour
2 cups milk
½ teaspoon salt

¼ teaspoon white pepper
1 teaspoon Worcestershire sauce
⅓ cup freshly grated Parmesan
   cheese

Melt butter over medium heat in a heavy saucepan. Add flour. Cook, stirring constantly, 4 to 5 minutes. Still stirring, preferably with a whisk or a wooden spoon, slowly pour in the milk. Simmer sauce 20 to 25 minutes, stirring occasionally to prevent scorching. Season with salt and pepper, add Worcestershire and grated cheese. Simmer 5 minutes longer, stirring frequently.

If completed sauce is thicker than desired, thin out with small additions of milk.

Seafood Curry Keaukaha

(Seafood Curry in Pineapple Boats)

Serves 8

Sheraton-Waiakea Village Hotel
Hilo, Hawaii

Curry Sauce:

1 cup chopped onions
1 teaspoon minced garlic
1 tablespoon oil
4 teaspoons curry powder
1 green cooking apple, peeled, cored, and chopped
2 tablespoons peeled, chopped cucumber
2 large carrots, peeled and chopped

2 tablespoons chopped pimentos
2 cups Chicken Stock (recipe, page 270)
4 tablespoons butter
4 tablespoons all-purpose flour
1 cup Coconut Milk (recipe, page 277)
1 cup heavy cream

Sauté chopped onions and garlic in hot oil for 2 to 3 minutes. Stir in curry powder and sauté 1 minute longer. Add chopped apple, cucumber, carrots, and pimento. Pour in chicken stock. Bring mixture to a boil, then lower heat and simmer 30 minutes. Purée mixture in food processor or blender until smooth, velvetlike consistency results. Set curry mixture aside.

Melt butter over medium-high heat in large heavy saucepan. Stirring constantly, blend in flour, cooking roux for 3 or 4 minutes, then stir in coconut milk and cream. Add curry mixture, reduce heat to medium, and simmer sauce for 20 minutes, stirring occasionally.

Seafood Keaukaha:

2 or more tablespoons butter
1½ pounds large raw shrimp, shelled and deveined
1½ pounds scallops, cut in half if large
1 pound firm white-fleshed saltwater fish, such as halibut, Mahi Mahi, or sea bass, skinned, boned, and cut into 1-inch chunks

4 small-sized pineapples
Garnish: shredded coconut toasted

Preheat oven to 375 degrees. Melt 2 tablespoons butter over medium heat in a large skillet. Add the shrimp and sauté just until shrimp turn pink. Remove and set shrimp aside. In the same pan, sauté scallops just until cooked through, adding more butter if necessary. Set scallops aside with the shrimp. Lastly, sauté fish, using more butter if necessary, until cooked through.

Continued

When all fish is cooked, pour off any fish juices that are in the pan. Return shrimp and scallops to the pan with the fish. Add 2 or more cups curry sauce to the seafood. Simmer approximately 5 minutes on low heat. Correct seasonings to taste.

Cut pineapples in half lengthwise. Remove ¾ of the pineapple meat from each side, saving the meat for other uses. Turn pineapples over and drain the shells briefly. Place shells in a 375-degree oven to warm through. Spoon equal amounts of filling into each shell. Serve immediately, garnish with toasted shredded coconut.

Baked Pork King Kalakaua

Serves 4

Sheraton-Maui Hotel
Maui, Hawaii

A creamy blend of sophisticated flavors makes this a dish for regal occasions.

2 cups Béchamel Sauce (recipe, page 275)
½ cup dry white wine
¼ teaspoon tarragon
1½ pounds pork tenderloin, cut into 8 (3-ounce) fillets
3 large garlic cloves, peeled
2 teaspoons salt
½ teaspoon pepper

¼ cup minced shallots
2 tablespoons butter
¼ pound small shrimp, shelled and cooked
⅓ pound shredded crabmeat
¼ teaspoon dry mustard
4 ounces cream cheese, cut into 8 slices

Combine béchamel sauce, white wine, and tarragon in a small saucepan and keep warm. Preheat the oven to 350 degrees.

Place fillets between two pieces of waxed paper. Pound each fillet on both sides until thin. Crush garlic cloves and mash them with the salt and pepper. Rub the garlic paste onto one side of each slice of meat.

Over medium heat, sauté shallots in butter briefly until tender. Add shrimp and crabmeat; sprinkle on the mustard. Stirring to blend, cook briefly to warm the shrimp and crabmeat. Then add ½ cup of the warm béchamel sauce. Remove from the heat.

To assemble, place a thin slice of cream cheese on each of four pieces of the pounded pork tenderloin. Spread equal amounts of shrimp and crab stuffing over the cheese-covered meat. Top the filling with another slice of the cream cheese, then cover with a second piece of pork.

Place the Pork King Kalakaua in a shallow greased baking dish. Pour over the remaining 1½ cups béchamel sauce. Bake in the preheated oven for 30 minutes, or until the pork is cooked through.

Lemon Chicken Royale

Serves 4–6

Royal Hawaiian Hotel
Honolulu, Hawaii

This dish has the clean, pure taste of well-prepared Oriental food. Make the sauce ahead to save your last-minute efforts for frying the chicken.

Chicken Royale:

2½ pounds chicken breasts, skinned
   and boned
1½ pounds chicken thighs, skinned
   and boned
4 tablespoons brandy
2 teaspoons minced fresh ginger root
1 teaspoon salt

⅛ teaspoon white pepper
1 egg, lightly beaten
¾ cup cornstarch (approximately)
Sufficient oil for deep frying
Lemon Sauce (recipe below)
Garnish: *Thin lemon slices*

Lightly pound the chicken, then cut into strips 1 inch wide. Put the chicken strips into a bowl. Mix in the brandy, ginger root, salt, and white pepper. Refrigerate 2 to 3 hours, allowing flavors time to permeate the chicken.

After marinating, drain the meat well and discard the marinade. Return chicken to the bowl. Stir in the egg, coating each chicken piece lightly. Take chicken out of the bowl and coat each strip with cornstarch.

Pour sufficient oil into a deep heavy saucepan to reach a depth of 2 or 3 inches. Deep-fry the chicken at approximately 375 degrees, until it is golden brown and cooked through. Drain well and keep warm.

Serve the chicken hot, with Lemon Sauce poured over it. Garnish with lemon slices.

Lemon Sauce

1 clove garlic, peeled
1 tablespoon vegetable oil
½ cup freshly squeezed lemon juice
½ cup Chicken Stock (recipe, page
   279)

½ cup sugar
1 tablespoon cornstarch
1 tablespoon water

In a small saucepan over medium heat, sauté the garlic clove in the oil for 2 or 3 minutes to flavor the oil. Remove and discard the garlic. Add the lemon juice, chicken stock, and sugar to the oil. Gently simmer for several minutes.

Dissolve the cornstarch in a tablespoon of water. Whisk this mixture into the hot sauce and simmer, stirring, several minutes longer to thicken the sauce. You will have a generous cup of sauce to serve warm over the chicken.

Desserts

Molokoff Cake

Makes one 8-inch cake

Royal Hawaiian Hotel
Honolulu, Hawaii

Cake:
40 ladyfingers sprinkled with cognac

Place a layer of 10 ladyfingers on the bottom of the cake pan. Cover with ½ inch of the filling (recipe below). Place another layer of ladyfingers on top of this, and cover again with ½ inch of filling. Repeat this procedure once more.

Press down on ladyfingers, so that cake will take form, then refrigerate for about 3 hours to allow cake to set.

Filling:

8 ounces unsalted butter	½ cup sugar
5 egg yolks	2 tablespoons honey
3 cups chopped, roasted	1¼ ounces cognac
macadamia nuts	1 cup whipped cream

Whip butter for about 10 minutes, until creamy and light. Add the egg yolks very slowly, one at a time, mixing them with the creamed butter. Blend the macadamia nuts, sugar, honey, and cognac into the mixture. Mix in the whipped cream. Do *not* overmix.

Frosting:

2 cups whipped cream	Chocolate truffles
Chopped macadamia nuts	

Take cake out of the cake pan. Use the whipped cream, beaten very stiff as frosting. Cover the frosting with chopped macadamia nuts and garnish the side of the cake with chocolate truffles.

Macadamia Nut Cream Pie

Makes one 9-inch pie

Royal Hawaiian Hotel
Honolulu, Hawaii

From the kitchens of this elegant "Grand Hotel" in the heart of Waikiki Beach comes a delicious dessert that combines Hawaii's famous macadamia nut with the smooth taste of coffee liqueur.

1 9-inch Rich Pastry Shell (recipe,
    page 281)
½ cup sugar
4 tablespoons sifted cornstarch
½ teaspoon salt
2 cups milk

4 egg yolks, lightly beaten
1 tablespoon butter
2 tablespoons Kahlua liqueur
¾ cup (4 ounces) macadamia nuts
2 cups whipped cream

Prepare and bake Rich Pastry Shell according to the recipe. Combine the sugar, cornstarch, and salt in top of a double boiler. Slowly add milk, stirring constantly. Place over gently boiling water and cook 10 to 15 minutes. Stir constantly until mixture thickens to a loose custard consistency.

Blend ½ cup of the hot sugar mixture into the beaten egg yolks, 1 tablespoon at a time. Slowly pour and beat the warm egg mixture back into the remaining sugar mixture. Continue cooking 3 to 5 minutes, until the custard is quite thick. Add the butter; cool to room temperature.

When cool, stir in the Kahlua liqueur and all but 1 tablespoon of the chopped nuts. Fold in 1 cup whipped cream. Fill the baked pastry shell; garnish with the remaining whipped cream and reserved nuts. Chill.

Strawberries Sabayon

Serves 6

Sheraton Waikiki Hotel
Honolulu, Hawaii

Strawberries Sabayon is another very special Sheraton dessert. Although it requires some last-minute attention, it is well worth the effort.

1 quart vanilla ice cream
1½ pounds fresh strawberries, rinsed
    and hulled
¾ cup sugar

2 tablespoons Grand Marnier
6 egg yolks
⅓ cup sweet Marsala wine
⅓ cup dry white wine

Advance Work:

Spoon approximately ½ cup ice cream into 6 large crystal bowls or goblets. Store in freezer until needed.

Place strawberries in a large bowl, sprinkle on ¼ cup sugar and the Grand Marnier. Cover and refrigerate at least 2 hours, turning occasionally.

Place egg yolks and ½ cup sugar in top of a large double boiler. Set aside. Measure out the Marsala and white wine.

Continued

Sabayon Preparation:

Beat yolks and sugar with portable electric mixer or whisk for 2 or 3 minutes, until thick and pale yellow. Pour in the wines; place pan over hot but not boiling water. Beat yolks constantly until you see them begin to foam and rise (about 5 minutes). Keep beating another 3 to 5 minutes until sabayon doubles or more in bulk and becomes quite thick and airy.

Distribute marinated strawberries over the ice cream, spooning on some of the strawberry juices. Top with generous portions of warm sabayon and serve immediately.

Menu Suggestions

An Elegant Luncheon

Pâté de Volaille Suprême
(page 29)

Cornichons   Radish roses

Watercress

Palace Court Salad
(page 35)

Peach Colada Frappé
(page 270)

An American Sunday Dinner

Pied Piper Sour
(page 270)

Fresh Broccoli Salad Royale
(page 34)

Slow-Roasted Prime Ribs of Beef
(page 41)

Baked potatoes   Sautéed string beans

New York Cheesecake
(page 70)

Continued

An Intimate Dinner

Fennel with Special Dressing
(page 34)

Homard du Ciel
(page 59)

Creamed rice   Kumquats

White Chocolate Mousse
(page 64)

That Special Dinner

Escargots en Croûte
(page 30)

Watercress Soup
(page 40)

Fillet of Pork with Pears
(page 48)

White rice   Young peas

Key Lime Pie
(page 66)

A Hawaiian Dinner

Hot and Sour Soup
(page 75)

Seafood Curry Keaukaha
(page 79)

White Rice

Waikoloa Coffee
(page 273)

The Cuisine of Latin America

Latin America

Appetizers

Ceviche
Lima-Sheraton Hotel
Lima, Peru

Salads

Rice Salad
Rio-Sheraton Hotel
Rio de Janeiro, Brazil

Soups

Black Bean Soup
Rio-Sheraton Hotel
Rio de Janeiro, Brazil
Sopa de Camarón
Lima-Sheraton Hotel
Lima, Peru
Gazpacho Maria Isabel
Maria Isabel-Sheraton Hotel
Mexico City, Mexico

Entrees

El Cid Tenderloin Fillets
Sheraton - San Cristobal Hotel
Santiago, Chile
Lomo à la Huancaina
Lima-Sheraton Hotel
Lima, Peru

Tournedos Martini
Guadalajara Sheraton
Guadalajara, Mexico
Fruit Carbonade
Buenos Aires-Sheraton Hotel
Buenos Aires, Argentina
Rio Grande Chili Beef
Maria Isabel-Sheraton Hotel
Mexico City, Mexico
Brazilian Feijoada
Rio-Sheraton Hotel
Rio de Janeiro, Brazil
Roast Loin of Pork à l'Ail
El Salvador-Sheraton Hotel
San Salvador, El Salvador
Macuto Chicken
Macuto-Sheraton Hotel
Caracas, Venezuela
Xim Xim Chicken
Rio-Sheraton Hotel
Rio de Janeiro, Brazil
Seafood Morsel
Sheraton - San Cristobal Hotel
Santiago, Chile
Shrimp Bahia Style
Rio-Sheraton Hotel
Rio de Janeiro, Brazil

Side Dishes

Ocopa à l'Arequipeña
Lima-Sheraton Hotel
Lima, Peru
Zucchini and Tomato Egg Scramble
Buenos Aires-Sheraton Hotel
Buenos Aires, Argentina
Continued

Sauces

Shrimp-Coconut Sauce
Rio-Sheraton Hotel
Rio de Janeiro, Brazil
Spicy Parsley Sauce
Lima-Sheraton Hotel
Lima, Peru

Desserts

Peach Meringue Cake
Sheraton-San Cristobal Hotel
Santiago, Chile

Pastelitos de Coco
La Paz-Sheraton Hotel
La Paz, Bolivia
Ambrosia
Buenos Aires-Sheraton Hotel
Buenos Aires, Argentina
Hot Kahlua Soufflé
Maria Isabel-Sheraton Hotel
Mexico City, Mexico
Paloma Blanca
Santo Domingo-Sheraton Hotel
Santo Domingo, Dominican Republic
Suspiros à la Limeña
Lima-Sheraton Hotel
Lima, Peru

The Cuisine of
Latin America

Latin America has been and continues to be a continent of diverse people and cultures. Each group has contributed the culinary art particular to its native environment and tradition. Most South American countries have two distinct types of cooking. One stems from European sources, and the other—*criolla,* or creole style—dates back to earlier days. In this book you will find a bit of both—from Kahlua Soufflé to Fruit Carbonade.

Mexico boasts its Rio Grande Chili Beef, Gazpacho (a delicious summer soup), and excellent seafood, and invites you to a typical fiesta with margaritas, tortillas, and Yucatan Black Bean Dip in the party chapter.

Brazilian cooking still possesses a distinct national character. Many of the dishes, while Portuguese in origin, are definitely African in seasoning and handling. Those who have tasted beef in Argentina claim, very justly, that its flavor and preparation there is unsurpassed. Chile offers a mixture of meats and excellent seafood. Ocean fish prepared Peruvian-style, known as Ceviche, combines the taste of lemon and lime with spices and onions. This, together with many other native dishes, will satisfy the most demanding gourmet. Then, there are recipes from Bolivia, Venezuela, the Dominican Republic—all in all a wealth of both innovative and traditional Latin dishes to sample.

Appetizers

Ceviche
(Marinated Raw Fish)

Serves 10

Lima-Sheraton Hotel
Lima Peru

Ceviche is a spicy raw fish mixture cooked by the chemical action of the lemon and lime juices. Peruvians typically serve this cold hors d'oeuvre with hot boiled corn and sweet potatoes. A special feature of this Ceviche is the "popped," or toasted, corn.

3 pounds firm, fresh white-fleshed saltwater fish	2 cups finely chopped onions
1¼ cups fresh lemon juice	1 pound sweet potatoes
1¼ cups fresh lime juice	4 ears fresh corn, cut into 2-inch-thick rounds
1¾ teaspoons salt	1 tablespoon vegetable oil
⅛ teaspoon pepper	½ cup fresh corn kernels, cut off the cob
2 fresh hot chilies, seeded and cut into thin strips	2 heads soft lettuce (Boston, redleaf, etc.)
1 tablespoon chili powder	

Peel, bone, and cut fish into small pieces. Place in a large deep strainer and pour 2 cups boiling water over fish. Let drain 2 or 3 minutes, then turn fish out into a deep glass or china bowl.

Make marinade out of lemon and lime juices, salt, pepper, chili strips, chili powder, and onions. Mix all together; pour over fish. If fish is not completely immersed, add more lemon and lime juices. Cover and refrigerate about 4 hours, until all fish is firm and white.

About 25 or 30 minutes before fish is through marinating, prepare the garnishes. Begin by boiling whole sweet potatoes 25 minutes, or until tender. Drain, peel, and slice into 2-inch-thick rounds. Boil cut corn rounds a few minutes until tender, then drain.

Heat 1 tablespoon oil in a heavy frying pan. When hot, add the fresh corn kernels. Stir frequently, until corn begins to brown and starts "popping" in the pan. Remove pan from heat.

Arrange lettuce leaves on a large serving platter or individual plates. Remove fish from marinade with slotted spoon and lay on lettuce leaves. Scatter sweet potato and corn rounds on edges of plates. Serve with toasted corn sprinkled on top.

Salads

Rice Salad

Serves 4–6

Rio-Sheraton Hotel
Rio de Janeiro, Brazil

2 cups cold cooked rice
1 tart green apple, julienned
½ avocado, peeled and sliced
1 cup canned peas, drained
1 tablespoon chopped pimento
1 tablespoon lemon juice
1 tablespoon vinegar

2 tablespoons olive oil
1 teaspoon prepared mustard
Salt and pepper, to taste
Heart of lettuce
Garnish: *Cooked beets, shrimp, or*
  hard-cooked eggs

Mix the rice with the fruits and vegetables. Make a dressing of lemon juice, vinegar, oil, and mustard; add it to the rice mixture. Season to taste. Refrigerate mixture at least 30 minutes to set the flavor.

Arrange rice in a pyramid on a bed of shredded lettuce, or press into a mold and then unmold. Garnish with cooked beets, shrimp, or eggs. Serve with your favorite salad dressing.

Soups

Black Bean Soup

Serves 6

Rio-Sheraton Hotel
Rio de Janeiro, Brazil

1 cup dried black beans
2 quarts Beef Stock (recipe, page
  278)
1 cup canned puréed pumpkin
Salt and pepper, to taste
1 onion, thinly sliced

½ cup tomato sauce
3 teaspoons tapioca
2 tablespoons butter
Garnish: *2 hard-cooked eggs, cut in*
  wedges

Pick over and wash beans. Soak overnight in 3 cups of water.

When ready to cook, discard the water and cover beans with 2 quarts of beef stock. Cook in covered saucepan over medium heat about 50 minutes, or until beans are tender, adding small quantities of water as necessary.

When beans are done, add pumpkin purée and cook about 15 minutes, uncovered. Add salt, pepper, sliced onion, and tomato sauce; cook until onion is tender and soup is of desired consistency.

Strain, add tapioca and butter, and reheat for about 2 minutes, until butter is melted. Do *not* bring to a boil.

Serve with the wedges of hard-cooked eggs.

Sopa de Camarón
(Lima Shrimp Soup)

Serves 10-12   *Lima-Sheraton Hotel*
                                                        Lima, Peru

Serve this shrimp soup with crispy Quesadillas (recipe, page 247) and enjoy an excellent Sunday night supper.

2 tablespoons olive oil
2 cups chopped onions
2 cloves garlic, peeled
3 tablespoons tomato sauce
6 cups boiling water
5 medium-sized potatoes, peeled and
  cut into ½-inch cubes
1 tablespoon salt
⅛ to ¼ teaspoon cayenne pepper, to
  taste

¼ teaspoon ground marjoram
4 ounces cream cheese
½ pound medium-sized shrimp,
  shelled and deveined
½ cup green peas
½ cup whole kernel corn
4 eggs

Pour the oil into a deep saucepan. Add onions and garlic and cook until browned, about 10 minutes, stirring frequently. Remove the garlic. Add the tomato sauce, water, potatoes, salt, cayenne pepper, and marjoram. Bring to a boil, lower heat, and simmer 20 minutes.

Cut the cream cheese into small pieces and purée with about 1 cup of the soup stock in a blender or food processor.

Add the cream cheese mixture, shrimp, peas, and corn to the soup and simmer 5 to 10 minutes. Remove the soup from the heat.

Beat the eggs. Very gradually, at first only a tablespoon at a time, add about 2 cups of the hot soup broth to the eggs while beating the eggs constantly to prevent curdling. Pour the egg mixture into the soup while stirring the soup. Reheat the soup but do not allow it to boil. Serve hot.

Gazpacho Maria Isabel

Serves 6

Maria Isabel-Sheraton Hotel
Mexico City, Mexico

This is a delicious soup for the summer when tomatoes are at their prime. If you do not have a blender, make the soup the way the Mexicans do it. Chop the vegetables very fine; beat the seasonings and liquids together with a rotary beater and mix them with the vegetables.

1 green pepper	*Dash of cayenne pepper*
3 large tomatoes	*1 tablespoon vinegar*
4 green onions, minced	*1 cup tomato juice*
1 cucumber, peeled	*¼ cup olive oil*
1 fresh parsley sprig	*Garnishes: 1½ cup bread cubes fried*
1 clove garlic, crushed	*in garlic and olive oil, cubes of*
Salt and pepper, to taste	*cucumber, green onions, frozen*
1 teaspoon cumin powder	*cubes of tomato juice*

Boil the green pepper 6 minutes, then cut it into small pieces. Skin and slice the tomatoes, mince the onions, and slice the peeled cucumber. Put the vegetables in a blender with the parsley, crushed garlic, seasonings, vinegar, tomato juice, and olive oil. After the ingredients are puréed, chill the mixture.

Sauté 1½ cups of ½-inch cubes of dry bread in crushed garlic and olive oil. Serve the bread cubes separately in a bowl, allowing guests to sprinkle them over their soup at the table. Peel and cube the cucumber and cut the green onions in ¼-inch lengths; pass them in bowls. Before serving the soup, freeze a tray of tomato juice and put 2 tomato cubes in each soup plate.

Entrees

El Cid Tenderloin Fillets

Serves 6

Sheraton-San Cristobal Hotel
Santiago, Chile

What could be easier or more elegant than this preparation of choice tenderloin fillets, served with a sauce laden with shallots and mushrooms.

6 beef tenderloin fillets, each 6 to 8
  ounces
4 tablespoons Clarified Butter (recipe,
  page 277)
¼ pound shallots, peeled and minced
  (about ½ cup)

½ pound mushrooms, cleaned and
  thinly sliced
¼ cup cognac
1½ cups heavy cream
½ teaspoon salt
¼ teaspoon freshly ground pepper

In a large heavy skillet, melt butter over high heat. Sear fillets 1 minute on each side. Lower heat and continue cooking, turning occasionally, until meat is done to your taste. Set aside on warm plates.

Using the same pan, sauté shallots 1 minute. Add mushrooms and sauté 1 or 2 minutes longer. Pour in cognac. Ignite and flambé, then add the cream. Stirring, reduce the sauce over high heat for 4 or 5 minutes, until a spoon dragged through the sauce leaves a trail that closes behind.

Season with salt and pepper to taste. Spoon sauce over each fillet.

Lomo à la Huancaina
(Tenderloin Fillets with Corn Sauce)

Serves 6

*Lima-Sheraton Hotel
Lima, Peru*

Most Peruvian cooks guard their Huancaina recipes like Texans guard their chili recipes. But the Lima-Sheraton has consented to part with its recipe so that we may all enjoy this sauce, served with its traditional accompaniments.

Huancaina Sauce:

½ pound feta cheese, very finely
  crumbled
½ pound Parmesan cheese, grated
2 tablespoons chopped fresh green
  chili peppers
4 egg yolks
3 tablespoons fresh lemon juice

1¼ pounds whole kernel corn
¾ cup olive oil
1 tablespoon olive oil
1 cup minced onions
⅛ teaspoon turmeric
1 cup heavy cream
Salt and pepper, to taste

In a medium-sized bowl, combine the cheeses, chili peppers, egg yolks, and lemon juice.

Grind the corn in a blender or food processor. Blend ground corn into cheese mixture. Very slowly drizzle in the ¾ cup olive oil, stirring constantly to keep sauce combined.

Pour 1 tablespoon olive oil into a large skillet and sauté onions until translucent. Stir in turmeric, corn mixture and cream. Season with salt and pepper to taste. Serve warm.

Huancaina Sauce keeps several days refrigerated. It is excellent on other meats, and on poultry and vegetables as well.

Continued

Presentation:

4 tablespoons Clarified Butter (recipe, page 277)

6 beef tenderloin fillets, each about 6 to 8 ounces

6 hard-cooked eggs, peeled and halved

Black olives
Slices of red bell pepper
Garnish: *Parsley*

In a large heavy skillet melt butter over high heat. Sear fillets 1 minute on each side. Lower the heat slightly. Continue frying, turning fillets once or twice, until meat is done to your satisfaction.

Place each steak on a warm plate, surround with eggs and olives, coat with Huancaina Sauce, and top with bell pepper slices and olives. Garnish with parsley.

Tournedos Martini

Serves 4

Guadalajara Sheraton
Guadalajara, Mexico

1 tablespoon (approximately) soft butter

4 slices of wide french bread, each ¾ to 1 inch thick, with crusts removed

2 tablespoons Clarified Butter (recipe, page 277)

4 (6- to 8-ounce) tournedos (filet mignon) of beef

Salt and freshly ground black pepper, to taste

1½ cups Béchamel Sauce (recipe, page 275)

½ cup Brown Sauce (recipe, page 276)

2 tablespoons fresh lemon juice

¼ teaspoon Worcestershire sauce

4 tablespoons (or more) dry vermouth, to taste

2 tablespoons butter

Garnishes: 4 large Spanish olives, 4 wide strips lemon peel

Butter both sides of the french bread slices and place them on a rack in a preheated 400-degree oven. Bake, turning them occasionally, until crisp and golden brown. (This can be done hours ahead.) Take bread out of the oven, and when ready to assemble the dish, place croutons in a shallow dish or on individual plates.

Heat the clarified butter in a skillet over medium-high heat. When sizzling, add the tournedos, seasoned to taste. Cook them, turning occasionally, until done to taste.

When done, place meat on top of croutons, pouring over butter from the pan, if desired. Place tournedos in a slow oven to keep warm.

Combine the Béchamel and brown sauces in the same skillet. When hot, add the lemon juice,

Worcestershire sauce, and vermouth. Take off the heat and swirl in the butter, 1 tablespoon at a time. Season further, if desired.

Pour vermouth sauce over the tournedos. Skewer an olive and a lemon peel onto each of 4 toothpicks and stick into the meat. Serve immediately.

Fruit Carbonade
(Meat, Vegetable, and Fruit Stew)

Serves 6

Buenos Aires-Sheraton Hotel
Buenos Aires, Argentina

All the colors of a Latin market are present in this unusual peasant stew. It is not too sweet and not too spicy, allowing the separate flavors of the fruits and vegetables to be appreciated alone and yet together. Though the list of ingredients seems to go on and on, a closer look will reveal that the dish is easily assembled and prepared.

3 cups boiling water
1¼ pounds ground beef
2 tablespoons lard or vegetable shortening
1 cup chopped onion
1 green bell pepper, seeded and diced into ½-inch pieces
1 red bell pepper, seeded and diced into ½-inch pieces
1 small sweet potato, peeled and diced into ½-inch pieces
1 large clove garlic, peeled and minced
1 tablespoon chopped fresh parsley
½ teaspoon paprika
½ teaspoon sugar

⅛ teaspoon cumin
1 teaspoon salt
⅛ to ¼ teaspoon freshly ground black pepper, to taste
3 cups Beef Stock (recipe, page 278)
½ pound zucchini, diced into ½ inch pieces; or ½ pound summer squash, diced into ½-inch pieces
1 cup whole kernel corn
2 tablespoons dark raisins
1 small firm but ripe peach, peeled and diced into 1-inch pieces
1 small firm but ripe pear, diced into 1-inch pieces
6 cups boiled white rice

Boil water in a large saucepan. Take pan off the heat. Add the ground beef, stirring to break the meat into little pieces. Let sit 5 minutes, stirring once or twice, until most of the pink disappears from the meat. Drain meat well, discarding the water.

Melt the lard (or shortening) in a large skillet over medium-high heat. Add the onions and fry 4 to 5 minutes, stirring constantly, until onions are limp and slightly brown. Mix in the blanched beef. Continue to fry, stirring constantly, until all liquid has evaporated from the pan and the meat is lightly browned, about 10 minutes. Scrape the pan frequently as you stir.

Continued

Lower the heat slightly; add the diced bell peppers, sweet potato, and garlic. Scraping and stirring, continue cooking the mixture 5 or 6 minutes longer, until peppers and potatoes are somewhat tender. Add the parsley, paprika, sugar, cumin, salt, and pepper. Stir and fry 1 minute longer to enliven the flavors.

Pour hot beef stock into the pan. Add the zucchini (or summer squash), whole kernel corn, and raisins. Simmer carbonade gently—do not boil—for 10 minutes. Add the diced peach and pear. Simmer 5 to 10 minutes longer, or until all vegetables and fruits are just tender. Correct the seasoning to taste.

Put 1 cup hot boiled rice into each of 6 dinner bowls. Ladle the carbonade over the rice. Serve hot.

Rio Grande Chili Beef

Serves 8–10   *Maria Isabel-Sheraton Hotel*
                                                                               Mexico City, Mexico

Serve this excellent chili with crusty French bread and frosty bottles of beer.

4 pounds beef chuck, cut into 2-inch	*1 teaspoon oregano*
cubes	*2 tablespoons vegetable oil*
⅓ cup all-purpose flour	*2 tablespoons butter*
1 teaspoon ground cumin	*1 cup chopped onions*
3 tablespoons chili powder	*4 cloves garlic, crushed*
1 tablespoon curry powder	*2 cups Beef Stock (recipe, page 278)*
1½ teaspoons salt	*1 cup dry red wine*
Freshly ground pepper, to taste	*Garnish: Pimento strips*

Dredge the meat in a mixture of flour, cumin, chili, curry, salt, pepper, and oregano. Set aside.

Place the oil and butter in a large heavy skillet. Add the onions and garlic and sauté several minutes, until soft. With a slotted spoon, remove the garlic and onions to an ovenproof casserole.

In the same pan, sauté the seasoned meat cubes, a few at a time, until they are browned on all sides. Add them to the casserole.

Deglaze the pan with the beef stock. Pour the stock and the red wine into the casserole. Cover tightly and bake in a 300-degree oven 2½ to 3 hours, until the meat is tender. Correct the seasonings and serve immediately, garnished with pimento, or let cool, refrigerate up to 24 hours, then reheat and serve.

Brazilian Feijoada

Serves 12

Rio-Sheraton Hotel
Rio de Janeiro, Brazil

Feijoada, Brazil's elaborate national party dish, takes advantage of the many smoked and dried meat products readily available there. In order for you to re-create this recipe, we have adapted it so that all ingredients can be obtained in local markets or from a butcher who specializes in German meats.

1 pound dried black beans
1 pound dried beef
¾-pound piece salted pork loin
¾ pound salted pork ribs
¾ pound fresh *linguica* sausage or other unsmoked pork link sausage
¾ pound smoked *linguica* sausage or other smoked pork link sausage
¼ pound lean smoked slab bacon
¾-pound boned fresh pork loin
2 tablespoons vegetable oil

2 cups chopped onions
½ teaspoon cayenne pepper
1 teaspoon ground black pepper
2 tablespoons minced fresh parsley
3 bay leaves
1 cup fresh orange juice
9 cups boiled long-grain white rice
Accompaniments: *sautéed collard greens, Tabasco sauce, orange slices*

Place the beans in a medium-sized pot. In another pot, place dried beef, salted pork loin, and salted pork ribs. Cover the ingredients of both pots with cold water and let soak overnight.

The next day, drain the beans and place them in a 6-quart pot. Pour in 4 quarts cold water. Bring beans to a gentle boil, reduce the heat, cover, and simmer the beans for about 2 hours. After the 2 hours, remove 1½ cups beans and 2 cups of the bean stock from the large pot. Set them aside.

Drain the dried beef, the salted pork loin, and the salted pork ribs. Add the drained meats, the fresh linguica, smoked linguica, slab bacon, and fresh pork loin to the large bean pot. Cover and simmer over medium heat about 1½ hours, or until meats are tender, skimming off any foam that forms now or at any time during the cooking process.

Meanwhile, heat 2 tablespoons oil in a skillet over moderate heat. Sauté chopped onions until they are softened, 3 to 5 minutes. Sprinkle on the peppers, parsley, and bay leaves. Cook 2 to 3 minutes more. Add the reserved 1½ cups partially cooked beans and 2 cups bean stock to the skillet. Cook onion-bean mixture at least 10 to 15 minutes, mashing the beans with a wooden spoon until mixture thickens substantially. Add more bean stock if necessary to prevent scorching.

Pour mashed bean mixture back into the bean pot. Add the orange juice. Simmer the
Continued

completed bean dish 30 minutes more, until beans are tender.

Remove the meats. Strip the ribs of the pork, discarding bones. Cut other meats in bite-sized pieces, and again mix the meat into the beans.

Serve the Feijoada with a bed of hot rice, sautéed collard greens, Tabasco sauce, and sliced oranges on the side.

Roast Loin of Pork a l'ail

Serves 6–8   *El Salvador-Sheraton Hotel*
San Salvador, El Salvador

Charles Lamb would be thrilled to get roast pork this good. We top this succulent viand with deep-fried pineapple slices; they add to the taste as well as to the appearance of the dish.

Roast Pork:

3- to 4-pound boned pork loin
2 tablespoons slivered garlic
1 teaspoon salt
¼ teaspoon freshly ground pepper
6 to 8 medium-sized potatoes, peeled and halved

Pineapples à l'Orly (recipe below)
Carrot and Apple Sauté (recipe follows)

Preheat oven to 350 degrees. With a sharp knife, make shallow slits in the meat and insert garlic. Rub the roast with a mixture of salt and pepper.

Place the meat on a rack in a shallow roasting pan. Pour in about ¼ cup water. Surround the meat with the potatoes. Turn the potatoes occasionally during the cooking process to help brown them. Roast the meat until cooked through, about 40 minutes to the pound or until internal temperature of the meat registers about 170 degrees.

When the roast is done, allow it to sit 10 to 15 minutes before carving. Serve pork slices topped with Pineapples à l'Orly, accompanied by pan roasted potatoes and Carrot and Apple Sauté.

Pineapples à l'Orly:

⅔ cup sifted all-purpose flour
1 tablespoon sugar
1 teaspoon baking powder
¼ teaspoon salt
1 beaten egg
½ cup milk

1 tablespoon melted butter
6 to 8 pineapple slices, each about ¼ inch thick, patted as dry as possible
Sufficient oil for deep frying

Sift together dry ingredients. Beat egg, milk, and butter. Pour wet ingredients into flour mixture and stir until smooth. Let sit 1 to 2 hours.

Preheat oil for deep frying to moderate temperature.

Coat the pineapple slices with the fritter batter and fry until they are golden brown and crispy, turning occasionally, about 1 minute.

Carrot and Apple Sauté:

2 tablespoons butter
2 pounds carrots, peeled and
    julienned
2 apples, peeled, cored, and
    julienned

1 teaspoon salt
⅛ teaspoon pepper
2 tablespoons dark rum
1 to 2 tablespoons dark brown sugar,
    to taste

Approximately half an hour before serving the roast pork, melt butter in a large skillet. Add carrots and apples, sprinkle with salt and pepper, and sauté briefly over medium-high heat until the carrots are just starting to get soft. Reduce heat to low, cover, and let braise about 15 minutes, or until carrots are just tender. Sprinkle in the rum and brown sugar. Simmer, stirring, until sugar melts. Serve hot.

Macuto Chicken

Serves 4

Macuto-Sheraton Hotel
Caracas, Venezuela

2 large chicken breasts, halved,
    skinned, and boned
¼ teaspoon salt
⅛ teaspoon pepper
2 ripe but firm bananas
1 teaspoon Angostura bitters

3 or 4 ounces cooked ham, thinly
    sliced
½ cup all-purpose flour
3 eggs, lightly beaten
1 cup freshly grated coconut
Sufficient oil for deep frying
Sweet and Sour Sauce (recipe follows)

Lay each chicken breast half between waxed paper and flatten out with a mallot until approximately ¼ inch thick. Season chicken with a portion of the salt and pepper. Peel, cut bananas in half or into pieces that are approximately the length of the breasts. Sprinkle bitters on sliced ham and wrap around bananas.

Continued

Place ham-wrapped bananas on each breast. Roll tightly to enclose filling completely. Secure with toothpicks. (Chicken rolls may be tightly encased in foil and refrigerated up to 24 hours at this point). Dredge breasts in flour, dip into beaten eggs, then roll in coconut. Deep-fry each chicken roll 5 to 7 minutes at 375 degrees, until golden brown and cooked through. Drain, remove toothpicks, and serve with Sweet and Sour Sauce.

Sweet and Sour Sauce:

1 cup orange juice
2 tablespoons vinegar
1 tablespoon dark brown sugar

1 tablespoon cornstarch
1 tablespoon dark rum
1 teaspoon Angostura bitters

In a small saucepan, whisk together orange juice, vinegar, sugar, and cornstarch. Place pan over heat, bring to a slow boil, and simmer for 1 minute. Take off heat; pour in rum and bitters. Serve warm.

Xim Xim Chicken

Serves 4

Rio-Sheraton Hotel
Rio de Janeiro, Brazil

This chicken recipe combines four key elements found in many Brazilian dishes: coconut milk, oil, peanuts, and dried shrimp. These items are obtainable in most large markets. If not, coconut milk and oil can be found in health food stores, dried shrimp in Chinese or Latin American markets.

¼ cup ground dry roasted peanuts
¼ cup ground cooked chestnuts
2 tablespoons ground dried and
  salted shrimp
½ cup coconut oil
1 chicken, cut into serving pieces
½ cup minced onions

1 teaspoon minced garlic
1¼ cups Coconut Milk (recipe, page
  277)
Salt and cayenne pepper, to taste
Garnish: Chopped fresh coriander
  (cilantro) or chopped fresh parsley

Grind together the peanuts, chestnuts, and dried shrimp in a blender or food processor until well combined. Set aside.

Heat oil in large heavy skillet over medium-high heat until a light haze forms over it. Fry chicken pieces for about 25 minutes in hot oil, turning to cook and brown evenly. Remove chicken, drain, and cool. When cool, tear meat off the bones, shred, and set it aside. Discard skin and bones.

Pour off all but 1 tablespoon of oil from the pan. Sauté onions and garlic briefly until translucent. Pour in coconut milk and the ground nuts and shrimp. Stir and gently boil 3 or 4 minutes until sauce starts to thicken. Lower heat, add shredded chicken, salt, and cayenne pepper to taste. Cover the pan and simmer 10 minutes longer to blend the flavors.

Serve on steamed or boiled white rice, garnished with a tablespoon of chopped coriander or parsley.

Seafood Morsel
(Cold Shellfish Salad)

Serves 8–10

Sheraton-San Cristobal Hotel
Santiago, Chile

Actually, "morsel" is a modest name for this imaginative combination of fish and vegetables. It is a light and yet satisfying salad, a wonderful treat for a hot summer night. Feel free to apportion the various seafood ingredients to your preference.

1 cup mayonnaise
2 tablespoons fresh lemon juice
1 teaspoon salt
Pinch of freshly ground white pepper
1 pound tomatoes, peeled, seeded,
*   and diced*
2 cups cooked whole corn kernels
2 pounds abalone, cooked and diced;
*   or 2 pounds cleaned and skinned*
*   squid, cooked and diced*
¼ pound medium-sized peeled
*   shrimp, deveined and cooked*

¼ pound cooked crawfish or lobster
*   meat*
2 green bell peppers, peeled, seeded,
*   and diced*
Garnishes: Lettuce leaves, hard-
*   cooked eggs cut in wedges, black*
*   olives; 1 pound mussels, scrubbed,*
*   steamed, and left in the shell*

Chill all ingredients well before assembling the salad. Mix the mayonnaise with lemon juice, salt, and pepper in a large bowl. Add tomatoes, corn, abalone, shrimp, crawfish, and bell peppers. Fold gently to combine. Correct seasoning.

Serve immediately on a bed of lettuce. Garnish with egg wedges, black olives, and if available, mussels still ensconced in their shells.

Shrimp Bahia Style

Serves 4

Rio-Sheraton Hotel
Rio de Janeiro, Brazil

The state of Bahia on the east coast of Brazil is known for the African influence found in its foods. Dishes such as this shrimp preparation are appreciated for their use of fine seafoods, brightly colored vegetables, and spicy ingredients. If ingredients are assembled in advance, it takes only about a quarter of an hour to prepare.

1 pound jumbo raw shrimp, shelled and deveined
2 tablespoons coconut oil or vegetable oil
⅓ cup minced onions
3 large green bell peppers, seeded and finely chopped
3 large tomatoes, peeled, seeded, and chopped

2 tablespoons chopped fresh chives
1½ cups Coconut Milk (recipe, page 277)
3 tablespoons chopped fresh coriander (cilantro) or chopped fresh parsley
½ teaspoon salt
¼ teaspoon pepper

Quickly sauté raw shrimp in hot oil, stirring until they turn pink. Remove, drain, and set them aside. Add the onions and bell peppers to the same pan, sautéing until they are tender. Stir in the tomatoes, chives, and coconut milk. Simmer the dish 4 to 5 minutes, then return shrimp to the pan and season with coriander, salt, and pepper.

Serve at once accompanied with rice or boiled potatoes.

Side Dishes

Ocopa à l'Arequipeña
(Potatoes with Cheese and Peanut Sauce)

Serves 10

Lima-Sheraton Hotel
Lima, Peru

This side dish of potatoes coated with a peanut-flavored cheese sauce is one of many classical Peruvian dishes. It dresses up ordinary potatoes beautifully. Use one, two, or more chilies, depending on how hot you want the sauce.

1 pound medium-sized shrimp,
    shelled, deveined, and cooked
3 tablespoons vegetable oil
½ pound mild Cheddar cheese,
    grated
1 cup skinned peanuts, ground
1 cup minced onions
2 teaspoons minced garlic
1 or more yellow chili peppers,
    seeded and minced

¼ teaspoon oregano
1 teaspoon salt
Milk
Ground soda crackers
10 soft lettuce leaves
10 hot boiled potatoes, peeled
10 hard-cooked eggs, peeled and
    halved
10 or more black olives

Put all but a few cooked shrimp in a blender or food processor, setting the remainder aside for a garnish. Blend or process until shrimp become pastelike. Pour in oil; blend briefly. Add the cheese, peanuts, onions, garlic, chili pepper, oregano, and salt. Blend and purée ingredients until a thick sauce (the consistency of peanut butter) results. If sauce is too thick, thin out with small additions of milk. If sauce is too thin, thicken with small additions of ground soda crackers. Sauce may be served warm or at room temperature.

Place lettuce leaves on 10 dinner plates. Set hot potatoes on top of the lettuce. Surround with eggs and olives. Pour approximately ½ cup sauce over each serving, garnishing with the reserved shrimp.

Zucchini and Tomato Egg Scramble

Serves 4

Buenos Aires-Sheraton Hotel
Buenos Aires, Argentina

½ cup olive oil
1 small onion, chopped
2 cups diced zucchini
½ cup chopped tomatoes

4 eggs, beaten
Salt and pepper to taste
⅛ teaspoon oregano

Heat the oil and fry the chopped onions until tender and transparent. Add the diced zucchini and brown; the edges must show some color. Add the tomatoes, stirring to blend well and help tomatoes dissolve a bit. Pour in eggs, beaten with seasonings, stirring until eggs are firmly set.

Serve immediately as a delicious accompaniment to beef, meat, or poultry dishes.

Sauces

Shrimp-Coconut Fish Sauce

Makes 3 large cups

Rio-Sheraton Hotel
Rio de Janeiro, Brazil

2 tablespoons butter
2 tablespoons all-purpose flour
1 cup Coconut Milk (recipe, page 277)
½ pound medium-sized raw shrimp, peeled, deveined, and coarsely chopped

1 tablespoon chopped onions
1 clove garlic, peeled and minced
¾ teaspoon salt
Pinch of freshly ground black pepper
Pinch or more of cayenne pepper, to taste
1 cup tomato sauce

Melt 1 tablespoon butter in a small heavy saucepan over medium heat. Add the flour; stir and simmer the roux 2 or 3 minutes. Gradually stir in the coconut milk. Simmer the coconut sauce, stirring occasionally, 10 to 15 minutes.

While sauce is simmering, sauté the shrimp, onions, and garlic for 3 or 4 minutes in remaining tablespoon of butter, until shrimp turn pink and onions soften nicely. Add the salt, freshly ground black pepper and cayenne pepper, to taste. Sauté the spiced shrimp a few moments to enliven the flavors. Finally, add the tomato sauce and let simmer a few minutes more.

Combine the shrimp sauce with the coconut sauce. Serve warm, over whole cooked fish or fish fillets.

Spicy Parsley Sauce

Makes 1 cup

Lima-Sheraton Hotel
Lima, Peru

A treat awaits you when you serve this spicy salsa with barbecued or roasted meats and fish.

½ cup minced onions
1½ teaspoon salt
1 teaspoon ground black pepper
¼ teaspoon cayenne pepper
½ teaspoon marjoram
½ teaspoon oregano

¼ to ⅓ cup red wine vinegar
2 medium-sized tomatoes, peeled, seeded, and puréed
¼ cup very finely minced fresh parsley

Place the minced onions in a bowl. Sprinkle on salt, black pepper, cayenne, marjoram, and oregano. Stir, then cover with vinegar. Let stand 1 to 2 hours at room temperature to meld flavors.

After mixture has stood 1 to 2 hours, drain and discard the vinegar. Add puréed tomatoes and parsley to the minced onions.

Desserts

Peach Meringue Cake

Serves 10

Sheraton-San Cristobal Hotel
Santiago, Chile

Meringues are not truly baked; they just dry out—thus the low oven. They are best made on dry days. If the weather is damp, keep them in the closed oven until ready to use.

6 egg whites, at room temperature
¼ teaspoon cream of tartar
1½ cups sugar
3 cups puréed ripe fresh peaches, at
*   room temperature*
¼ cup fresh lemon juice

2 tablespoons gelatin
2 cups heavy cream
1 teaspoon vanilla
¼ to ⅓ cup sugar, to taste
Garnish: Sliced peaches, honey, and
*   lime juice*

Preheat the oven to 225 degrees. Place egg whites in a copper or stainless-steel bowl and beat them on a slow speed until foamy. Sprinkle in the cream of tartar, raise the beating speed, and beat egg whites until they form soft peaks. Add the sugar 1 tablespoon at a time, beating until all sugar is incorporated and peaks are stiff and shiny.

Using an 8-inch cake pan or plate as a guide, outline 3 circles on parchment paper. Adhere the paper to baking sheets with dabs of meringue. Once in position, fill a pastry bag with meringue. Pipe out meringue in a circular fashion, filling the 8-inch circles on the parchment paper. Smooth tops of meringue circles with a spatula.

Bake in the preheated oven 1½ to 2 hours, or until meringues are dry. Turn oven off. Leave meringues inside the oven until they have cooled down, usually several hours.

When meringues are cool, peel off the parchment paper. (Do not despair if meringues crack or break. The fruit mousse will cover all flaws so that no one will be the wiser.) If meringue discs are not used immediately, store them in airtight containers to keep them crisp.

Several hours before serving, purée the peaches and pour peach purée into a large bowl.

Continued

111

Pour lemon juice into a small saucepan and stir in the gelatin. Let sit 1 minute to soften. Gently warm this mixture over low heat, stirring constantly, until gelatin melts and mixture clears in color, about 1 or 2 minutes. Pour and stir the gelatin into the puréed fruit. If, at this point, peach purée is not the consistency of softly whipped cream, place peach bowl in a larger bowl of ice water. Stir frequently until purée reaches correct consistency. Take out of the ice water and set aside briefly while whipping cream.

Whip the cream and vanilla until slightly thickened.   Drizzle in ¼ to ⅓ cup sugar and beat until soft but firm peaks form. Do not overbeat, or cream will dry out. Fold the whipped cream into the thickened peach purée. Refrigerate peach mousse, covered, until well chilled.

When ready to serve, place 1 meringue disk on a cake stand. Spread peach mousse generously on top of it. Cover with a second meringue disc, more mousse, then top with the third meringue disc. Spread remaining peach mousse on the sides and top of the cake.

Garnish with slices of fresh peaches dipped in a mixture of honey and lime juice, made to your taste. Decorate crown of the cake with the slices and serve immediately. The completed cake cannot be refrigerated because meringues soften very quickly.

Pastelitos De Coco
(Coconut Pastries)

Makes 1½ dozen pastries

La Paz-Sheraton Hotel
La Paz, Bolivia

Coconut Filling:

½ cup sugar
1 cup grated coconut, preferably
   freshly grated
½ cup light cream or ¼ cup heavy
   cream plus ¼ cup half and half

1 tablespoon all-purpose flour
3 egg yolks
2 tablespoons butter
Coconut Pastry Dough (recipe follows)

Preheat oven to 450 degrees. Prepare the filling by mixing the sugar, coconut, cream, and flour in a saucepan. Place over medium heat and cook, stirring constantly, until mixture thickens nicely, about 8 to 10 minutes.

Place 2 egg yolks in a small bowl. Whip them lightly with a fork. Then, whipping constantly, add 4 tablespoons of the hot coconut cream, 1 tablespoon at a time. Be careful not to add the hot mixture too quickly or the eggs may scramble. Once ingredients are well combined, pour warm mixture back into the saucepan, again stirring constantly. Finally, swirl in the butter, 1 tablespoon at a time. Cook about 3 minutes longer. Take filling off the heat. Cool to room temperature.

While custard is cooling, roll out the Coconut Pastry Dough (recipe below) to a thickness of approximately ⅛ inch. Lightly flour the work surface if necessary. Cut dough into 3-inch circles. Place a scant 1 tablespoon filling on half of the circles. Cover with remaining circles, pressing the edges together well to seal pastries tightly shut.

Place coconut pastries on baking sheets. Lightly beat the remaining egg yolk and brush on top of the pastries to help them brown. Place pastries in preheated oven. Immediately lower oven heat to 425 degrees and bake 10 to 12 minutes, or until pastries are crisp and lightly browned. Remove and cool pastries on wire rack.

Coconut Pastry Dough:

2 cups sifted all-purpose flour
½ teaspoon baking powder
1 teaspoon salt

½ cup solid vegetable shortening,
   well chilled
4 to 6 tablespoons ice water

Sift the dry ingredients together into a chilled bowl. Cut in the cold shortening until mixture resembles coarse meal. Drizzle in only as much ice water as needed for the dough to come together and clean the sides of the bowl. Wrap and refrigerate the dough for at least 1 hour before using.

Ambrosia

Serves 6

Buenos Aires-Sheraton Hotel
Buenos Aires, Argentina

1 cup sugar
1 well-rounded tablespoon cornstarch
2 cups boiling water
2 whole eggs beaten with 2 egg yolks
4 tablespoons freshly made orange
   juice, strained

Pinch of grated nutmeg or vanilla, to
   taste
Optional: 2 tablespoons Grand
   Marnier
Garnish: Chopped nuts

Mix sugar and cornstarch in a small saucepan, stirring to make sure that ingredients are well blended to avoid lumps. Pour boiling water over mixture; continue stirring and slowly bring to a boil. Cook 3 minutes, and remove from the heat .

Beat together eggs with egg yolks, freshly pressed orange juice, and a pinch of nutmeg (or a little vanilla).

Continued

Stirring vigorously, pour the beaten egg mixture gradually into cornstarch preparation. Return pan to the heat and simmer gently 2 minutes. If desired, add the Grand Marnier just before taking Ambrosia off the heat.

Serve cold, in stemmed glasses and sprinkled with chopped nuts. Honey biscuits are a delicious accompaniment.

Hot Kahlua Soufflé

Serves 4–5

Maria Isabel-Sheraton Hotel
Mexico City, Mexico

This lovely froth of a dessert may be served successfuly at the end of any meal. The semisweet chocolate garnish is excellent, but if you can find some chocolate-covered coffee beans to chop and sprinkle on top, you will have something superb.

Soufflé:

3 tablespoons butter
3 tablespoons all-purpose flour
4 tablespoons sugar
1 cup light cream or ½ cup heavy
* cream plus ½ cup half and half*

6 eggs, separated
¼ cup Kahlua liqueur
Garnish: Chocolate-covered coffee
* beans or semisweet chocolate*
* shavings*

Preheat oven to 375 degrees. Melt the butter in the top of a double boiler over simmering water. Blend in the flour, then the sugar, and slowly add the cream. Cook, stirring constantly, until the mixture is thick and smooth, about 5 minutes.

Beat the egg yolks. Slowly, a tablespoon at a time, pour ½ cup of the warm mixture into the beaten egg yolks, stirring constantly to prevent curdling. Pour the cream and eggs back into the double boiler and continue to cook until the custard is thick, 3 to 5 minutes.

Remove mixture from the heat and let cool for about 5 minutes before adding the Kahlua. (This soufflé base may be made up to 1 hour in advance of baking.)

Butter a 1½-quart soufflé dish and dust with sugar. Beat the egg whites until stiff but not dry. Stir ¼ of the whites into the soufflé base to lighten it, then lightly fold in the rest. Empty into the prepared soufflé dish and set it in a large shallow pan filled with 1 to 2 inches of hot water. Bake 10 minutes at 375 degrees, then lower heat to 325 degrees and bake about 35 minutes longer, until the soufflé has puffed up and become a golden brown in color. Serve with the following sauce.

Kahlua Sauce:

⅓ cup water
¼ cup sugar
1 tablespoon freshly grated orange
   rind
1 tablespoon cornstarch

1 tablespoon water
1 cup light cream or ½ cup heavy
   cream plus ½ cup half and half
5 or more tablespoons Kahlua, to
   taste

Simmer ⅓ cup water, sugar, and orange rind very gently for 10 minutes. Dissolve the cornstarch in 1 tablespoon water. Add the dissolved cornstarch and the cream to the pan containing the water, sugar, and orange rind mixture. Cook over medium heat until the mixture has thickened, about 10 to 15 minutes. Remove from heat and let cool to room temperature. When ready to serve, add the liqueur. Pass the sauce.

Paloma Blanca

Serves 4

Santo Domingo-Sheraton Hotel
Santo Domingo, Dominican Republic

Diced pineapple, swimming in rum, served in its own shell, and cloaked in a cloud of guava-flavored meringue—a small heavenly slice of tropical paradise, brought to you via Santo Domingo.

It may be difficult to find small pineapples to cut and serve as four separate desserts. Don't fret; be friendly and serve half of a large pineapple to every two people. This will certainly end the meal on a cozy note.

2 small pineapples, about 2 pounds
   each; or 1 large pineapple, about 5
   pounds
¾ pound diced pineapple
1 small papaya, peeled, seeded and diced
1 cup (8 ounces) dark rum

4 egg whites, at room temperature
¾ cup (6 ounces) guava jelly
1 tablespoon fresh lime juice
1 cup (2½ ounces) loosely packed
   grated coconut

Cut the pineapples in half lengthwise. Cut out the fruit, leaving a sturdy shell. Chill the shells until serving time.

Dice the fruit, discarding the tough core. Set fruit in a bowl. Mix in the additional diced pineapple and about ½ of the diced papaya. Pour the rum over the fruit. Cover and refrigerate the fruit 1 hour at most or the rum will completely mask the fruit flavors.

When ready to serve, beat the egg whites in a stainless-steel or copper bowl until soft peaks form. Add the guava jelly, a scant tablespoon at a time, until all jelly is incorporated and meringue

Continued

is stiff and smooth. Beat in the lime juice.

Fill chilled pineapple shells with fruit and rum. Spoon on generous amounts of meringue, completely covering the fruit. Top with reserved papaya and sprinkle on grated coconut.

Place filled pineapples in a preheated 350-degree oven and bake 8 to 10 minutes, until meringue is lightly browned. Serve at once.

Suspiros à la Limeña
("Daydreams of Lima")

Serves 8   *Lima-Sheraton Hotel*
                                                              Lima, Peru

Suspiros can mean to daydream or sigh, and sigh you will when you see and taste this colorful Peruvian specialty. A rich golden custard base, a thin layer of ruby red wine, and a white cloud of meringue make this dessert a dramatic end to any dinner party.

2 cups milk	*1 cup Port wine*
2 cups condensed milk	*¾ cup dark brown sugar, loosely*
½ cup sugar	*packed*
2 3-inch cinnamon sticks	*3 egg whites*
8 egg yolks	*⅔ cup powdered sugar*
	1½ teaspoons ground cinnamon

Pour both milks into a pan; add sugar and cinnamon sticks. Boil gently 20 minutes. Remove cinnamon sticks.

In the top of a double boiler, beat the yolks lightly, then gradually drizzle in hot milks, stirring constantly. Place top pan over hot but not boiling water, simmer, and stir custard at least 10 minutes, until fairly thick. (*Never* allow custard to boil or it will curdle.) Set aside until cool, then pour into 8 stemmed glasses. Chill.

Heat the wine and brown sugar until the sugar melts. Cool and chill.

Just before serving, prepare meringue. Beat the egg whites until soft peaks form. Sprinkle on powdered sugar and continue beating until peaks become stiff and shiny.

Spoon 2 tablespoons chilled Port mixture over each custard, top with generous tablespoons of meringue, sprinkle on ground cinnamon, and serve.

Menu Suggestion

A Latin American Dinner

Gazpacho Maria Isabel
(page 98)

El Cid Tenderloin Fillets
(page 98)

Asparagus Tips

Pastelitos De Coco
(page 112)

The Cuisine of
Europe

Europe

Appetizers

Bavarian Cheese Croquettes
Sheraton-Munich Hotel
Munich, West Germany

Soups

Soupe aux Escargots
Atlantis Sheraton Hotel
Zurich, Switzerland

Cream of Chick-Pea with Spinach
Lisboa-Sheraton Hotel
Lisbon, Portugal

Salads

Cheese Salad
Frankfurt-Sheraton Hotel
Frankfurt, West Germany
Warmer Krautsalad
Frankfurt-Sheraton Hotel
Frankfurt, West Germany
Salade "Le Trianon"
Sheraton Park Tower Hotel
London, England

Salade Niçoise
Paris-Sheraton Hotel
Paris, France

Entrees

Rôti de Pintade
Paris-Sheraton Hotel
Paris, France
Chicken Suprême Castle Sandizell
Sheraton-Munich Hotel
Munich, West Germany
Poule au Pot Henry IV
Sheraton-Heathrow Hotel
London, England
Portuguese Chicken and Vegetable Stew
Lisboa-Sheraton Hotel
Lisbon, Portugal
Cold Braised Beef Provençal
Paris-Sheraton Hotel
Paris, France
Le Riz Colonial
Sheraton-Skyline Hotel
London, England
Délice de Veau
Sheraton-Schiphol Inn
Amsterdam, The Netherlands
Kalvemørbrad Hirtshals
Sheraton-Copenhagen Hotel
Copenhagen, Denmark

Continued

Desserts

Emincé de Volaille Homardine
Sheraton-Skyline Hotel
London, England
Homard des Mandarins
Aerogolf Sheraton Hotel
Luxembourg, Luxembourg
Poached Salmon with Mousseline Sauce
Sheraton-Stockholm Hotel
Stockholm, Sweden
Fisherman's Stew
Lisboa-Sheraton Hotel
Lisbon, Portugal
Kalbsbries in Champagnersauce mit Spinat
Frankfurt-Sheraton Hotel
Frankfurt, West Germany
Pancakes, Poached Pears, and Parmesan Sauce
Brussels-Sheraton Hotel
Brussels, Belgium

Rødgrød med Fløde
Sheraton-Copenhagen Hotel
Copenhagen, Denmark
English Sherry Trifle
Sheraton-Skyline Hotel
London, England
Pruneaux Glacés au Cognac
Paris-Sheraton Hotel
Paris, France
Salade de Figues Monte Carlo
Aerogolf Sheraton Hotel
Luxembourg, Luxembourg
Zitronen Quark
Frankfurt-Sheraton Hotel
Frankfurt, West Germany

The Cuisine of Europe

The spectrum of cooking in Europe varies from the elegant world of subtle sauces, high-rise soufflés, and delicate pastries to the rugged taste of northern fish cookery that blends the seasonings of fresh ingredients.

Whether you travel to the southern, western, or northern lands of Europe, all culinary roads lead to France—the bastion of classic cooking. The French *haute cuisine* came into its own in the magnificent *châteaux* of pre-revolutionary France and provides the ultimate pleasure for both eye and palate. No other cooking in the world demands more precision than classic French cooking. The Paris Sheraton offers you its version of this elegant fare. You can find variations on the classic French theme in almost all major European restaurants along with their own distinct flavors geared toward the climate of the locale.

In Germany, the "typical" fare of Sauerkraut and Wurst is representative only of the southern region; flavorful game dishes and fish preparations are more customary as you travel along the Rhine to the north. Included here is a marvelous sweetbread dish, Kalbsbries in Champagnersauce mit Spinat, as well as tasty Bavarian Cheese Croquettes.

The cooking of the British Isles—often regarded as tasteless by their continental neighbors—has of late made significant culinary gains and can today match most modern-day fare anywhere in the world. We have included samples of this new British cuisine, as well as some more traditional recipes, such as English Sherry Trifle.

In the far north, Scandinavia has created an inter-Nordic kitchen, as the four Viking fellowships share a common cuisine. The emphasis here is on a plain and simple diet. The well-known Smorgasbord—a buffet of cold and hot meat and fish dishes with a variety of preparations—combines many Scandinavian flavors. Sandwiches of roast beef, smoked eel, and roast pork featured in the sandwich chapter are individual samples of such Smorgasbord.

These recipes provide you with the best of Europe's culinary tradition while familiarizing you with the improvisations of highly skilled chefs who masterfully create a cuisine of their own.

Appetizers

Bavarian Cheese Croquettes

Makes 24 croquettes

Sheraton-Munich Hotel
Munich, West Germany

Much-requested hot hors d'oeuvres at the Munich Sheraton are these crisp, malt-flavored cheese croquettes.

Croquette Dough:

4 cups light German beer
1 cup all-purpose flour
½ pound Swiss cheese, grated
½ teaspoon salt
⅛ teaspoon pepper

1 egg yolk
2 to 3 teaspoons Dijon-style mustard
⅓ pound cooked ham, diced into 2
  dozen ½-inch cubes

Pour beer into a 6- or 8-cup pan. Boil approximately 45 minutes until beer is reduced to 1½ cups. (This intensifies the malt flavor considerably.) When reduced, take pan off the heat. Add all the flour at once, beating into a thick, fairly dry dough. Add grated cheese, salt, and pepper. Quickly beat in the egg yolk. Cool and refrigerate dough at least 12 hours.

When properly chilled, roll dough into 24 small balls, about 1 inch thick. Make a depression in center of each ball and put in a touch of mustard and a piece of ham. Close dough around the filling and again shape into a ball. Set aside or refrigerate until ready to fry.

Beer Batter Coating:

1⅓ cups light German beer
2 tablespoons oil
1 egg yolk

2 cups all-purpose flour
3 egg whites

Combine beer, oil, and egg yolk. Gradually stir them into the flour, beating until a smooth batter results. Whip the egg whites just until stiff. Stir ¼ of the whites into the beer batter to lighten it, then gently fold in remaining ¾ egg white. Use the batter immediately, lest the whites fade.

Continued

Final Preparations:

Sufficient oil for deep frying

Fill a pan with 3 or 4 inches of oil. Bring heat to 375 degrees on a deep-fry thermostat. Dip filled croquettes into the beer batter. Fry 3 or 4 minutes, until golden brown and cooked through. Drain and serve.

Finished croquettes are at their best when eaten right away, but they can be set aside after frying for a short while and then reheated in a 400-degree oven for 3 or 4 minutes.

Soups

Soupe aux Escargots

Serves 6

*Atlantis Sheraton Hotel
Zurich, Switzerland*

Curried Soup Base:

½ chicken breast, skinned and boned
½ cup mixture of chopped carrot, celery, and onion
2 cups Beef Stock (recipe, page 278)
2 tablespoons butter
½ cup chopped onions
½ cooking apple, peeled, cored, and chopped

1 banana, peeled and sliced
3 tablespoons all-purpose flour
1½ tablespoons curry powder
2 cups Chicken Stock (recipe, page 279)
1 cup canned turtle soup

Poach the chicken breast and chopped vegetables in beef stock for 30 minutes. Remove the breast, cool, and finely dice the meat. Set meat aside. Save the beef stock.

Melt butter in a heavy pan over medium-high heat. Sauté onions until translucent. Add chopped apple and banana, sautéing briefly 1 to 2 minutes. Quickly sprinkle on flour and curry powder, stirring and sautéing for 1 or 2 minutes. Pour and whisk in the chicken stock. Lower heat and simmer the mixture for 30 minutes, stirring occasionally.

Add turtle soup and diced chicken, and simmer another 5 minutes. Purée the soup, then pass it through a chinois or fine-meshed sieve, pressing down on the curried soup mixture with a spoon before discarding any residue.

Escargot Mixture:

2 tablespoons minced shallots
1 tablespoon butter
1 dozen escargots (snails), finely
   chopped
2 tablespoons brandy

1½ cups reserved beef stock
½ cup heavy cream
Salt and pepper to taste
Topping: *1 cup heavy cream,*
   whipped

Quickly sauté shallots in butter over high heat. Add the escargots. Pour in the brandy, ignite, and flambé. Add and stir in 1½ cups of the reserved beef stock and ½ cup heavy cream. Pour the escargot mixture into the curried soup base. Heat the soup gently; add salt and pepper to taste.

Pour into 6 ovenproof cups or bowls, top with whipped cream, and quickly brown under a preheated broiler. Serve immediately.

Cream of Chick-Pea with Spinach

Serves 6-8

Lisboa-Sheraton Hotel
Lisbon, Portugal

2 medium-sized onions, chopped
1 clove garlic
2 tablespoons olive oil
2 cups puréed chick-peas
3 cups cooked potatoes, cubed

2 cups cooked chopped spinach
4 cups Béchamel Sauce (recipe,
   page 275)
Optional: *Grated Parmesan cheese*

Fry the onions and garlic in oil 4 to 5 minutes, until golden brown. Combine puréed chick-peas, potatoes, and spinach and add to the béchamel sauce. Stir and bring to a quick boil. Add the onions and garlic, and simmer for about 5 minutes.

Sprinkle with Parmesan cheese, if desired, and serve.

Salads

Cheese Salad

Serves 6

Frankfurt-Sheraton Hotel
Frankfurt, West Germany

10 ounces Gouda cheese
5 ounces cooked ham
1 cup mushrooms
1 cup canned peas, drained
1 cup chopped pimentos

4 ounces oil
1½ ounces vinegar
2 tablespoons brandy
Salt and pepper, to taste

Cut the cheese and ham into ½-inch strips. Slice the mushrooms, sauté, and add them, the peas, and the pimentos to the ham and cheese strips.

Mix all ingredients thoroughly with the oil, vinegar, brandy, salt, and pepper, and let stand in the refrigerator for 1 hour before serving.

Warmer Krautsalad
(Warm Cabbage Salad)

Serves 4

Frankfurt-Sheraton Hotel
Frankfurt, West Germany

½ head white cabbage (about 1
    pound cabbage)
2 medium-sized onions
6 strips bacon

1 cup white wine vinegar
1 tablespoon sugar
Dash of salt

Cut cabbage into thin strips, then set aside.

Chop the onions finely and the bacon in bite-sized pieces, then sauté both on low heat until onions are golden brown. The bacon should be quite crisp.

Pour the vinegar, sugar, and salt into a pan; insert vegetable steamer, layer it with the cabbage, onions, and bacon, and steam vegetables 10 minutes, or until cabbage is soft.

Mix everything together in a salad bowl. Let cool for about 10 minutes, until salad is lukewarm, and then serve.

Wintermelon Soup *(Far East)*

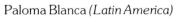

Paloma Blanca *(Latin America)*

Oriental Chicken Salad
(North America)

Macadamia Nut Cream Pie *(Hawaii)*

International Holiday Party. Left to right: Christmas
Stollen, Venezuelan Hallacas, Holiday Salad, Soufflé
Potatoe Pancakes, Roast Goose, Egg Nog *(Parties)*

Strawberry Cheese Chantilly *(Parties)*

Bavarian Cheese Croquettes *(Eur*

Bavarian Village Bread *(North America)*

mp Omelet with Hot Gingered Fruits *(North America)*

Baked Rainbow Trout
(North America)

Melon Bow Gad *(Middle East)*

Salade "Le Trianon"

Serves 4

Sheraton Park Tower Hotel
London, England

2 tablespoons olive oil
2 tablespoons white wine vinegar
1 tablespoon lemon juice
Touch of crushed garlic, to taste
Freshly ground black pepper, to taste
2 coddled eggs
¼ head crisp iceberg lettuce

½ bunch watercress, picked
½ head chicory, chopped finely
1 cup sliced raw white button
   mushrooms
2 ounces smoked salmon, cut into
   strips
Garnish: *Diced deep-fried croutons*

Prepare a dressing of olive oil, vinegar, and lemon juice, seasoned to taste with crushed garlic and pepper. Break and stir coddled eggs into the dressing while you prepare salad.

Wash and drain salad greens. Break lettuce roughy and place in a bowl; add watercress, chicory, and mushrooms. Pour salad dressing with the eggs over the greens and mushrooms, toss lightly, and correct seasoning if necessary. Place on serving plates topped with smoked salmon. Sprinkle with croutons.

Salade Niçoise

Paris-Sheraton Hotel
Paris, France

Serves 4-6

Salad:

1 heart romaine lettuce
1 heart Bibb lettuce
3 medium-sized boiled potatoes,
   cubed
3 large tomatoes
3 hard-cooked eggs, peeled and
   quartered

1 can (6½ ounces) tuna fish, drained
½ cup black olives
8-12 anchovy fillets
8 ounces cooked green beans
Vinaigrette Sauce (recipe follows)
1 tablespoon chopped fresh parsley

Continued

Cover the bottom of a salad bowl with the lettuce and mound the potatoes on top of it. Surround with the tomatoes, eggs, tuna fish, olives, anchovies, and green beans. Pour the Vinaigrette Sauce over the salad, sprinkle with parsley, and serve.

Vinaigrette Sauce:

4 tablespoons red wine vinegar	*1 tablespoon dry mustard*
Salt and pepper to taste	*2 tablespoons olive oil*

Mix vinegar, salt, pepper, and mustard until smooth. Add the oil and mix until oil is absorbed.

Entrees

Rôti de Pintade

(Rock Cornish Hen Roast)

Paris-Sheraton Hotel
Paris, France

Serves 6

Guinea hen (pintade), much prized by the French for its delicate gamy flavor, is a difficult bird to find in most American markets. Therefore, we have substituted the readily available American hybrid, the Rock Cornish hen that, although slightly smaller, has tender, moist white meat and a subtle flavor.

Hens:

6 (approximately 1 ½ pounds each)	*3 teaspoons salt*
Rock Cornish hens	*1 teaspoon pepper*
Seasoned Stuffing (recipe follows)	*4 tablespoons butter, softened to*
4 medium-sized cloves garlic,	*room temperature*
peeled and chopped	

Preheat oven to 350 degrees. Wash the Rock Cornish game hens and pat dry. Place ¼ cup stuffing into each cavity. Truss the hens. Place remaining stuffing in a small baking dish and set aside.

Make a paste of the garlic, salt, and pepper. Work in the butter. Rub an equal portion of this mixture onto each of the birds. Place the hens breast side down on a rack set in a shallow pan.

Roast for 30 minutes. Turn the chicken breast side up. Baste with the pan drippings. Roast 20 minutes longer. Baste again. Raise the temperature to 400 degrees and cook about 10 minutes longer, until the hens are a dark golden brown. Place the casserole of reserved stuffing into the oven for the last 5 to 10 minutes that the hens are roasting, to heat through. Serve the Rock Cornish hens garnished with small portions of the warmed stuffing.

Seasoned Stuffing:

4 tablespoons butter
2 tablespoons olive oil
4 cups day-old French bread, crusts
   removed, cut into ¼-inch cubes
1 or 2 teaspoons minced anchovies,
   to taste

½ cup minced fresh parsley
½ cup minced green onion
½ teaspoon dried thyme leaves
2 tablespoons boiling water or
   Chicken Stock (recipe, page 279)

In a large heavy skillet, melt 2 tablespoons butter in 1 tablespoon olive oil over medium-low heat. Add the bread cubes and stir well to coat all with butter. Pan-fry until the bread cubes are golden and crispy, 15 to 20 minutes, stirring occasionally. Remove and set aside. Wipe out the skillet.

Return the pan to heat. Melt the remaining butter in the remaining olive oil. Add the anchovies, mashing them with the back of a spoon. Stir in the parsley, onion, and thyme leaves. Sauté them until the onions are tender, about 5 minutes.

When the onions are tender, return the sautéed cubes to the pan. Sprinkle on the water or stock and stir to moisten all the cubes. Set aside until ready to use.

Chicken Suprême Castle Sandizell

Serves 6

*Sheraton-Munich Hotel
Munich, West Germany*

Macaire Potatoes (recipe follows)
6 chicken suprêmes (3 whole chicken
   breasts, split, skinned, and boned)
3 shallots, peeled and chopped
1 teaspoon salt
⅛ teaspoon pepper
¼ cup cognac or brandy
2 cups heavy cream
½ pound mushrooms, cleaned and
   sliced
¼ teaspoon Dijon-style mustard

¼ teaspoon salt
Pinch of white pepper
3 medium-sized ripe tomatoes,
   skinned, seeded, and chopped
12 asparagus spears (about 10
   ounces)
3 tablespoons butter
1 cup Hollandaise Sauce (recipe,
   page 275)
¼ cup freshly grated Parmesan
   cheese

Continued

Make the Macaire Potatoes as described in the recipe below.

Place the 6 chicken supremes in a shallow dish. Sprinkle the shallots, 1 teaspoon salt, and ⅛ teaspoon pepper on them. Pour the cognac over the seasoned chicken. Turn the breasts several times to distribute the marinade ingredients evenly. Cover and refrigerate 1 or 2 hours, turning occasionally.

Pour cream into a saucepan; add mushrooms, mustard, ¼ teaspoon salt, and a pinch of white pepper. Gently boil cream and mushrooms about 25 minutes (until cream has reduced by half), stirring frequently. (Cream and mushrooms should measure about 2 cups at this point.)

To take the edge of rawness off the tomatoes, place them in a hot pan and fry them for no more than 30 seconds. Scrape them out of the pan and set aside.

Steam or poach the asparagus until they are just a little underdone. Plunge them into cold water to stop their cooking and set their color. Drain and set them aside.

Take the breasts out of the marinade when enough time has passed (see above) and wipe them dry. Discard the marinade.

Melt 3 tablespoons butter in a large frying pan over medium heat. Sauté all the breasts, covered, 2 to 3 minutes on each side, until just done. Do not overcook or breasts will lose their tenderness.

Place the sautéed chicken breasts in a shallow baking dish, fitting them together closely. Pour the reduced mushroom sauce over the breasts. Top each breast with about 2 tablespoons chopped tomatoes and place 2 asparagus spears on each breast. (Dish may be covered at this point and refrigerated several hours before serving.)

Shortly before serving, prepare the Hollandaise Sauce and keep it warm.

Place the covered chicken dish in a cold oven and turn it on to 300 degrees. Heat the dish just long enough to warm all ingredients through. While dish is warming, fry the Macaire Potatoes (recipe below).

Take the hot chicken dish out of the oven and top each serving with 2 or 3 tablespoons warm Hollandaise Sauce. Sprinkle on the grated Parmesan cheese. Run chicken under the broiler just long enough to lightly brown the cheese. Serve immediately, accompanied with Macaire Potatoes.

Macaire Potatoes:

2¼ pounds baking potatoes	1 teaspoon salt
6 tablespoons (approximately) softened butter	⅛ teaspoon white pepper

Early in the day, or as much as 24 hours ahead, bake the potatoes until cooked through. Let cool just until they can be handled, then peel potatoes or scoop out their flesh and place it in a bowl. While potatoes are still hot, mash them well, stirring in 2 tablespoons butter, salt, and pepper. Cool, cover, and refrigerate the potatoes until needed.

When you are ready to fry them, form the potatoes into 12 balls and flatten them slightly with the palms of your hands. Fry potatoes in enough remaining butter, 2 to 3 minutes on a side, until crisp golden crusts develop. Drain briefly. Serve immediately, 1 or 2 per person.

Poule au Pot Henry IV
(Poached Chicken and Vegetables)

Serves 4

Sheraton-Heathrow Hotel
London, England

Poached chicken in a pot was such a favorite of King Henry IV that it now bears his name. It is a simple dish to prepare, looks beautiful with its vegetable garnish, and most important, tastes delicious. It can easily be refrigerated and reheated.

4-pound chicken, trussed
(tied)
6 to 8 cups Chicken Stock (recipe,
page 279)
2 tablespoons fresh lemon juice
2 carrots, peeled and julienned into
1½-inch pieces
2 celery stalks, julienned into 1½-inch
pieces
3 green onions, trimmed and
julienned into 1½-inch pieces
¼ pound fresh mushrooms, cleaned
and quartered

¼ cup chopped onions
1 large garlic clove, minced
2 bay leaves
2 whole cloves
¼ teaspoon ground cardamom
¼ teaspoon oregano
¼ teaspoon pepper
4 large tomatoes, quartered and
seeded
1 teaspoon chopped fresh mint leaves
or ½ teaspoon dried mint
¼ teaspoon rosemary
Garnish: *Chopped parsley* (optional)

Place trussed chicken in a large pot. Pour in enough stock to cover the bird. Bring to a boil, then lower heat to simmer. Add remaining ingredients, except tomatoes, mint, and rosemary. Poach, partially covered, for 35 minutes.

After 35 minutes, add the tomatoes, mint, and rosemary. Simmer the dish 25 minutes longer, or until juices in the bird run clear when pierced with a knife.

To serve, place chicken on a large platter, untie, and surround it with the vegetables. Spoon over it 1 cup cooking stock, then garnish with chopped parsley, if desired. Strain and degrease additional cooking stock for a natural gravy.

Portuguese Chicken and Vegetable Stew

Serves 6–8

Lisboa-Sheraton Hotel
Lisbon, Portugal

2 chickens, cut into serving-sized
  pieces
2 teaspoons salt
½ teaspoon pepper
2 tablespoons olive oil or vegetable
  oil
8 tablespoons (approximately) butter
½ pound small white boiling onions,
  peeled and parboiled
2 cups chopped onion
2 large cloves garlic, peeled and
  minced
2 shallots, peeled and minced
¾ pound medium-sized mushrooms,
  cleaned and quartered

¼ pound ham
2 pounds small white potatoes,
  peeled and parboiled
2 medium-sized tomatoes, cut into
  wedges
1 cup whiskey
1 cup dry white wine
1 cup Chicken Stock (recipe, page
  279)
3 tablespoons chopped fresh parsley
1 teaspoon dried oregano
Optional: ½ cup Port wine

Rinse the chicken well and pat dry. Sprinkle with a mixture of the salt and pepper.

Place a large frying pan over medium-high heat. Add the olive oil and 2 tablespoons butter. When oil and butter are hot, fry batches of chicken until golden brown but not necessarily cooked through. This should take about 20 minutes. Drain and place chicken and parboiled onions in a large casserole, preferably earthenware.

Clean the frying pan and place it back on the stove over medium-high heat. Add three tablespoons butter. When hot, sauté the chopped onions, garlic, and shallots 8 to 10 minutes, until onions are soft. Add to the casserole.

Melt an additional tablespoon butter in the pan and toss in the mushrooms. Sauté 1 to 2 minutes to glaze and soften the mushrooms. Add to the casserole.

Melt another tablespoon butter in the pan and sauté the ham several minutes, until lightly browned. Remove, dice the meat, and add to the casserole.

Sauté the potatoes, quartered if necessary, until golden brown, adding more butter if the pan is dry. When potatoes are brown, add them to the casserole. Finally, top the casserole with tomato wedges.

Pour the whiskey into the hot frying pan; stir and scrape the pan bottom well. Boil the whiskey about 1 minute to cook out the alcohol. Pour in the wine, then the chicken stock, parsley, and oregano. Simmer mixture 1 or 2 minutes to blend the flavors, then pour it into the casserole.

Cover and bake the dish in a 375-degree oven at least 1½ hours, until chicken is fork tender and the broth is rich in flavor. (If you are using an earthenware casserole, do not preheat the oven or the casserole may break.) Just before serving, pour in ½ cup Port wine, if desired.

The stew may be made in advance, refrigerated, then reheated.

Cold Braised Beef Provençale

Serves 6

Paris-Sheraton Hotel
Paris, France

This dish looks very impressive when it is unmolded and served. The julienned beef is suspended in a lovely light beef aspic.

4 tablespoons olive oil
4 large onions, peeled and sliced
4 medium-sized carrots, peeled and
  sliced
5 cloves garlic, peeled and minced
2 cracked veal shanks or knuckles
2 pounds lean beef, cut into 2-inch
  pieces
4 cups dry red wine
2 sprigs parsley
1 teaspoon thyme
2 whole cloves

2 bay leaves
¼ pound bacon, blanched and diced
Zest of 1 orange
1 tablespoon salt
½ teaspoon ground pepper
2 cups Beef Stock (recipe, page 278)
1 tablespoon unflavored gelatin
8 to 10 jumbo Spanish olives stuffed
  with pimentos
3 large carrots, peeled, sliced, and
  cooked
Garnish: *Sprigs of fresh parsley*

In a large heavy kettle set over medium-high heat, warm 2 tablespoons olive oil. Add the onions, 4 sliced raw carrots, and garlic. Sauté all until onions are golden, about 10 to 15 minutes. Remove the vegetables with a slotted spoon, place in a large bowl, and set aside.

Add the other 2 tablespoons oil to the kettle along with the veal shanks (or knuckles). Fry the shanks, turning frequently, until brown. Using a slotted spoon, remove the veal and place it with the vegetables.

Brown the beef in the oil remaining in the kettle. When the beef is browned on all sides, return the vegetables and the veal bones to the pan. Pour in the red wine.

Make a bouquet garni by combining parsley, thyme, cloves, and bay leaves. Tie up in cheesecloth. Add this to the kettle along with the bacon, orange zest, salt, and pepper. Bring the

Continued

contents of the pan to a boil, cover, then simmer over very low heat for about 6 hours or until the meat is tender.

After the cooking has been completed, skim off all fat, or chill the contents of the kettle until the fat has hardened, thus simplifying its removal.

Remove vegetables, meat, bouquet garni, and orange zest from the broth. Save the broth and the braised beef. Discard all other ingredients.

Strain the broth through a piece of cheesecloth to clarify it. Then boil it, uncovered, over high heat to reduce to 2 cups. Add 1 cup of the beef stock. Take pan off the heat.

Soften 1 tablespoon gelatin in 1 cup remaining stock for 5 minutes. Add this to the flavored beef broth combination and stir over low heat until gelatin has completely dissolved. Correct seasoning.

Julienne the braised beef into ¼-inch strips. Place the Spanish olives in a 5 × 9 × 4-inch loaf pan. Add ½ of the julienned meat to create the first layer. Place the cooked carrot slices evenly over the meat to create the second layer. The third layer is composed of the rest of the meat.

Fill the loaf pan with the flavored beef broth. Cover and refrigerate to set, about 5 hours or overnight. Unmold onto a serving platter and garnish with fresh parsley. Serve at once.

Le Riz Colonial
(Veal, Sole, and Shrimp in Curry Sauce)

Serves 2

Sheraton-Skyline Hotel
London, England

2 (3-ounce) veal scallops, pounded and cut into pieces 3 inches by 4 inches

4 ounces fillet of sole, cut into pieces 3 inches by 4 inches

4 ounces large shrimp, peeled, deveined, and split lengthwise

½ teaspoon salt

Pinch of white pepper

4 tablespoons Clarified Butter (recipe, page 277)

2 teaspoons minced shallots

¼ pound fresh mushrooms, cleaned and quartered

½ green bell pepper, thinly sliced

¼ cup dark raisins

¼ cup pine nuts

¾ cup dry white wine

1 cup heavy cream

1 teaspoon curry powder

⅛ scant teaspoon cayenne pepper

1 teaspoon fresh tarragon or ½ teaspoon dried tarragon

Season veal, sole, and shrimp with salt and white pepper. Melt 3 tablespoons clarified butter in heavy frying pan over medium-high heat. Quickly sauté the veal, then the sole, then the shrimp, until the veal is browned, the sole cooked through, and the shrimp pink. Transfer them, when done, to an ovenproof platter. Keep warm.

Add 1 more tablespoon clarified butter to the pan. Sauté shallots, mushrooms, bell pepper, raisins, and pine nuts for 2 to 3 minutes, until nuts are brown and bell peppers crisp but tender. When done, set aside in their own dish.

Deglaze the frying pan with white wine. Add cream, curry powder, cayenne pepper, and tarragon. Bring to a boil, then reduce heat to low. Simmer the sauce gently for about 5 minutes, stirring occasionally. Season with additional salt and pepper if desired.

Pour the hot curry sauce over the veal, sole, and shrimp, then top with the vegetables, raisins, and nuts. If necessary, reheat whole dish in a 350-degree oven for 3 to 4 minutes. A side dish of white rice would be appropriate.

Délice de Veau

Serves 2

Sheraton-Schiphol Inn
Amsterdam, Netherlands

³/₄- to 1-pound veal tenderloin, trimmed of all fat and membranes
1 tablespoon butter, melted
2 tablespoons fine dry white bread crumbs with crusts removed
½ teaspoon salt
Generous pinch of freshly ground black pepper
3 tablespoons butter
1 clove garlic, peeled and minced
1 large shallot, peeled and minced

1 tablespoon all-purpose flour
³/₄ cup light cream or half and half
½ cup Chicken Stock (recipe, page 279)
⅛ to ¼ teaspoon dried rosemary, to taste
2 teaspoons or more fresh lemon juice, to taste
Garnishes: Minced fresh parsley, thin lemon wedges

Preheat the oven to 350 degrees. Brush the tenderloin with 1 tablespoon melted butter. Pat all over with a mixture of the bread crumbs, salt, and pepper.

Melt 2 tablespoons butter in a small heavy frying pan over medium heat. Sauté the tenderloin about 5 minutes, turning frequently, until bread crumbs are crisp and brown. Take tenderloin out of the frying pan and place on a small ovenproof platter or in a baking dish. Scrape browned crumbs and butter left in the pan onto the top of the tenderloin fillet. Cover the fillet and bake 40 to 50 minutes, until cooked through.

While the tenderloin is baking, place the frying pan back on the heat and proceed with the lemon sauce. Add the remaining 1 tablespoon butter to the pan and sauté the garlic and shallots, stirring, until tender, about 1 or 2 minutes. Sprinkle in the flour, cook, and stir the roux 2 or 3 minutes. Whisk in the light cream and the chicken stock. Bring sauce to a boil, reduce heat, and simmer 10 minutes, stirring occasionally. Add the rosemary and lemon juice. Season with additional salt and pepper, if desired, then simmer 5 to 10 minutes longer. (Sauce may be made ahead and refrigerated if desired.)

To serve, pour warm sauce over the tenderloin, sprinkle with parsley, and garnish with lemon wedges.

Kalvemørbrad Hirtshals
(Veal Tenderloin Stuffed with Lobster)

Serves 4

Sheraton-Copenhagen Hotel
Copenhagen, Denmark

A delightfully simple yet elegant dish. It is as impressive as an entrée that takes hours to prepare.

4 (6-ounce) veal tenderloin fillets or 4
  (6-ounce) loin boneless chops,
  trimmed of all fat
½ pound cooked lump lobster meat

Salt and freshly ground black pepper,
  to taste
¼ cup Port wine
4 tablespoons butter

Place each tenderloin fillet between sheets of waxed paper and pound to flatten slightly. Cut a pocket into the side of each fillet and stuff with lobster meat.

Rub the outside of stuffed fillets with a moderate amount of salt and pepper. Melt 2 tablespoons butter in a large heavy skillet over a moderate heat. Sauté the fillets until well browned all over and cooked through, about 15 minutes.

When done, take fillets out of the pan and set on a warm platter or individual plates. To the same pan, add the Port wine, stirring and scraping 1 to 2 minutes to deglaze the pan. Remove pan from heat and swirl in the remaining butter, 1 tablespoon at a time. Pour the sauce over the veal fillets and serve immediately.

Emincé de Volaille Homardine
(Chicken and Lobster in Brandy Cream Sauce)

Serves 2

Sheraton-Skyline Hotel
London, England

In culinary terms, *émincé* usually implies a dish of thinly sliced precooked meats or poultry topped with a complementary sauce. The Sheraton-Skyline has adapted this technique to create an elegant entrée.

2 tablespoons butter
1½ tablespoons minced shallots
1 cup brandy
1 cup dry white wine
2 tablespoons condensed Chicken
  Stock (recipe, page 279)
2 cups heavy cream
½ pound cooked chicken breast, cut
  into ½-inch-wide slivers

½ pound cooked lobster, cut into
  ½-inch-wide slivers
1 teaspoon fresh tarragon or
  ½ teaspoon dried tarragon
½ teaspoon salt
¼ teaspoon white pepper
Garnish: Chopped fresh parsley

Melt the butter over medium-high heat in a large heavy skillet. Sauté the shallots for 1 to 2 minutes, until translucent. Pour in the brandy and flambé. (Be prepared for the flames to jump quite high.)

As soon as the flames die down, blend in the wine, chicken stock, and cream. Simmer and stir the brandy cream sauce about 20 minutes, until it has reduced to a smooth, fairly thick consistency.

Lower the heat. Add chicken, lobster, tarragon, salt, and pepper. Simmer gently until chicken and lobster are heated through. Serve on a bed of white rice, garnished with 2 tablespoons parsley.

Homard Des Mandarins
(Lobster in Brandy-Orange Sauce)

Serves 8

Aerogolf Sheraton Hotel
Luxembourg, Luxembourg

4 lobsters, each 1 to 1½ pounds
   cooked and split in half
6 tablespoons Clarified Butter (recipe,
   page 277)
¼ cup finely minced shallots
1 tablespoon brandy
1 teaspoon Cointreau
2 tablespoons dry white wine

2 cups heavy cream
½ teaspoon salt
⅛ teaspoon white pepper
¼ cup Hollandaise Sauce (recipe,
   page 275)
½ cup whipped cream
Garnish: *Mandarin orange sections*

Remove meat from the lobster shell in whole pieces and set aside. Clean out, wash and dry the shells. Fit shells snugly together in one or two shallow baking dishes.

Melt clarified butter in a large frying pan over medium heat. When hot, sauté the lobster meat for 1 to 2 minutes, thus flavoring the butter with lobster juices and coating the lobster with butter. Remove the meat from the pan and set aside briefly.

Add shallots to the pan and sauté until soft. Raise the heat to medium high, pour in the brandy, then the Cointreau, then the white wine. Simmer briefly to deglaze the pan. Pour in the cream; season with salt and pepper. Stirring occasionally, boil the cream until reduced to 1 cup, about 15 minutes. When reduced, strain the hot cream into a bowl. Let cool completely until it is at room temperature.

Once cool, spread 1 tablespoon reduced cream sauce into the bottom of each lobster shell. Place sautéed lobster meat back in the shells, on top of the sauce. (At this point the lobsters and remaining cream sauce can be covered and refrigerated several hours before proceeding with the final preparations.) To the remaining cool sauce, stir in the hot sauce, then fold in whipped cream.

Spoon the brandy-orange sauce over the lobsters. Top each lobster with mandarin orange sections.

Bake at 400 degrees in upper third of a preheated oven, 6 to 8 minutes, until heated through. Dish can be run under the broiler to lightly brown, if desired. Serve immediately.

Poached Salmon with Mousseline Sauce

Serves 12

Sheraton-Stockholm Hotel
Stockholm, Sweden

Poached Salmon:

¼ cup chopped celery
¾ cup chopped carrots
1 onion, sliced
1 teaspoon peppercorns
1 tablespoon salt
*2 sprigs fresh dill or 1 teaspoon dried
  dill*

¼ cup white wine vinegar
2 quarts water
*1 whole salmon, 7 to 8 pounds,
  cleaned*
Garnish: *Fresh dill sprigs, lemon
  wedges*

Place all ingredients except salmon and garnish in a fish poacher or large pan. Boil gently 25 to 30 minutes. Take pan off the heat and cool bouillon to room temperature.

Wipe fish with a damp cloth. Lay fish on its side and measure the height of the fish at its thickest or highest point (for timing purposes).

Place fish on poaching rack and lower into the pan. Add more cold water if necessary to ensure that fish is covered.

Set pan over medium-high heat and bring to a simmer. Reduce heat to low, cover pan, and poach the fish 10 minutes for each inch of thickness (measured as above). For example, a fish 3½ inches high would poach for 35 minutes. (This technique for measuring fish is called the "Canadian" method.) Do not allow bouillon to boil or salmon may break.

When done, remove pan from the heat, uncover, and allow the fish to cool down in the bouillon for 1 hour.

Carefully lift out the poaching rack and slide salmon onto a large platter. With a small knife, cut through skin near the head and slit skin down the backbone and belly. Starting at the head, pull whole top layer of skin off the fish. Scrape off any darkish brown meat so that exposed flesh is uniformly pink.

Serve at room temperature or chilled, decorated with fresh dill sprigs and lemon wedges. Accompany with the following sauce.

Mousseline Sauce:

1½ cups mayonnaise
*2 tablespoons fresh dill or 1
  tablespoon dried dill*

Finely chopped fresh chives
½ cup heavy cream, whipped

Whisk together mayonnaise, dill, and 1 tablespoon chives (if desired). Let stand. Lightly fold in whipped cream. Refrigerate until ready to serve. You will have about 2½ cups sauce.

Fisherman's Stew

Makes 5 quarts

Lisboa-Sheraton Hotel
Lisbon, Portugal

Even if you haven't enjoyed a successful piscatory venture recently, you can still revel in fish stew. Choose the "catch of the day" at your fish market. Using a variety of fish adds greatly to the flavor of this stew. Do be a little adventurous and enjoy.

3 medium-sized onions, peeled and sliced ¼ inch thick
2 cloves garlic, peeled and mashed
3 large green bell peppers, seeded and diced
2 bay leaves
¼ cup olive oil
1 pound tomatoes, peeled and diced
⅓ cup tomato paste
1 cup dry white wine
1 tablespoon salt

½ teaspoon white pepper
⅛ teaspoon dried basil
⅛ teaspoon dried thyme
6 pounds varied fish fillets, preferably lean white fish such as red snapper, cod, bass, perch, or flounder, cut into 2-inch pieces
Tabasco sauce, to taste
Garnish: *Chopped fresh parsley*

In a large soup pot, sauté onions, garlic, bell peppers, and bay leaves in olive oil over medium heat until onions are soft, about 8 to 10 minutes. Add the diced tomatoes, tomato paste, wine, and seasonings. Bring to a gentle boil.

When the broth is boiling gently, add the fish to the pot, stirring carefully and thoroughly. Bring the broth to a gentle boil, cover, reduce heat to medium, and continue to cook, stirring occasionally, 20 to 25 minutes, or until fish is opaque and flakes when gently scraped with a fork. The fish will emit juices as they cook, producing a lovely stew broth.

When stew is done, remove the kettle from the heat. Add Tabasco sauce to taste. Serve the stew in large bowls, sprinkling it with chopped fresh parsley. Accompany with hot French bread or steamed potatoes and additional Tabasco sauce.

Kalbsbries in Champagnersauce mit Spinat

(Sweetbreads in Champagne Sauce on Spinach Bed)

Serves 4

Frankfurt-Sheraton Hotel
Frankfurt, West Germany

The subtle flavor of sweetbreads finds a perfect match in this superb champagne sauce. The combination is sure to please sweetbread lovers and make devotees of those who will be eating them for the first time.

1½ pounds fresh sweetbreads
1 quart cold water
1 tablespoon fresh lemon juice
½ teaspoon salt
2½ cups champagne
8 tablespoons unsalted butter
⅓ cup all-purpose flour
2 cups hot Chicken Stock (recipe,
*   page 279)*

½ cup heavy cream
3 tablespoons Hollandaise Sauce
*   (recipe, page 275)*
2½ pounds fresh spinach, washed,
*   stemmed, and dried*
½ teaspoon salt
¼ teaspoon pepper

Soak fresh sweetbreads in cold water 2 to 3 hours. Drain, then transfer them to a large pan. Pour in 1 quart cold water, lemon juice, and ½ teaspoon salt. Bring to a boil, reduce heat, and simmer 5 minutes. Drain and cool.

Remove tough sinews and membranes surrounding cooled sweetbreads and separate them into small sections. Wrap sections in toweling and place between 2 flat surfaces, such as small cheese boards. Weigh down with a few pounds (cans work well for this) if flat objects do not exert any pressure on the sweetbreads. Refrigerate several hours or overnight, allowing sweetbreads time to exude undesirable pink juices.

When thoroughly pressed, put sweetbreads in medium-sized pan and pour in 1¾ cups champagne. Cover and simmer gently for 30 minutes. While the sweetbreads are poaching, prepare champagne sauce and spinach bed.

For sauce, melt 6 tablespoons butter in a medium-sized pan over medium heat. Add flour and blend with a whisk for 3 or 4 minutes. Slowly pour in chicken stock, stir, and simmer 20 minutes longer. Just before serving, pour in cream, remaining champagne, and Hollandaise sauce. Heat through.

Make spinach bed by melting remaining 2 tablespoons butter in a large pot; add cleaned, stemmed spinach, ½ teaspoon salt, and ¼ teaspoon pepper. Cover and cook over medium heat, stirring occasionally, until spinach has wilted and is tender.

To present, place spinach on a serving dish, remove sweetbreads from champagne with a slotted spoon, and arrange on spinach. Coat with champagne sauce. *Note:* Small fried potato balls served on the side would be appropriate.

Pancakes, Poached Pears, and Parmesan Sauce

Serves 6

Brussels-Sheraton Hotel
Brussels, Belgium

If you are looking for an unusual breakfast or brunch dish, this is it!

Pancakes:

2¼ cups sifted all-purpose flour
1 teaspoon baking powder
3 eggs, lightly beaten
1⅓ cups milk
4 tablespoons melted butter, cooled
   to room temperature
3 egg whites

6 ounces Cheshire cheese, thinly
   sliced
Warm Poached Pears (recipe below),
   sliced
Warm Parmesan Sauce (recipe follows)
Garnish: Ground cinnamon

Preheat the oven to 225 degrees. Mix together the flour and baking powder and sift them into a bowl. Lightly stir in a mixture of the 3 whole eggs and milk, followed by 3 tablespoons melted butter. Do not overbeat the batter or the pancakes will not be as tender as when lightly beaten. (It is best, but not necessary, to let this batter rest several hours, refrigerated, before proceeding. If after resting, batter has thickened substantially, thin out with small additions of milk.)

Beat the 3 egg whites until stiff but not dry. Gently fold into the pancake batter.

Grease a griddle or frying pan with a small amount of remaining tablespoon of butter. When hot, pour in about ¾ cup batter to make 1 pancake 6 to 7 inches wide. Cook until lightly browned on the bottom and fairly dry on the top. Flip over and lightly brown the other side. Proceed making the remaining 5 or 6 pancakes in the same fashion, greasing the skillet as necessary.

As they are cooked, place pancakes on a rack in the slow oven to keep warm.

When all pancakes are cooked, take them out of the oven and place on warm plates. Top with thin slices of Cheshire cheese, then warm pear slices arranged in a pinwheel design, and finally with 2 or 3 tablespoons of the warm Parmesan cheese sauce. Sprinkle with a small amount of ground cinnamon and serve.

Poached Pears:

4 large firm but ripe pears
2 cups sugar

1½ cups water
1 cinnamon stick, broken up

Continued

Peel, slice in half lengthwise, and core the pears. Combine the sugar and water and bring to a simmer. Add the pears to the simmering sugar syrup. Poach the pears until slightly translucent and just tender. Take pan off the heat. Allow the pears to cool down in their syrup enough to handle them. (Pears can be kept, set to the side, or refrigerated until time to reheat.)

When ready to serve, remove warm pears from their syrup and cut them into slender, long wedges. Save the pear syrup for other uses.

Parmesan Sauce:

3 egg yolks
½ cup sour cream
½ cup hot melted butter
¼ cup freshly grated Parmesan
    cheese

1 tablespoon lime juice
Salt and white pepper, to taste

Place egg yolks and sour cream in a heavy saucepan. Using a wire whisk the whole time, stir until yolks and sour cream are well combined.

Place the pan over a very low heat, stir, and cook yolks and cream 3 to 4 minutes until warmed through. Very slowly, drizzle in the melted butter, whisking the entire time, until all butter is added and sauce is very smooth.

Begin adding the grated cheese, 1 tablespoon at a time, waiting until each tablespoon is well dissolved before adding the next. Add the lime juice, and salt and pepper to taste. Let sauce cook a few minutes longer, stirring occasionally. Set sauce to the side, or cover and refrigerate until needed. Serve warm, reheating over a low fire. Thin out with small additions of heavy cream if necessary to achieve a thick pouring consistency.

This recipe makes about 1 cup of sauce.

Desserts

Rødgrød Med Fløde
(Red Fruit Pudding with Cream)

Makes 2 large cups

Sheraton-Copenhagen Hotel
Copenhagen, Denmark

Ruby red, a color for kings and queens, can bring a regal dessert to your table in the form of Denmark's red fruit pudding. Fresh red raspberries or strawberries, or a combination of both, will produce this pudding. If fresh berries are out of season, unsweetened frozen berries may be substituted with success.

1½ pounds raspberries or
  strawberries
1 to 2 teaspoons fresh lemon juice
3 to 4 tablespoons sugar
2 tablespoons plus 1 teaspoon
  arrowroot

⅓ cup water
3 tablespoons blanched, slivered
  almonds
⅔ cup light cream or equal portions
  heavy cream and half-and-half

Place berries in a chinois or other fine mesh strainer and set over an enamel or stainless-steel saucepan. Press berries through the sieve into the pan, discarding any seeds or residue that cannot pass through the sieve.

Stir 1 or 2 teaspoons lemon juice into fruit purée, depending on the tartness of the berries.

Sweeten the berries by adding 3 to 4 tablespoons sugar to the pan. Place saucepan over medium-high heat and bring to a gentle boil, stirring constantly. Let boil 1 or 2 minutes, then remove pan from heat to stop the boiling.

Combine the arrowroot and water, stirring to make a smooth mixture. Stir arrowroot into the hot berry purée. Lower the heat and continue cooking at a simmer, again stirring constantly, 2 to 3 minutes, until pudding thickens slightly and becomes a little clearer in color. Do not let the pudding boil.

Cool slightly before pouring pudding into 6 small individual dishes or a small crystal bowl. Chill well, then serve garnished with slivered almonds. Pass the cream on the side.

English Sherry Trifle

Serves 8

Sheraton-Skyline Hotel
London, England

A tiny change in the presentation of this traditional English dessert makes it appear a "trifle" more interesting than usual.

1 9-inch Sponge Cake (recipe, page
  281)
½ cup (approximately) raspberry jam
½ cup dry sherry
⅓ cup sugar
2 tablespoons cornstarch

¼ teaspoon salt
3½ cups milk
6 egg yolks
1 teaspoon vanilla
Garnish: 1 cup sweetened whipped
  cream

Cut the sponge cake into 8 wedges. Coat the sides of each wedge with jam. Select a deep serving dish or crystal bowl and re-form the cake in it. Sprinkle thoroughly with the sherry. Set aside

Continued

briefly while preparing the custard sauce.

Mix sugar, cornstarch, and salt together in a heavy saucepan. Slowly stir in the milk. Place the pan over medium heat and bring to a gentle boil. Cook and stir about 1 minute. Remove pan from heat.

Place the egg yolks in a small bowl and beat them lightly with a fork or a whisk. Stirring constantly, very slowly at first, drizzle in 1 cup hot milk. When the cup of milk is added, reverse the process and, stirring constantly, slowly pour the warmed eggs into the pan of hot milk. Bring custard just up to a gentle boil. Simmer 1 minute longer, stirring constantly. Take off the heat. Stir in the vanilla. Let custard cool slightly.

Pour warm custard sauce over the sponge cake. Cover with plastic wrap (to prevent a film from forming on the custard) and refrigerate until well chilled.

To serve, top the trifle with rosettes of whipped cream and small dollops of raspberry jam.

Pruneaux Glacés au Cognac

(Marinated Prunes on Ice)

Serves 12

Paris-Sheraton Hotel
Paris, France

A wonderful dessert—so easy, so elegant, so good!

2 cups water
1½ cups sugar
12 extra large, pitted prunes
½ cup cognac

3 pints rich vanilla ice cream
Optional: *2 cups sweetened whipped cream*

Pour water into a medium-sized saucepan. Stir in the sugar. Bring to a boil over high heat, stirring until the sugar dissolves. Add the prunes, lower the heat, cover, and simmer 10 to 15 minutes to plump, soften, and sweeten the prunes. Take pan off the heat.

Remove prunes from the syrup with a slotted spoon. Place prunes in a bowl, pour the cognac over them, cover, and refrigerate several hours or several days. Refrigerate the syrup also.

To serve, take prunes out of the cognac. Pour cognac into the sugar syrup. Scoop the ice cream into 12 chilled dessert bowls or goblets. Place a marinated prune on top of each serving. Pour as much cognac syrup as desired over each serving. Dollop with whipped cream if you wish. Serve immediately.

Salade de Figues Monte Carlo
(Marinated Figs)

Serves 8   *Aerogolf Sheraton Hotel*
                                              Luxembourg, Luxembourg

24 figs, peeled   8 ounces heavy cream
2 cups orange juice   ¼ cup grated bitter chocolate
¼ cup sugar   8 thin, crisp rolled butter cookies
1 ounce Curaçao

Quarter the figs and let them marinate in the orange juice, sugar, and Curaçao about 8 hours.
   Just before serving, whip the heavy cream until it holds peaks. Serve the figs with the marinade in 8 individual dessert bowls. Cover the figs with a big dollop of whipped cream. Sprinkle grated chocolate on top of the whipped cream and serve with a butter cookie on the side.

Zitronen Quark

Serves 4   *Frankfurt- Sheraton Hotel*
                                              Frankfurt, West Germany

16 ounces cottage cheese   Juice of 1 lemon
3 egg yolks   ¼ teaspoon grated lemon rind
4 tablespoons sugar   3 egg whites
Dash of salt   1 cup raisins
1 teaspoon vanilla

Beat cottage cheese until creamy; add egg yolks, sugar, salt, vanilla, lemon juice, and lemon rind. Blend these ingredients until smooth. Beat egg whites until peaks form.

   Blend cottage cheese mixture gradually with the beaten egg whites. Stir in raisins. Chill for 1 hour. Serve.

Menu Suggestions

A Gracious Luncheon

Salade "Le Trianon"
(recipe, page 129)

Chicken Suprême Castle Sandizell
(recipe, page 131)

Macaire Potatoes
(recipe, page 132)

English Sherry Trifle
(recipe, page 145)

A Hearty Dinner

Soupe aux Escargots
(recipe, page 126)

Kalvemørbrad Hirtshals
(recipe, page 138)

Mixed Green Salad

Zitronen Quark
(recipe, page 147)

The Cuisine
of The
Middle East

Middle East

Appetizers

Lahem-Muqadad
Kuwait-Sheraton Hotel
Kuwait City, Kuwait
Mutabal
Kuwait-Sheraton Hotel
Kuwait City, Kuwait
Dolmas
Istanbul-Sheraton Hotel
Istanbul, Turkey
Hot Artichoke Soufflés
Dubai-Sheraton Hotel
Dubai, United Arab Emirates
Hot Gingered Croquettes with Apricot Sauce
Abu Dhabi-Sheraton Hotel
Abu Dhabi, United Arab Emirates
Circassian Chicken
Istanbul-Sheraton Hotel
Istanbul, Turkey
Raw Kebbah
Kuwait-Sheraton Hotel
Kuwait City, Kuwait
Sambousek
Jeddah-Sheraton Hotel
Jeddah, Saudi Arabia

Soups

Shoubet Sbaanegh
Damascus-Sheraton Hotel
Damascus, Syria

Salads

Fattoush
Abu Dhabi-Sheraton Hotel
Abu Dhabi, United Arab Emirates
Tabbouleh
Abu Dhabi-Sheraton Hotel
Abu Dhabi, United Arab Emirates
Tunisian Salad
Hammamet-Sheraton Hotel
Hammamet, Tunisia

Entrees

Roast Leg of Lamb
Hammamet-Sheraton Hotel
Hammamet, Tunisia
Da Bamia
Sheraton-Nile Boats
Aswan and Luxor, Egypt
Maghrebia
Abu Dhabi-Sheraton Hotel
Abu Dhabi, United Arab Emirates
Mozat Bellaban
Kuwait-Sheraton Hotel
Kuwait City, Kuwait
Melon Bow Gad
Tel Aviv-Sheraton Hotel
Tel Aviv, Israel
Sea Wolf Twelve Tribes
Tel Aviv-Sheraton Hotel
Tel Aviv, Israel

Continued

Desserts

Gâteau Hobza Baskutu
Hammamet-Sheraton Hotel
Hammamet, Tunisia
Marak Perot Kar
Tel Aviv-Sheraton Hotel
Tel Aviv, Israel
Meghlie
Dubai-Sheraton Hotel
Dubai, United Arab Emirates

The Cuisine of the Middle East

The Middle East is the cradle of civilization where people first learned to produce their own food. In the early days, the hostile desert offered a meager existence of gathered fruits, nuts and seeds, roots, snails, and the odd tortoise. The introduction of domesticated sheep made a dramatic change in the food supply. The primitive diet was slowly replaced with sheep and wheat, the basic foods of the modern Arabic world.

Lamb served in this part of the world is seldom more than a day old. The animals are usually slaughtered shortly before the meal at which they are to be consumed. As a rule, the lamb is spitted whole and roasted until succulent over a roaring, open fire.

Middle Easterners drink coffee on almost every conceivable occasion. The tiny cup of coffee forms an essential part of life and everyday hospitality. By Western standards the coffee is extremely strong, but a frequent traveler to the Middle East slowly acquires the taste.

Arak, a clear white liquor that turns to a milky white when mixed with water, is served before most meals. Hors d'oeuvres are always offered when arak is an aperitif.

In the Middle East, as in Europe, food is a delight to the eye. Scented coriander leaves of bright green often garnish the main dish. The Arab manner of eating is considerably different from that of the West. Bite-sized pieces are torn from a disc of flat Arabic bread and used to scoop morsels from the plate.

In all the Arab states hospitality is lavish and food is the key ingredient. The *mazza,* a traditional Arab avalanche of hors d'oeuvres, often includes thirty kinds of delicacies at a time, usually far more than is necessary for the group to be entertained. Favored dishes in the *mazza* include Tabbouleh, Fattoush, Dolmas, Raw Kebbah, Mutabal, Sambousek, and Lahem Muqadad. With these and other recipes in this chapter, you will be able to create an Arabian feast of your own!

Appetizers

Lahem Muqadad
(Ground Lamb Shish Kebabs)

Makes 24 kebabs   *Kuwait-Sheraton Hotel*
                                                       Kuwait City, Kuwait

These plump cigar-shaped lamb kebabs make an excellent appetizer for outdoor parties of all kinds. As they sizzle and pop over a hibachi, giving off a spicy aroma, they are bound to attract many hungry admirers. They are wonderfully spicy, so be sure to provide your guests with plenty of refreshing drinks, such as the Blizzard (page 267).

1½ pounds finely ground lamb   *⅓ cup minced onion*
½ teaspoon thyme leaves   *2 eggs, lightly beaten*
1 teaspoon salt   *1 cup loosely packed minced fresh*
¼ to ½ teaspoon pepper, to taste   *parsley*
2 tablespoons finely minced garlic   *¼ cup olive oil*

Combine all ingredients except olive oil in a medium-sized bowl. Work together well. Shape meat mixture into 24 cigar or elongated egg shapes, each containing 1 ounce (2 tablespoons) meat. Thread kebabs lengthwise onto slender greased skewers. Refrigerate until ready to grill. Baste with olive oil and grill 12 to 15 minutes for medium to well done.
   Ungrilled Lahem Muqadad freezes beautifully.

Mutabal
(Puréed Eggplant Dip)

Makes about 4 cups   *Kuwait-Sheraton Hotel*
                                                       Kuwait City, Kuwait

2 eggplants, each weighing about 1   *2 large garlic cloves, minced*
*   pound*   *1½ teaspoons salt*
⅓ to ½ cup fresh lemon juice, to taste *Freshly ground black pepper, to taste*
1 cup (8 ounces) sesame tahini   *Garnish: 2 tablespoons toasted*
1 cup (8 ounces) plain yogurt   *sesame seeds*

Continued

If you are using a gas stove, grill the eggplants over a low gas flame, turning them slowly until they soften substantially, begin to collapse, and all their skin is crisped and charred, about 15 minutes.

If you are using an electric oven, place the eggplants on a baking sheet and position them 5 to 6 inches below the broiling element. Broil with oven door ajar 15 to 25 minutes, turning frequently until eggplants collapse and are evenly charred. Remove and cool.

When eggplants are cool, cut or tear off and throw out the charred skins. Place the softened eggplant meat in a blender, food processor, or large bowl. Add the remaining ingredients. Mash or purée well, until a smooth, fairly firm eggplant dip results.

Transfer the completed Mutabal dip to a serving dish. Chill well before serving garnished with toasted sesame seeds, surrounded by pieces of pita bread.

Dolmas
(Stuffed grape leaves)

Makes 3 dozen

Istanbul-Sheraton Hotel
Istanbul, Turkey

Dolmas (or *Dolmades*) are a well-known appetizer that can be served hot, at room temperature, or even cold. Here they are presented while still hot with a thin sauce of beaten yogurt. They are perfect for buffets or cocktail parties since they can be made well in advance.

4 dozen (1 8-ounce jar) grape leaves	*1½ teaspoons minced fresh dill or*
1½ cups minced onions	*1 teaspoon dried dill*
4 tablespoons butter	*½ teaspoon salt*
⅓ cup white rice	*1 teaspoon freshly ground black*
3 cups water	*pepper*
1¾ pounds lean ground beef	*1 pint plain yogurt, well beaten*

Blanch grape leaves in hot water for 30 seconds to remove excess brine, then quickly drain and submerge them in cold water. Pat dry with paper towels. Select 36 of the best leaves for stuffing.

Lightly brown onions in 2 tablespoons butter over medium heat. Add and stir rice for 2 minutes to thoroughly coat with butter. Pour in 1 cup water, cover pan, and simmer approximately 10 minutes, until rice absorbs all liquid. Remove pan from the heat, stir in ground beef, dill, salt, and ½ teaspoon freshly ground pepper. Stir for several minutes, making sure filling is well combined.

To stuff and shape dolmas, start by laying leaves shiny side down, tips pointing away from you.

Place a teaspoon or two of meat mixture in the center, fold over the sides, then roll gently but firmly away from you toward the tip until you have neat little cylindrical dolmas.

Cover bottom of a large heavy casserole with unused leaves. Place dolmas side by side, seamside down, in layers in the casserole. Top with 2 tablespoons butter and 2 cups water. Weigh down lightly with a plate to keep them from unrolling. Cover, place over moderate heat, and simmer 40 minutes. Remove, drain, and serve on a platter with remaining freshly ground pepper and yogurt.

Hot Artichoke Soufflés

Serves 4

*Dubai-Sheraton Hotel
Dubai, United Arab Emirates*

Your reputation as a cook will rise to its greatest height when you present your guests with these hot artichoke soufflés, individually served in trimmed artichoke shells.

Artichoke Shells:

4 large fresh artichokes
6 to 8 cups water
2 tablespoons lemon juice

1 teaspoon salt
Garnish: *Lemon wedges*

Cut off stems of artichokes even with bases. Lay on their sides and trim approximately 2 inches off the tops, leaving each artichoke about 2 inches high. Place trimmed artichokes in 6 to 8 cups boiling water, seasoned with lemon juice and salt. Weigh down with a small plate or towel to keep them submerged. Gently boil 40 to 50 minutes or until the leaves can just barely be pulled out of the shells. Cool and drain.

When cool, remove all inner leaves and hairy chokes, exposing the hearts and leaving only 3 or 4 outer layers of leaves. Pat each one dry inside and out. To protect and prevent the shells from shriveling during baking, encase the outsides of the artichokes in tinfoil. Set aside until ready to use.

Soufflé Base:

1 cup milk
4 tablespoons butter
6 tablespoons all-purpose flour
4 egg yolks
½ pound artichoke bottoms, chopped
    (preferably freshly poached, but
    can be frozen or packed in water)

¼ teaspoon cayenne pepper
⅛ teaspoon nutmeg
¼ teaspoon salt
5 egg whites

Continued

Bring milk and butter to a boil. Pour in the flour and stir vigorously until mixture leaves the sides of the pan. Take pan off the heat. Beat in the egg yolks, one at a time, blending them well. Add the chopped artichoke hearts, cayenne pepper, nutmeg, and salt. Set aside.

Preheat oven to 375 degrees. Place foil-encased artichoke shells in oven for 3 or 4 minutes to heat through. While they are warming up, beat egg whites just until stiff. Mix one-third of the whites into the soufflé base, then gently fold in the remaining two-thirds egg whites. Fill hot artichoke shells four-fifths the way up with the soufflé mixture.

Place filled artichokes on a baking sheet in lower third of the oven. Bake 40 to 50 minutes, until the soufflés rise and brown nicely on top. Remove tinfoil and serve immediately, garnished with lemon wedges.

Hot Gingered Croquettes with Apricot Sauce

Makes about 40 croquettes   *Abu Dhabi-Sheraton Hotel*
                                                               Abu Dhabi, United Arab Emirates

Croquettes:

4 cups milk	*4 teaspoons grated fresh ginger root*
¾ cup sugar	*½ cup ground blanched almonds*
1 cup white rice	*Sufficient oil for deep frying*
1 teaspoon vanilla	

Over high heat and stirring constantly, bring milk, sugar, and rice to a boil. Lower heat to medium and cook, uncovered, for 45 minutes or until mixture forms a thick rice paste, stirring frequently to prevent scorching.

When rice is properly cooked, add the vanilla and grated ginger, cool, then shape rice into small balls (about 1 tablespoon each) and coat thoroughly with ground almonds. Deep fry the croquettes at 375 degrees until very crisp and brown. Serve hot with the following cold sauce.

Apricot Sauce:

*1 can (29 ounces) pitted apricots in
   heavy syrup*
2 tablespoons apricot brandy

Purée apricots with their syrup. Pour purée into a heavy saucepan, bring quickly to a boil, then lower heat and simmer until the sauce reduces to 2 cups. Remove sauce from heat, cool, and stir in the brandy. Chill well.

Circassian Chicken
(Chicken in Walnut Sauce)

Serves 8

Istanbul-Sheraton Hotel
Istanbul, Turkey

Circassian Chicken is shredded chicken masked by an absolutely sublime walnut sauce. A flat bread like pita, torn into pieces, goes well with this dish.

*3 pounds chicken pieces (breasts,
   thighs, drumsticks)*
1 small onion, peeled and quartered
*1 carrot, peeled and coarsely
   chopped*
4 teaspoons salt
6½ cups water

3 slices day-old white bread
*3¾ cups (14 ounces) walnuts, finely
   ground*
*1 small onion, peeled and finely
   chopped*
4 teaspoons paprika

Place chicken, quartered onion, chopped carrot, and 2 teaspoons salt in a large pot. Pour in 6 cups water and bring to a boil over high heat. When boiling, reduce heat to low, partially cover, and simmer chicken 45 minutes or longer, until tender. Take pan off heat and allow chicken to cool down, uncovered, in the pan.

When cool, take chicken pieces and vegetables out of the broth. Set chicken aside and discard vegetables. Put broth back on the fire and boil, uncovered, over high heat for 30 minutes, until liquid is reduced to approximately 3 cups.

Skin and bone the cooked chicken. Shred or cut meat into thin pieces 1 inch long. Set aside.

To prepare the sauce, begin by soaking bread briefly in ½ cup water until soft. When soft, put bread into a food processor or blender. Add most of the ground walnuts, saving a small amount for garnish. Also add the finely chopped onion, 3 teaspoons paprika, and remaining 2 teaspoons salt. Purée until the mixture forms a thick paste. (Depending on the size of your processor or blender, this may have to be done in batches.)

Place walnut paste in a large bowl. Slowly pour in 2 or more cups reduced chicken stock and beat until the sauce has the consistency of thin mayonnaise.

Pour half of the walnut sauce over the shredded chicken and mix thoroughly. Select a shallow serving dish on which to mound the masked chicken. Pour as much remaining walnut sauce as desired over the chicken. Sprinkle with 1 teaspoon paprika and reserved walnuts. Serve at room temperature.

Raw Kebbah
(Minced Meats, Tartare Style)

Serves 12

Kuwait-Sheraton Hotel
Kuwait City, Kuwait

Since this Kebbah is to be served raw, it is imperative that all ingredients be very cold, very fresh—and that the completed dish be served promptly. If portions of the Kebbah go untouched, it makes a delicious snack, sautéed in a small amount of butter or olive oil.

1 cup plus 2 tablespoons (6 ounces) *finely ground burghul (bulgur)*	*1 pound lamb, finely ground*
¾ cup water	*1 pound beef tenderloin, finely* *ground*
4 teaspoons salt	*½ cup finely chopped red onion*
½ teaspoon freshly ground black *pepper*	*1 cup loosely packed, finely chopped* *fresh mint*
¼ teaspoon cinnamon	*4 tablespoons olive oil*
¼ teaspoon turmeric	*¾ cup finely chopped pine nuts*
⅛ teaspoon cardamom	*⅓ cup finely chopped walnuts*

Place burghul in a large bowl, pour water over it, mix with a fork, then let stand 10 minutes. While burghul is softening, mix together salt, pepper, cinnamon, turmeric, and cardamom.

Once burghul has stood 10 minutes, fluff and lighten it with your fingers. Knead in the well-chilled ground meats, sprinkle over and knead in the spices. Finally, mix in the chopped onion, mint, 2 tablespoons oil, and all but a few of the nuts (saved for garnish).

Shape Kebbah into 12 individual patties, or mound attractively on a serving dish. Sprinkle remaining oil and reserved nuts over patties. Refrigerate briefly to chill through. Serve with split, toasted pieces of flat bread.

NOTE: Burghul, more commonly known to us as bulgur, is a staple in Middle Eastern diets. It is wheat that has been boiled, dried, then crushed. It is sold in 3 different milling sizes, ranging from finely ground (#1), medium grind (#2), to coarsely ground (#3).

Sambousek
(Jeddah Meat Pastries)

Makes 12–15 pastries

Jeddah-Sheraton Hotel
Jeddah, Saudi Arabia

These mild meat pastries are an excellent idea for informal luncheons, late-night suppers, or whenever something simple yet filling is wanted for an appetizer or snack. Sambousek freezes beautifully. When ready to use, defrost in the refrigerator, then fry and serve.

Pastry Dough:

4 cups sifted all-purpose flour	*4 teaspoons olive oil*
2 teaspoons baking powder	*2 eggs, lightly beaten*
2 teaspoons salt	*¾ to 1 cup water*

Mix the dry ingredients together in a medium-sized bowl. Beat in the olive oil and eggs. Starting with ¾ cup water, work in enough water for dough to come together and clean the sides of the bowl. It will be very tight and elastic at this point. Place dough on a floured surface and knead 8 to 10 minutes.

Return kneaded dough to the bowl, cover, and refrigerate 12 to 24 hours, allowing dough to relax and soften.

Filling, Assembly, and Frying:

¼ teaspoon salt	*1 hard-cooked egg, finely chopped*
⅛ teaspoon freshly ground black pepper	*½ cup finely chopped fresh parsley*
½ pound ground lamb or ground lean beef	*Sufficient oil for shallow frying*

Place frying pan over medium-high heat. Sprinkle in salt and pepper. When the pan is hot, add ground meat and sauté, stirring constantly until meat is browned and cooked through. Remove pan from heat and cool contents down to room temperature. Once cool, mix in the chopped eggs and parsley. Correct seasoning to taste.

To assemble, divide rested dough in half. Roll first half out approximately 12 inches square. Place one generous teaspoon of the meat filling every 2 to 3 inches along the pastry dough.

Using a pastry brush dampened with water, brush around each teaspoon of filling. Roll out second half of dough, again approximately 12 inches square, and place it on top of the filled section. Press down between each meat filling.

Take a pastry wheel or sharp knife and cut out the individual pastries. Crimp the edges of each one tightly with your fingers or a fork.

Pour oil into a large heavy frying pan to a depth of ½ inch. Bring up to medium heat (approximately 325 degrees). Add Sambousek to the pan 3 or 4 at a time and fry 2 to 3 minutes on a side until puffed, golden brown, and cooked through. Drain on paper towels.

Serve hot or at room temperature.

Soups

Shoubet Sbaanegh
(Spinach Soup with Lamb Patties)

Makes 15 cups

Damascus-Sheraton Hotel
Damascus, Syria

Spinach Soup:

¼ cup Clarified Butter (recipe, page 277)
¾ cup finely chopped onions
1 stalk celery, finely chopped
2 cloves garlic, peeled and minced
3 quarts Beef Stock (recipe, page 278)

½ cup long-grain white rice
1½ pounds spinach, cleaned, stemmed, and finely chopped
Sautéed Kibbi Patties (recipe below)
Salt and pepper, to taste

Heat clarified butter in a heavy skillet. Add the onions and stir and sauté them 4 to 5 minutes, until they just begin to brown. Add the celery and garlic. Cook 2 to 3 minutes longer, until celery is soft.

Pour the beef stock into a large pot. Add the sautéed vegetables and bring the mixture to a boil. Add the raw rice, lower the heat, and simmer the soup base about 10 minutes. Return the soup base to a boil; add the spinach and Kibbi Patties. Lower the heat once more and simmer the soup another 10 minutes or until the rice is tender. Correct seasonings to taste. Serve hot.

Makes approximately 50 miniature patties.

Kibbi Patties:

¾ pound finely ground lamb
¼ teaspoon thyme leaves
½ teaspoon salt
⅛ teaspoon pepper
1 tablespoon finely minced garlic

¼ cup minced onions
1 cup loosely packed minced fresh parsley
3 tablespoons (or more) Clarified Butter (recipe; page 277)

Combine the lamb, thyme, salt, pepper, garlic, onions,and parsley. Form the mixture into small balls, about the size of large marbles. Press them between the palms of your hands to form patties about ¼ inch thick.

Place the 3 tablespoons clarified butter in a large skillet over medium-high heat. Add a portion of the meatballs and fry, turning very gently, until patties are browned all over. Remove with a slotted spoon and drain. Continue sautéeing until all the patties are browned, approximately 10 minutes, adding more butter if necessary.

Salads

Fattoush
(Mixed Salad)

Serves 6

Abu Dhabi-Sheraton Hotel
Abu Dhabi, United Arab Emirates

1 heart of romaine lettuce
3 medium-sized tomatoes, cubed
2 cucumbers, peeled and diced
1 green bell pepper
1 medium-sized onion, chopped
4 tablespoons finely chopped fresh
  parsley
1 tablespoon fresh mint, finely
  chopped; or 2 teaspoons dried
  mint

1 clove of garlic, mashed with a pinch
  of salt
½ cup olive oil
¼ cup lemon juice
Salt and pepper, to taste
1 piece pita bread, toasted and cut
  into small pieces

Combine and toss gently in a wooden salad bowl the lettuce, the vegetables, the parsley, and the mint. Mix the mashed garlic, olive oil, lemon juice, and salt and pepper; add to salad and toss well.

Chill for approximately 1 hour before serving, then add the pieces of pita bread, mix them through the salad, and serve.

Tabbouleh
(Crushed Wheat, Tomato, Mint, and Parsley Salad)

Serves 4–6

Abu Dhabi-Sheraton Hotel
Abu Dhabi, United Arab Emirates

⅔ cups fine burghul (bulgur)
3 medium-sized tomatoes, finely
  chopped
¾ cup finely chopped fresh parsley
1 medium-sized onion, finely
  chopped

4 tablespoons fresh lemon juice
1½ teaspoons salt
4 tablespoons olive oil
1½ tablespoons finely chopped fresh
  mint, or 2½ teaspoons dried mint

Place the burghul (crushed wheat) in a bowl or pan and pour in enough cold water to cover it completely. Let it soak for about 10 minutes, then drain in a sieve or colander lined with a double thickness of dampened cheesecloth. Wrap the burghul in the cheesecloth and squeeze it vigorously until dry. Drop the burghul into a deep bowl; add the tomatoes, parsley, onions, lemon juice, and salt and toss gently but thoroughly, mixing together with a fork.

Just before serving, stir in the olive oil and mint and taste for seasoning.

Tunisian Salad

Serves 6

Hammamet-Sheraton Hotel
Hammamet, Tunisia

2 medium-sized tomatoes, cubed
1 medium-sized green bell pepper,
   chopped
1 small onion, chopped
1 tablespoon finely chopped fresh
   mint, or 2 teaspoons dried mint

½ cup olive oil
1 tablespoon vinegar
1 can (6½ ounces) tuna fish in oil,
   drained
Salt and pepper to taste
Garnish: *Green olives*

Combine the vegetables and the mint; mix well. Add the olive oil, vinegar, and crumbled tuna fish, and mix once again. Season to taste.

Serve in a salad bowl, garnished with about 6 green olives.

Entrees

Roast Leg of Lamb

Serves 8

Hammamet-Sheraton Hotel
Hammamet, Tunisia

Saffron, considered by some to be the most precious of spices, is used sparingly but effectively in this roast lamb recipe. Just a scant two pinches of saffron will not only give your lamb a deep golden color but will fill the meat with subtle perfume.

6-pound leg of lamb, trimmed of all
   fell
1 teaspoon salt
½ teaspoon freshly ground black
   pepper
2 pinches saffron
⅛ teaspoon cinnamon

2 tablespoons butter
1 cup dry white wine
1 pound artichoke bottoms
1 pound cherry tomatoes
2 tablespoons fresh lemon juice
Garnish: *Chopped fresh parsley*

Preheat oven to 450 degrees. Place lamb, fat side up, in a shallow roasting pan. Rub both sides of the lamb well with salt, pepper, saffron, and cinnamon. Dot butter on top of the meat and pour wine into the pan. Place lamb in the oven and reduce heat immediately to 350 degrees. Roast approximately 1½ hours for rare (140 degrees on a meat thermometer), 2 hours for medium rare (160 degrees). Closer to 3 hours will produce a well-done leg of lamb.

During the last 15 minutes of roasting, place artichoke bottoms in the pan. Roll them in the pan drippings to help them pick up additional color as they bake. Add the cherry tomatoes 4 or 5 minutes before removing meat from the oven, just long enough to heat them through.

Take lamb out of the oven when done to taste and let rest 10 to 15 minutes. To serve, carve the lamb and place slices on serving platter. Scatter artichoke bottoms around the lamb, filling them with cherry tomatoes. Sprinkle lemon juice over all; garnish with chopped parsley.

Da Bamia
(Meat and Okra Stew)

Serves 4

Sheraton-Nile Boats
Aswan and Luxor, Egypt

In Egypt, meat and okra dishes are as common and as well liked as meat and potato dishes are in North America. Here, the okra imparts a lovely earthy flavor to the Da Bamia.

1 pound fresh okra
2 tablespoons olive oil
1 cup chopped onion
2 garlic cloves, minced
1 pound lamb or beef, cut into bite-sized pieces
½ pound tomatoes, peeled and coarsely chopped

¼ to ½ cup water
2 tablespoons lemon juice
3 tablespoons chopped fresh parsley
1 teaspoon salt
¼ teaspoon freshly ground black pepper
Garnishes: Black olives, thin lemon wedges

Wash okra well; cut off stems and gently rub dry. Set aside.

Pour oil into a large heavy skillet and place over a medium-high heat. When oil is hot, add onions and garlic. Sauté a few minutes until onions are translucent and garlic is lightly browned.

Remove onions and garlic from pan or push to the sides. Add meat and brown well over high heat. Lower heat, stir in the okra and tomatoes. Simmer gently, 5 to 6 minutes, stirring frequently.

Pour in ¼ cup water and all the lemon juice. Mix in the parsley, salt, and pepper. Cover and simmer 1½ hours or more, until meat is tender, occasionally adding more water if stew is too thick or too dry. Adjust the seasoning to taste. Serve garnished with black olives and lemon wedges.

Da Bamia can be placed in a covered casserole for serving. If made ahead, it is easily refrigerated, reheated, then garnished.

Maghrebia
(Couscous)

Serves 6

Abu Dhabi-Sheraton Hotel
Abu Dhabi, United Arab Emirates

Maghrebia, more commonly known to us as couscous, is a shining example of fine Middle Eastern cuisine. Couscous consists of finely crushed semolina grains, traditionally steamed to perfection over a flavorful stew or broth, that provide a light, tender base for meats (usually lamb or chicken) and a variety of vegetables. Chick-peas are frequently added to couscous, sometimes with raisins as well. Many spices are used, but usually so sparingly that one can hardly discern each individual taste. Often, as we do here, a hot sauce is prepared to be served on the side for those who wish to be further "inflamed and intoxicated."

The actual process of cooking the couscous grain is very simple, but it calls for ample time and a subtle handling of the grain. The aim is to make it swell and become extremely light, each grain soft, delicate, and separate from its neighbor. We provide a recipe for preparing couscous in a traditional fashion, but there are packaged instant couscous grains that require a shorter cooking time. Feel free to use whichever method suits your time and interests.

1 pound lamb or lean beef, cut into hearty chunks
1 bay leaf
1 teaspoon cinnamon
2 teaspoons salt
¼ teaspoon pepper
2½ to 3 cups water
3 pounds chicken pieces (breasts, thighs, drumsticks)
10 small white onions, peeled
1 tablespoon butter

1 teaspoon caraway seeds, crushed
6 carrots, scraped and cut into hearty chunks
1½ cups canned cooked chick-peas (garbanzo beans)
10 ounces fresh or frozen green peas
Steamed Couscous (recipe follows)
Garnish: Finely chopped parsley
Optional: Hot Pepper Sauce (recipe page 170)

Place lamb, bay leaf, cinnamon, salt, and pepper in a large pot and cover with 2½ to 3 cups water. Bring to a boil, reduce heat, and simmer partially covered for 30 minutes. Add the chicken and more water, if necessary, to cover the chicken and meat. Bring to a boil, reduce heat, and simmer partialy covered an additional 20 minutes.

Meanwhile, lightly sauté the onions in butter. Add them to the meat pot and continue simmering 15 minutes longer. Finally, add crushed caraway seeds, carrots, chick-peas, and green peas. Simmer gently 10 to 15 minutes, adjusting the seasoning to taste. Meat and chicken should be cooked through and very tender by this time. If not, simmer slightly longer.

Prepare couscous grain according to the recipe given below or use recipe given on packaged instant couscous. When ready to serve, place hot buttered couscous on a large shallow serving platter, pushing the grains to the sides to create a well in the center. Remove meats and vegetables from broth and arrange in the center of the well. Sprinkle with parsley. Serve broth as gravy and add our Hot Pepper Sauce if desired.

Steamed Couscous:

Best results are obtained by using a special 3-part couscous steamer *(couscousière)*, but you may also use a metal steamer or colander and a large stock pot, as we explain below.

1 carrot, coarsely chopped
1 large onion, quartered
1 bay leaf
2 sprigs fresh parsley
1 pound couscous (crushed wheat
  semolina), sold in packages in
  stores or Middle Eastern markets

1 teaspoon salt
1 cup water
2 to 3 tablespoons butter

Select a metal steamer or colander that fits snugly into a large heavy pot that has a cover. There should be several inches of clearance between the bottom of the pan and the bottom of the colander so that the stock added to the pan can boil without touching the couscous steaming in the bottom of the colander. Line the colander with several layers of cheesecloth to prevent couscous from slipping through. Set colander aside.

Put the carrot, onion, bay leaf, and parsley into the pot and cover with several inches of water, but not so much that it will touch the bottom of the colander when it is inserted in the pan. Cover the pot and cook vegetable broth 30 minutes over medium heat.

Place dry couscous in a bowl and mix in salt. Sprinkle 1 cup water over couscous and stir until all grains are dampened. Let sit 10 minutes, until the water is well absorbed. Then, using your fingertips, lift and rub the compact, swollen couscous grains to loosen and break up all lumps. It is very important to the final outcome of this dish that you spend several minutes doing a thorough job of separating and lightening all the grains.

When vegetables have cooked for 30 minutes, and couscous has been soaked and aerated, place cheesecloth-lined colander in the pot over the vegetable broth. Check again to be sure the broth does not touch the bottom of the colander. Gently transfer the couscous to the colander with your fingertips, being careful not to pack it down.

Seal any open spaces between the edges of the colander and the pan with tinfoil or cheesecloth so that all the broth's flavorful steam is forced up through the couscous sitting in the colander. Tightly cover or seal over the colander and pan. Steam the couscous for 1 hour. Check periodically to see if water should be added to the pot to complete steaming. Turn out cooked couscous and toss with 2 or 3 tablespoons butter. Serve immediately.

Continued

Hot Pepper Sauce:

4 or more small chili peppers, seeded
 and diced; or 3 or more
 tablespoons canned diced green
 chili pepper

2 small garlic cloves, mashed
6 or more dashes Tabasco
6 tablespoons olive oil

Combine all ingredients, adding hot peppers and tabasco to taste, in a blender or food processor. Purée well. Serve at room temperature, advising guests to taste with caution.

Mozat Bellaban

(Braised Lamb Shanks in Yogurt Sauce)

Serves 6

Kuwait-Sheraton Hotel
Kuwait City, Kuwait

6 lamb shanks
⅔ cup peanut oil
1 onion, quartered
1 carrot, peeled and chopped
2 bay leaves
4 cloves
½ teaspoon peppercorns

2 quarts plain yogurt
2 egg yolks
¼ cup sifted cornstarch
½ teaspoon salt
4 tablespoons minced garlic
½ cup chopped fresh mint

Heat 3 tablespoons peanut oil in a large heavy skillet over medium-high heat. Brown the lamb shanks well on all sides. When brown, transfer shanks to a large stock pot. Cover them with water. Add the onion, carrot, bay leaves, cloves, and peppercorns. Bring to a boil, then lower heat and simmer shanks 30 to 45 minutes until done.

While shanks are simmering, prepare the yogurt sauce. Mix the yogurt, egg yolks, cornstarch, and salt together in a large enameled or stainless-steel pan. Gently boil the sauce for 10 minutes, stirring constantly to prevent lumping and scorching. Keep warm.

When ready to serve, fry the garlic and mint in remaining ½ cup oil over medium-high heat, stirring well, until garlic browns and mint turns crisp.

Place the braised lamb shanks on a large serving platter. Coat with hot yogurt sauce, top with crisp garlic and mint mixture.

Melon Bow Gad

(Chicken and Rice Stuffed Cantaloupe)

Serves 6

Tel Aviv-Sheraton Hotel
Tel Aviv, Israel

Melon Bow Gad is typical of Israel's culinary ingenuity, yet is practically unknown in America. The combination of hot chicken and rice stuffed in a melon shell is bound to delight and surprise luncheon or dinner guests.

*3 large ripe cantaloupes, each about
    3 pounds*
2 cups long-grain white rice
3 tablespoons olive oil
2 cups Chicken Stock (recipe, page 279)
2 cups water
2 teaspoons salt
1 cup chopped onions
*2 large, whole chicken breasts
    (about 2 pounds chicken),
    skinned and boned, meat diced
    into ½-inch pieces*

¼ cup brandy
*¼ pound mushrooms, cleaned and
    coarsely chopped*
1 cup black olives, coarsely chopped
Optional: *¼ cup Brown Sauce
    (recipe, page 276)*
Garnishes: *Red leaf or Boston lettuce
    leaves; 1 cup roasted unsalted
    pistachio nuts, coarsely chopped*

Halve the cantaloupes, using a decorative zigzag cut. Remove seeds. Scoop out balls of fruit with a small melon baller, leaving a sturdy shell for stuffing. Set aside melon shells and fruit.

Sauté rice in 1 tablespoon olive oil over medium-high heat until golden brown. Pour in the chicken stock, water, and salt and bring to a boil. Cover pan, reduce heat, and simmer 20 to 25 minutes, until rice has absorbed all liquid and is tender. Fluff with a fork and set aside.

In a large heavy frying pan, sauté onions in remaining 2 tablespoons oil 2 to 3 minutes over medium heat, until onions are tender and translucent. Add diced chicken meat and sauté 3 or 4 minutes longer until chicken turns white and is cooked through. Pour in the brandy and flambé.

When flames die out, add the chopped mushrooms and olives. Continue cooking 1 to 2 minutes more. For a final lift in flavor, add brown sauce, if desired.

Stir the boiled rice and melon balls into the chicken mixture and heat until all components are hot. Taste and correct seasoning if necessary.

To serve, line 6 small dinner plates with leaf lettuce. Place a melon shell on each lettuce bed and fill loosely, mounding high, with hot rice mixture. (Enough filling is provided to allow those with heartier appetites a second serving.) Sprinkle chopped pistachios over the mixture and serve while filling is still hot.

Sea Wolf Twelve Tribes

(Sea Bass in Sesame Sauce)

Serves 6

Tel Aviv-Sheraton Hotel
Tel Aviv, Israel

Near Tel Aviv are large saltwater fish that swim in the depths of the ocean, using their strong jaws to procure food. They are aptly called sea wolves. For this recipe, they can easily be replaced by sea bass.

Here the fish is covered with a sesame-seed sauce typical of the region, then encased in tinfoil to hold in all the aromatic juices until the moment of presentation.

*3 pounds sea bass or similar fish cut
   into 6 (8-ounce) pieces*
1½ cups fresh lemon juice
¼ teaspoon salt
⅛ teaspoon pepper
1½ cups Tahini Sauce (recipe follows)

3 large potatoes, unpeeled
½ cup all-purpose flour
1 cup vegetable oil
*6 small sprigs fresh dill or ⅓ teaspoon
   dried dill*
Garnish: Lemon wedges

A day ahead: Place the sea bass in a medium-sized stainless-steel, glass, or enamel bowl. Pour fresh lemon juice over the fish and sprinkle on salt and pepper. Mix lightly to incorporate spices, then cover and refrigerate 24 hours until lemon flavor permeates the fish. The Tahini Sauce (recipe follows) can also be made a day ahead and refrigerated until ready to use.

Shortly before serving, cut out 6 pieces of tinfoil, each about 12 inches square, and set aside. Boil potatoes in their jackets until just done, 25 to 30 minutes. Drain, cool, peel, and slice potatoes into ¼-inch slices. Set aside.

Preheat oven to 350 degrees. Remove sea bass from its marinade and pat fairly dry. Dredge the fish through the flour lightly.

Pour oil into a large heavy skillet and place over medium-high heat. When oil is hot (375 degrees), deep-fry fish until cooked, about 7 to 8 minutes. Remove fish from skillet and drain on a paper towel.

Place a layer of potato slices evenly over each tinfoil square, cover with a portion of fried fish, then spoon on 3 to 4 tablespoons Tahini Sauce. Season further with salt and pepper if desired. Top with dill. Seal each tinfoil square tightly. Bake at 350 degrees 15 to 20 minutes, until piping hot. Serve the fish in the tinfoil squares immediately, accompanied by lemon wedges. Allow each guest to open his own package of fish.

Tahini Sauce:

1 cup (8 ounces) sesame tahini
¾ cup water
¼ cup fresh lemon juice

3 large garlic cloves, mashed
¾ teaspoon salt
¼ teaspoon pepper

Tahini (also spelled *tehina*) is a ground, hulled sesame-seed paste sold in cans in some markets and most health food stores.

Place all ingredients in a bowl, blender, or food processor. Mix until well combined. The end result should be a sauce with the consistency of a thick mayonnaise.

Desserts

Gâteau Hobza Baskutu
(Pistachio Cake)

Serves 8–10

Hammamet-Sheraton Hotel
Hammamet, Tunisia

The success of this lovely gâteau depends on a lengthy beating of the eggs. Have all your ingredients out and ready to use so that the cake can be quickly assembled and baked. It is the perfect cake to serve with tea or coffee.

¼ pound (roughly 1 cup) roasted
    unsalted pistachio nuts
1½ cups sifted cake flour
2 teaspoons baking powder
⅓ cup blanched almonds, toasted
6 large eggs, at room temperature

2½ cups sifted confectioners' sugar
¼ cup butter, melted and cooled to
    room temperature
¼ cup water
2 tablespoons fresh lemon juice
2 tablespoons orange flower water

Preheat oven to 350 degrees. Butter a 10-inch spring-form pan or a 10-inch cake pan.

Shell the pistachios, then grind them finely with a food processor, blender, or rolling pin. Lightly mix ground pistachios into the flour, along with the baking powder. Set aside. Finely grind the toasted almonds that will be used as a topping, and set them aside also.

Continued

Using an electric mixer, set on medium speed and beat the eggs 2 to 3 minutes. Sprinkle in ½ cup sugar. Raise speed to medium-high and beat eggs another 8 to 10 minutes, until they are thick, light-colored, and doubled or more in volume.

When eggs are thickened, sprinkle over them and gently fold in the flour-nut mixture, using a spatula or wooden spoon. Once the flour-nut mixture is lightly incorporated into the eggs, drizzle over and quickly fold in the melted butter. Immediately pour gâteau batter into the greased cake pan and place in preheated oven. Bake 25 to 30 minutes, until the gâteau is cooked through and golden brown on top.

While gâteau is baking, make sugar syrup. Mix remaining sugar with ¼ cup water in a small saucepan. Place over low heat and stir constantly until sugar dissolves, and all lumps disappear. Keep thick syrup warm.

Remove gâteau from oven when done. While still warm, turn out and place browned side up on a cake rack. Brush top of the cake first with lemon juice, then with orange flower water. Pour over as much of the sugar syrup as desired. Sprinkle liberally with ground almonds.

Serve gâteau at room temperature.

Marak Perot Kar
(Cold Fresh Fruit Soup)

Serves 12

Tel Aviv-Sheraton Hotel
Tel Aviv, Israel

2 pounds (1 medium-sized)
  cantaloupe, peeled, halved,
  seeded, and coarsely chopped
1½ pounds fresh strawberries, rinsed
  and hulled
½ pound green grapes, rinsed
4 medium-sized firm cooking apples,
  peeled, cored, and coarsely
  chopped

½ cup sugar
5 cups water
¾ to 1 cup fresh lemon juice
1½ cups fresh orange juice
Garnishes: Sour cream, sliced fresh
  fruit

Combine all the fresh fruits, sugar, water, and ½ cup lemon juice in a 4- to 6-quart enameled or stainless-steel pan. Bring quickly to a boil, reduce heat, and simmer uncovered for 15 minutes.

Purée the fruit mixture, then pass it through a chinois or large, fine-meshed sieve, forcing fruits through with the back of a spoon. Press down hard before discarding any remaining pulp.

Stir orange juice and as much of the remaining lemon juice as desired into the fruit mixture. If soup seems too thick, thin out with small additions of water. Refrigerate until thoroughly chilled.

Serve in glass bowls topped with sour cream and fresh fruits.

Meghlie
(Rice Pudding)

Makes 8 cups

Dubai-Sheraton Hotel
Dubai, United Arab Emirates

For years, Meghlie has been made with rice flour. Now the many contemporary cooks in the Middle East substitute the more readily available cream of rice cereal, as you may choose to do.

This soft rice pudding is frequently served to visitors who come to call on newborn infants.

1 tablespoon caraway seeds
2 teaspoons fennel seeds
1½ teaspoons anise seeds
1 cup rice flour or ¾ cup cream of
 rice cereal
2 cups sugar
1½ teaspoons ground cinnamon

7 cups water
Garnishes: ½ cup shredded dried
 coconut; ¼ cup slivered almonds;
 ½ cup roasted unsalted pistachios;
 2 tablespoons pine nuts (pignola or
 piñon nuts)

Crush all the whole seeds in a food processor, blender, or with a rolling pin. Make a spice bag by placing crushed spices on several small layers of cheesecloth. Knot the ends of the cheesecloth together, firmly tying in the spices. Stir together rice flour, sugar, and ground cinnamon.

Bring water to a boil in a large heavy saucepan, then reduce heat to simmer. Stirring constantly, slowly drizzle in the rice-sugar mixture, taking approximately 1 minute in all. Pudding will thicken in 2 to 4 minutes, at which time big bubbles will begin to break the surface. Add the spice bag; stir frequently over the next 20 to 25 minutes to prevent scorching and allow flavors in the spice bag to permeate the pudding. A loose custard consistency is the desired result.

Allow mixture to cool down; remove spice bag, and pour mixture into 8 one-cup serving dishes or a 2-quart dessert bowl. Chill well before serving topped with coconut, almonds, pistachios, and pine nuts.

Menu Suggestion

A Middle Eastern Dinner

Mutabal
(page 157)

Fattoush
(page 165)

Maghrebia
(page 168)

Gâteau Hobza Baskutu
(page 173)
Serve fresh figs with cake

The
Cuisine of
The Far East

and India

Far East

Appetizers

Sashimi Raratonga
Sheraton-Walker Hill
Seoul, South Korea
Bagna Cauda
Century Park Sheraton Singapore
Singapore, Republic of Singapore
Kilawing Isda
Century Park Sheraton
Manila, Philippines
Sang Choy Um Chum Soong
Sheraton-Hong Kong Hotel
Hong Kong, B.C.C.

Soups

Winter Melon Soup
Sheraton-Hong Kong Hotel
Hong Kong, B.C.C.
Tinolang Manok
Century Park Sheraton
Manila, Philippines

Salads

Gado-Gado
Hotel Ambarrukmo Sheraton
Yogyakarta, Indonesia
Roast Beef Chili Salad
Sheraton-Bangkok Hotel
Bangkok, Thailand

Side Dishes

Banana Bread
Century Park Sheraton Singapore
Singapore, Republic of Singapore

Entrees

Rack of Lamb with Mint and Honey
Sheraton-Perth Hotel
Perth, Western Australia
Escalopes de Veau au Xérès
Sheraton-Perth Hotel
Perth, Western Australia
Peking Duck with Doilies
Century Park Sheraton Singapore
Singapore, Republic of Singapore
Ayam Panggang Ketjap
Hotel Ambarrukmo Sheraton
Yogyakarta, Indonesia
Poularde à la Pattaya
Sheraton-Bangkok Hotel
Bangkok, Thailand
Lobster Play Pan
Sheraton-Hong Kong Hotel
Hong Kong, B.C.C.

Desserts

Sari-Saring Sa Buko
Century Park Sheraton
Manila, Philippines
Crêpes Surprises au Chartreuse
Sheraton-Hong Kong Hotel
Hong Kong, B.C.C.
Coco Chana
Sheraton-Bangkok Hotel
Bangkok, Thailand

The Cuisine of the Far East

The food of the Pacific is as diverse and exciting as its people—combining the western influence with the Far East's natural wealth of flavorful ingredients, ranging from the aromatic flavor of garlic, and the zest of chili or curry, to the natural tang and sweetness of fresh fruits. The cuisine of Singapore reflects the influence of both the English and the Chinese. The dishes of Manila and Indonesia frequently combine tropical fruits, herbs, and spices with the delicate flavors of chicken or fish. Korea utilizes the resources of the sea in a raw fish salad, Sashimi Raratonga, a delicious departure from traditional western cooking.

A close neighbor, Australia, with its strong English heritage, makes use of its abundant livestock production by highlighting veal and lamb, represented here by Escalopes de Veau au Xérès and Rack of Lamb with Mint and Honey.

The meeting of East and West in the Pacific has truly found a most delightful manifestation in its cuisine.

Appetizers

Sashimi Raratonga
(Raw Fish Salad)

Serves 10–12

Sheraton Walker Hill
Seoul, South Korea

Absolutely fresh saltwater fish must be used for this colorful dish. Use the raw fish listed below or substitute other suitable saltwater fish.

Fish Salad:

½ pound fresh salmon fillet
½ pound fresh sea bass fillet
½ pound fresh yellowfin tuna fillet
½ teaspoon salt
⅛ teaspoon pepper
2 teaspoons minced shallots
*2 teaspoons canned green
    peppercorns, drained*

2 tablespoons olive oil
Zest of 1 lemon, finely shredded
*2 ounces fresh ginger, peeled and
    finely shredded*

Assembly:

2 small heads iceberg lettuce
½ teaspoon salt
⅛ teaspoon pepper
⅓ cup fresh lemon juice

2 or more tablespoons red caviar
Grated horseradish
Soy sauce

Using a very sharp, heavy knife, slice the raw fish fillets on an angle into paper thin, almost transparent slices. Place fish in a rimmed dish and sprinkle with ½ teaspoon salt, ⅛ teaspoon pepper, shallots, peppercorns, and olive oil. Refrigerate 15 minutes.

Blanch shredded lemon zest and ginger in a small amount of water for 3 minutes. Drain, cool, and set aside.

When ready to assemble, slice the lettuce into fine strips. Arrange on a large serving dish, mounding slightly in the middle. Season the lettuce with ½ teaspoon salt, ⅛ teaspoon pepper, and lemon juice.

Alternately arrange marinated fish slices on lettuce folded to simulate petals of a flower. Decorate with blanched lemon peel, ginger, and caviar. Chill whole dish 15 minutes. Serve with grated fresh horseradish and soy sauce.

Bagna Cauda
(Hot Anchovy and Garlic Dip)

Makes 2 cups

Century Park Sheraton Singapore
Singapore, Republic of Singapore

2¼ cups heavy cream
2 tablespoons butter
2 tablespoons olive oil
10 or more anchovies, mashed
2 tablespoons minced fresh parsley
1½ teaspoons minced garlic
⅛ teaspoon white pepper

Assorted cold fresh vegetables
(carrots, celery, scallions,
fennel, mushrooms, peppers,
etc.), peeled, seeded, and cut
into strips where appropriate
Italian bread sticks

Pour cream into a small heavy saucepan and boil, stirring frequently, until reduced to about 1 cup. Set aside.

Melt butter in olive oil over low heat. Add anchovies, parsley, garlic, and pepper. Stirring constantly with a wire whisk, slowly pour in reduced cream. Stir and simmer sauce 1 to 2 minutes. Do not allow the sauce to boil. (Dip should have the consistency of thin mayonnaise.)

Serve hot in a fondue pot or chafing dish accompanied by cold fresh vegetables and Italian bread sticks.

Kilawing Isda
(Pickled Fish Appetizer)

Makes 1 quart

Century Park Sheraton
Manila, Philippines

This is an appetizer that not everyone will like. But for those who enjoy new experiences, it will be a treat. It is imperative to use very fresh (preferably deep) saltwater fish for Kilawing Isda.

¾ pound fresh saltwater fish, such as
sea bass, red snapper, or halibut
¼ cup chopped fresh ginger root
½ cup chopped onions
6 cloves garlic, peeled and finely
chopped
¾ cup fresh lime juice
⅓ cup white wine vinegar

4 or 5 small hot fresh chilies, to taste
¼ green bell pepper, julienned
¼ red bell pepper, julienned
¾ teaspoon salt
¼ teaspoon freshly ground black
pepper
Garnishes: Lettuce leaves, chopped
fresh parsley

Cut the fish fillets in paper-thin slivers about 2 inches long and put them into a glass, or ceramic bowl.

Place ginger root, onions, and garlic in a blender or food processor with the lime juice and vinegar. Blend or process to purée these ingredients. Pour this marinade on top of the slivered fish.

Slice as many hot chilies as desired into very thin strips. Add the chilies and the julienned green and red peppers to the fish. Stir in the salt and pepper.

Cover and chill Kilawing Isda for at least 4 hours, stirring once or twice. When "cooked," remove the fish from the bowl with a slotted spoon, allowing excess liquids to drain.

Serve on lettuce leaves; sprinkle with chopped parsley.

Sang Choy Um Chum Soong
(Minced Quail in Lettuce Leaves)

Makes about 30 hors d'oeuvres

Sheraton-Hong Kong Hotel
Hong Kong, B.C.C.

2 quail, each about 5 ounces, or 1 Cornish game hen, skinned, boned, and finely minced
1 egg, lightly beaten
1 teaspoon salt
3 tablespoons vegetable oil
Generous pinch of cayenne pepper
½ teaspoon finely minced fresh ginger

1 medium clove peeled garlic, finely minced
½ pound bamboo shoots, finely minced
3 tablespoons dry sherry
30 bite-sized pieces of lettuce
Garnishes: Minced green onion, cayenne pepper

Mix quail with egg and salt and set aside. Heat 2 tablespoons oil in a heavy skillet over medium-high heat. Stir in cayenne pepper, ginger, and garlic and cook 1 to 2 minutes. Add bamboo shoots and continue stir-frying 3 to 4 minutes longer. Allow spiced shoots to cool, then rapidly mix them into the quail and egg mixture.

Heat the remaining tablespoon of oil in the pan over high heat; stir in the minced quail mixture, then sprinkle with dry sherry. Sauté 3 to 4 minutes, stirring constantly, until quail is cooked and is beginning to brown.

Mound hot minced quail in the center of a platter and surround with cold, bite-sized lettuce leaves. Garnish quail with minced green onions and a small pinch of cayenne pepper for color.

Guests serve themselves by scooping minced quail onto lettuce leaves.

Soups

Winter Melon Soup

Makes 2¾ quarts

Sheraton-Hong Kong Hotel
Hong Kong, B.C.C.

¼ *pound pork loin*
¼ *pound good-quality smoked ham*
   such as Smithfield or prosciutto
¼ *pound dark chicken meat, skinned*
   and boned
4 cups Chicken Stock (recipe, page 279)
2 cups water
2 tablespoons dry sherry
1 pound winter melon, peeled,
   seeded, and cut into ½-inch pieces

1 teaspoon salt
⅛ *teaspoon white pepper*
1½ teaspoons minced fresh ginger root
¼ *pound cooked crabmeat, shredded*
¼ *pound mushrooms, cleaned and*
   thinly sliced
2 ounces dried lotus seeds

Blanch pork, ham, and chicken in 1 quart boiling water for about 5 minutes. Drain and cool. Cut the pork, chicken, all but 1 tablespoon ham into ¼- to ½-inch pieces. Mince reserved tablespoon ham to be used for garnish later.

Pour chicken stock and water into a 5- to 6-quart pot. Add sherry, diced pork, chicken, ham, and melon. Season with salt, pepper, and minced ginger root. Bring to a boil, lower heat, and simmer, partially covered, for 10 minutes.

Stir in shredded crab, sliced mushrooms, and lotus seeds, and simmer 10 minutes longer. Serve in heated soup bowls, sprinkled with minced ham.

For more festive occasions, serve out of a whole steamed winter melon. Cut top from melon and clean inside; decorate melon if desired. Set melon in a heatproof bowl on a rack in a large kettle. Have enough water in the kettle to reach the upper rim of the bowl. Steam for about 1 hour, then remove bowl from kettle. Fill melon with soup.

To serve, cut slices of melon from the top edge and ladle soup over them.

Tinolang Manok
(Gingered Chicken Soup with Papaya)

Makes about 6 cups

Century Park Sheraton
Manila, Philippines

There are many recipes for gingered chicken soup in Indonesia, but this one stands out from the rest because of its subtle yet skillful blend of flavors. Tart and tangy without being overly so, it has colorful chunks of chewy papaya for taste as well as for appearance.

2 pounds chicken breasts, skinned
   and boned
1 teaspoon salt
½ teaspoon white pepper
1 tablespoon fresh lime juice
2 tablespoons oil
¾ cup finely chopped onion

2 cloves garlic, minced
4 teaspoons minced fresh ginger root
3 cups water
1 small (about 1 pound), fairly firm
   papaya, peeled, seeded, and cut
   into 1-inch pieces

Lightly pound the chicken breasts, then cut them into bite-sized pieces. Season all sides with salt, pepper, and lime juice. Set aside briefly.

Pour oil into a heavy frying pan and place over medium-high heat. When the oil is hot, add the onion and garlic. Sauté, stirring constantly, until onions are golden and garlic is crisp. Add the chicken and minced ginger. Continue sautéeing, stirring constantly, until chicken has whitened.

Transfer sautéed ingredients to a saucepan and add 3 cups water. Bring soup to a boil, cover, lower the heat, and simmer until chicken is tender, about 15 minutes. When chicken is tender, add the diced papaya and simmer 5 to 6 minutes longer. Correct seasonings, to taste. Serve hot.

Salads

Gado-Gado

(Vegetable Salad with Peanut Sauce)

Serves 6–12

Hotel Ambarrukmo Sheraton
Yogyakarta, Indonesia

Indonesians are great salad lovers. Here, Gado-Gado, one of their heartier salads, is prepared in the Javanese style, with a slightly sweet peanut sauce. This recipe will serve six as a main course, or as many as twelve as an appetizer.

Continued

Vegetable Salad:

2 soybean curd cakes (about 1 pound
   in all), drained
3 small boiling potatoes
¾ pound fresh green beans, washed,
   trimmed, and cut into 2-inch pieces
½ pound fresh bean sprouts
Sufficient oil for frying

1 large head cabbage or iceberg
   lettuce, shredded
3 large ripe tomatoes, sliced
6 hard-cooked eggs, sliced
1 cucumber, scrubbed, scored, and
   sliced
Peanut Sauce (recipe below)

Wrap bean cakes in paper towels and place them between two flat, fairly lightweight objects, such as small cheese boards, to squeeze out any remaining water. Let sit 20 to 30 minutes, replacing or adding towels as they become saturated.

Steam or boil the potatoes just until done. Drain, cool, peel, and slice fairly thick. Steam or boil green beans until tender but still crisp. Remove, cool, and set them aside. Steam or boil the bean sprouts 8 to 10 minutes. Remove and cool them down.

Pour several inches of oil into a deep heavy pan. When oil is hot (about 365 degrees on a deep-fry thermometer), add the lightly pressed soybean cakes and fry each one several minutes, until crisp and golden brown on all sides. Remove, drain, cool, and cut the bean cakes into thick slices or cubes.

The salad is now ready to be assembled and served. On a large platter or individual salad plates, arrange the cooked ingredients in a decorative fashion, adding the shredded cabbage or iceberg lettuce, sliced tomatoes, eggs, and cucumber. Serve the salad at room temperature with the following Peanut Sauce.

Peanut Sauce:

4 tablespoons minced shallots
½ teaspoon minced garlic
2 tablespoons vegetable oil
2 cups unsalted roasted peanuts,
   hulled
4 teaspoons light brown sugar, loosely
   packed

1 tablespoon fresh lime juice
1 teaspoon or more finely chopped
   hot chilies, to taste; or Tabasco
   sauce, to taste
1½ cups water

Sauté the shallots and garlic in the oil 2 to 3 minutes to soften. When softened, scrape shallots, garlic, and oil into a blender or food processor and add all other ingredients. Purée or process until sauce is fairly smooth.

Pour sauce back into the frying pan and cook over a low heat, stirring constantly, about 5 to 6 minutes, long enough to blend flavors and thicken the sauce.

The sauce is usually served quite thick. If you prefer a thinner sauce, it is easily thinned down with small additions of water. Serve sauce warm or at room temperature.

Roast Beef Chili Salad

Serves 6–8

Sheraton-Bangkok Hotel
Bangkok, Thailand

This recipe from Thailand uses hot chilies and cool cucumbers to balance the sweet taste of the roast beef. Nampla, a Thai fish sauce, is salty like soy sauce, but has a definite, delightful fish taste to it. Just a few tablespoons give this salad extra life. You can buy Nampla (sometimes *Nam Pla*) in Indonesian or Oriental markets.

2 pounds lean, boneless beef,
  preferably tenderloin, top loin, or
  rib eye
3 to 4 medium-sized cucumbers
1 large onion
½ cup red wine vinegar
5 garlic cloves, peeled
1 tablespoon coarse salt
1 teaspoon sugar
4 or more small hot chilies, seeded
  and diced

1 large green bell pepper, seeded and
  diced
2 tablespoons fresh lemon juice
1 head Boston or Bibb lettuce
Optional: *2 to 3 tablespoons Nampla*
  (Thai fish sauce), 4 bacon strips
Garnishes: *Small red bell pepper,*
  julienned; chopped fresh mint
  leaves

Preheat the oven to 425 degrees. If using a piece of beef with little or no exterior fat, such as a tenderloin, lay a few strips of bacon over it. Place beef in preheated oven, lower the heat to 350 degrees, and bake about 1 hour, until meat is rare (140 degrees on a meat thermometer). Remove, let roast cool down, then chill well.

When chilled, cut the roast beef into thin slices and place them in a deep bowl. Scrub cucumbers, cut off the ends, and score the peel with a fork. Cut cucumber into thin slices and add to the roast beef.

Peel the onion. Cut into thin slices and combine with the meat and cucumbers.

Place vinegar, garlic, salt, sugar, hot chilies, and green pepper in a blender or food processor. Blend until well combined. Pour vinaigrette over the beef mixture and toss well.

Line a salad bowl or individual plates with soft lettuce. Distribute the salad. Sprinkle with lemon juice and with Nampla, if desired. Garnish with julienned red bell pepper and chopped fresh mint. Serve at once.

Side Dishes

Banana Bread

Makes 1 loaf

Century Park Sheraton Singapore
Singapore, Republic of Singapore

2 large eggs
1/3 cup heavy cream
1/3 cup vegetable oil
2 cups all-purpose flour
1 teaspoon baking powder

1 teaspoon baking soda
1/2 teaspoon salt
3 ripe medium-sized bananas
1 1/2 cups sugar

Preheat oven to 350 degrees. Grease a 1½-quart loaf pan.

Mix eggs, cream, and oil together with a whisk or beater until well combined. Set aside.

Combine flour, baking powder, baking soda, and salt. Set aside.

Whip up the ripe bananas and sugar until watery. Slowly pour the egg mixture into the sugared bananas, bit by bit. Beat for 1 or 2 minutes. Add the flour mixture and continue beating 1 or 2 minutes longer. Pour batter into greased pan and bake at 350 degrees for 1 hour, or until done.

Entrees

Rack of Lamb with Mint and Honey

Serves 2–3

Sheraton-Perth Hotel
Perth, Western Australia

This rack of lamb is absolutely succulent. The honey and mint coating not only gives it a look of glazed perfection but imparts a slightly sweet flavor that is sheer inspiration!

Roast Lamb:

Rack of lamb, 6 to 7 bones (about
2½ pounds)
1/2 teaspoon salt

1/4 teaspoon black pepper
2 tablespoons honey
1 tablespoon chopped fresh mint

Have the butcher trim the rack of the fell and any excess fat, as well as partially crack the back bone for easier serving.

Preheat oven to 325 degrees. Season the lamb with a mixture of the salt and pepper. Place lamb on a rack in a shallow roasting pan. Put lamb in preheated oven and roast approximately 1 hour, or until it reaches an internal temperature of 140 degrees on a meat thermometer. The lamb will be rare.

Mix honey with mint and spread over the lamb. Lower the oven temperature to 250 degrees. Roast lamb an additional 10 minutes to set the glaze. Remove rack of lamb from the oven and let rest several minutes before carving. Serve with mint jelly or with the following Mint Sauce.

Mint Sauce:

¼ cup chopped fresh mint leaves
⅓ cup white wine vinegar
¾ cup boiling water
1 tablespoon sugar

¼ cup cold water
1 tablespoon lemon juice
⅓ cup chopped fresh mint leaves

Place ¼ cup mint leaves, vinegar, and boiling water in a small saucepan. Boil the mixture about 5 minutes, until it reduces to ½ cup. Remove from heat and strain liquid into a bowl. Discard the discolored mint. Add sugar to reduced vinegar, and stir to dissolve. Then add cold water, lemon juice, and fresh chopped mint leaves.

Escalopes de Veau au Xérès
(Scallops of Veal with Sherry Sauce)

Serves 6

Sheraton-Perth Hotel
Perth, Western Australia

These veal scallops are perfect for those evenings when you want an elegant entrée that takes only minutes to prepare. Assemble all ingredients in advance, then plan on about 15 minutes of cooking time from start to finish.

12 slices veal scallops, each slice
   about 2 ounces
4 tablespoons Clarified Butter (recipe,
   page 277)
3 tablespoons minced onions
½ teaspoon minced garlic
½ pound fresh mushrooms, cleaned
   and sliced

⅓ cup dry sherry
3 tablespoons brandy
3 tablespoons Beef Stock (recipe,
   page 278)
1 cup heavy cream
Salt and pepper, to taste

Trim scallops of any remaining fat or membrane. Place each scallop between sheets of waxed paper and pound well to flatten out and tenderize. Flattened scallops should be very thin.

Continued

Melt the butter over high heat in a large heavy skillet. Quickly sauté flattened veal scallops, 4 to 6 at a time, until golden brown. Remove the scallops and keep warm.

Add onions, garlic, and mushrooms to the skillet, stirring and cooking 2 to 3 minutes, until onions turn light golden brown. Pour in sherry and brandy, then add beef stock and cream. Reduce heat and simmer until sauce begins to thicken. Season to taste. Pour sauce over veal and serve.

Peking Duck with Doilies
(Roasted Duck with Mandarin Pancakes)

Serves 4

Century Park Sheraton Singapore
Singapore, Republic of Singapore

Peking Duck, known for its crisp, crackling skin, is one of China's most famous culinary dishes. Unfortunately, there is no elegant way to dry out the skin of the duck and produce the crisp skin that is so highly prized. Whether you hang the duck by its neck for hours somewhere in your home, perhaps using a fan to speed the process, or use the even easier method we propose, anyone who sees the duck prior to roasting is sure to wonder just what's cooking in your kitchen!

Since it is difficult at times to obtain ducks with their necks left on, we provide a modified method that allows for propping up the duck rather than hanging it out to dry.

Peking Duck:

5- to 6-pound duck	*¾ cup boiling water*
1 generous teaspoon Chinese five-spice powder	*3 star anise*
	Doilies (recipe follows)
1 cup golden syrup or 1 cup light corn syrup plus 3 tablespoons light molasses	*Hoisin Sauce (recipe follows)*
	Scallion Fans (recipe follows)

Clean and wash the duck, drying the inside and outside thoroughly. Rub the duck well with Chinese five-spice powder, again both inside and out.

Pour the golden syrup into the boiling water. Add the 3 star anise and bring back to a boil.

Place the duck in a pan and pour the boiling syrup mixture over it. Marinate the duck in this solution 4 or 5 minutes, turning occasionally. Remove the duck, cool, and refrigerate some of the marinade.

Insert a large heavy bottle into the body cavity of the duck. Place the propped-up duck in a shallow pan, to catch the drippings. Place in the refrigerator for 12 to 24 hours. Exposure to the cold air will dry the skin out quite effectively.

When duck is ready to be cooked, preheat the oven to 325 degrees. Take the duck off the bottle. Brush well with reserved marinade. Place breast side down on a rack in a shallow roasting pan. Bake for 45 minutes. Turn the bird breast side up and bake an additional 45 minutes. (Total roasting time is 1½ hours.) If at any time during the roasting process the skin begins to blacken on top, cover the blackened areas with small pieces of tinfoil. Do *not* cover the whole bird with foil, or skin may lose its crispness.

To serve, slice off the crisp hot skin of the duck and cut it into attractive bite-sized pieces. Do the same with the meat. Arrange skin and meat on separate warm platters. Serve immediately accompanied by Doilies, bowls of Hoisin Sauce and Scallion Fans.

Eat the duck by dipping a Scallion Fan into the Hoisin Sauce and brushing on a doily. Place onion in the doily, if desired, and top with crisp skin and/or duck meat. Fold the doily over and eat with your fingers.

Hoisin Sauce:

> 1 cup hoisin sauce (sweet soy-bean
>   paste)
> ¼ cup water

Pour thick, hoisin sauce into a small saucepan. Stir in the water. Bring to a boil, take off the heat, and cool. Pour into 4 small bowls. Serve sauce at room temperature.

Scallion Fans:

> 12 or more scallions (green onions)

Trim off the root end of the scallions. Cut green leaves down to the top of the white bulb base. Halve large-scallions lengthwise. Shred the tops and bottoms of each scallion vertically with a knife. Drop into a bowl of ice water. Refrigerate 1 hour, or until onions fan out. Drain, pat dry, and serve.

Doilies:

> 2 cups all-purpose flour   2 teaspoons sesame oil
> 1 cup boiling water   (approximately)

Sift flour into a mixing bowl and pour in the boiling water. Stir with a wooden spoon until dough is completely mixed and comes together. (Add a little more water if dough seems too dry.) When cool enough to handle, place dough on a lightly floured surface and knead briskly for about 10 minutes, until smooth. Cover with a damp towel and let rest 15 minutes.

Continued

Roll the rested dough out into a 12-inch-long cylinder. Cut into 12 1-inch pieces. Roll each piece into a ball, then flatten it out until about ¼ inch thick. Brush one side of the doilies with sesame oil. Place two doilies together, oiled sides meeting, making 6 pairs of pancakes. Roll the pairs of doilies out until paper thin. They will be about 5½ to 6 inches in diameter.

Place a heavy frying pan over medium heat. When pan is hot, add a pair of pancakes. Cook them until lightly browned on the bottom, about 1½ minutes, then flip them and brown the other side. Take out of the pan and peel doilies apart. Do *not* cook the inside surfaces. Continue cooking remaining doilies in the same fashion. Keep doilies wrapped in a cloth until ready to serve.

If they are made ahead, doilies may be wrapped in foil, refrigerated, then reheated in a moderate oven, still wrapped in foil.

Ayam Panggang Ketjap
(Indonesian Baked Chicken)

Serves 4

Hotel Ambarrukmo Sheraton
Yogyakarta, Indonesia

The Indonesian sweet soy sauce, Ketjap, distinctly different in taste from Japanese or Chinese soy sauce, is the key ingredient in this baked chicken preparation. It can be found in Indonesian or Oriental markets.

¼ cup dark brown sugar, firmly
*   packed*
1 tablespoon boiling water
3 tablespoons Ketjap Manis
*   (Indonesian sweet soy sauce)*
3 tablespoons paprika
2 tablespoons (about 7 cloves)
*   mashed garlic*

2 tablespoons fresh lime juice
1 teaspoon salt
3-pound chicken, cut into serving-
*   sized pieces*

Place brown sugar in a small bowl. Stir in boiling water, then add the remaining marinade ingredients. Mix well. Brush chicken pieces with this sauce. Refrigerate, if possible, for several hours, allowing the flavors in the sauce time to permeate the chicken.

Bake prepared chicken in a preheated 350-degree oven about 1 hour, or until chicken is cooked through.

The sauce is equally good on broiled or barbecued chicken.

Poularde à la Pattaya

(Thailand Chicken in Curry Broth)

Sheraton-Bangkok Hotel
Bangkok, Thailand

Serves 4

1 cup freshly grated coconut
1 cup boiling water
2 large chicken breasts, skinned,
    boned, and cut into bite-sized
    pieces
¼ ounce or more Thai curry paste
1 tablespoon soy sauce
1 teaspoon salt

⅛ teaspoon pepper
3 cups Chicken Stock (recipe, page
    279)
1½ teaspoons fresh basil leaves (or
    1 teaspoon dried basil leaves)
Accompaniments: Fried rice,
    peanuts, raisins, papaya balls, diced
    fresh pineapple, chutneys

Several hours ahead, or the day before, prepare the coconut milk necessary to the taste of this dish.

Place grated coconut and hot water in a blender. Blend on high speed about 2 minutes, scraping down the sides of the container occasionally.

Line a strainer with a double thickness of cheesecloth and place it over a bowl. Pour coconut mixture into the strainer, allowing the hot liquid to drain through. When cheesecloth is cool enough to handle, pick it up, twist, and squeeze out as much remaining liquid as possible. Discard the cheesecloth and the depleted coconut.

Pour pressed coconut milk into a slender container and refrigerate several hours or overnight (but not much longer or coconut milk will spoil), until thick coconut milk rises and forms a creamy white layer on top.

When you are ready to begin frying, skim off the thick white layer and place it in a large pan over medium-high heat. (Freeze the remaining coconut milk for other uses.) Stir for 1 to 2 minutes until hot, then add the diced chicken, curry paste, soy sauce, salt, and pepper. Sauté these ingredients about 1 minute to blend flavors and partially cook the chicken. Pour in the chicken stock; add the basil. Bring to a gentle boil, then lower the heat and simmer gently 10 minutes longer, or until chicken is cooked through.

Serve hot Poularde à la Pattaya in coconut shells or bowls, accompanied by fried rice, peanuts, raisins, papaya balls, diced fresh pineapple, chutneys, and the like. Dinner guests add the rice and other accompaniments according to their taste.

Lobster Play Pan

Serves 2

Sheraton-Hong Kong Hotel
Hong Kong, B.C.C.

Nothing could be more tempting to see or eat than a plump mango stuffed to the brim with curried lobster. This whole dish takes less than 10 minutes to prepare if ingredients are assembled in advance.

Curried Lobster:

2 large mangoes
2 teaspoons butter
1 teaspoon minced shallots
½ pound cooked lobster meat
¼ cup brandy
1 cup Heavy Béchamel Sauce (recipe below)
3 teaspoons curry powder
2 teaspoons mango chutney

½ cup pineapple juice
4 teaspoons tomato catsup
¼ cup white wine
¼ cup heavy cream
2 drops Tabasco sauce
½ teaspoon salt
Pinch of white pepper

Cut each mango in half, remove the seed, and scoop out most of the orange-colored fruit, leaving a sturdy shell for stuffing. Slice scooped-out fruit into thin slivers. Set aside.

Melt butter in a large heavy skillet over medium-high heat. Sauté shallots 1 or 2 minutes until soft. Add lobster and sauté briefly just until meat is warmed through. (Overcooking the lobster will toughen it.) Pour in the brandy and flambé. As soon as flames die out, remove the lobster and set aside.

To the hot pan, add béchamel sauce, curry powder, chutney, pineapple juice, catsup, wine, and cream. Simmer curry sauce 2 to 3 minutes. Season with Tabasco, salt, and pepper. Fold back in the lobster, simmering just long enough to warm meat through.

Divide curried lobster evenly between the mango shells; top with reserved slices of mango. Serve with buttered rice mixed with green and red peppers.

Heavy Béchamel Sauce:

3 tablespoons butter
3 tablespoons all-purpose flour
1 cup half-and-half, heated

Melt butter over low heat in small heavy saucepan. Add flour, stir, and simmer for 3 to 4 minutes. Slowly stir in hot half-and-half. Let sauce simmer 20 minutes, stirring frequently.

Desserts

Sari-Saring Sa 'Buko
(Hot Brandied Fruit in Coconut Shells)

Serves 4

Century Park Sheraton
Manila, Philippines

An easy-to-prepare dessert fruit sauce with a rich, inviting brandy and caramel flavor.

3 tablespoons butter
¼ cup dark, firmly packed brown
    sugar
½ cup papaya or pineapple juice
¼ cup orange juice
2 tablespoon grated coconut
8 ounces diced fresh pineapple
1 banana, peeled and sliced

1 fresh mango, peeled, seeded, and
    diced
¼ cup brandy
1½ pints coconut or vanilla ice cream
¼ cup unsalted roasted peanuts,
    coarsely chopped

Melt the butter over low heat in a heavy pan. Add the brown sugar and stir until dissolved. Mix in the juices, raise the heat, and bring to a boil. Lower the heat, add the fruit, and simmer until the fruit is warmed through, about 3 to 5 minutes. Heat brandy in a small pan and ignite.   When flames die out, stir brandy into fruit sauce.

Pour hot Sari-Saring into 4 dessert bowls or coconut shells. Top with ice cream and chopped nuts. Serve immediately.

Crêpes Surprises au Chartreuse

Serves 4

Sheraton-Hong Kong Hotel
Hong Kong, B.C.C.

Timing is crucial when preparing Crêpes Surprises au Chartreuse. You must work very quickly to keep the ice cream hidden inside frozen.

8 thin dessert crêpes
1 pint chocolate or vanilla ice cream
3 tablespoons Clarified Butter (recipe,
    page 277)

1 cup blueberries
⅓ cup yellow Chartreuse
¼ cup Cherry Heering

Continued

Fill the center of each crêpe with approximately ¼ cup ice cream; roll, wrap in cellophane, and freeze until hard.

Just before serving, melt butter in a large skillet over high heat. Working quickly, add all the frozen crêpes, turning them over once to coat with butter. Pour in Chartreuse, ignite, and flambé. Flames will jump quite high. As soon as flames begin to die out, remove crêpes and place 2 per person on dessert plates. Quickly pour blueberries into the pan, heat briefly, then add Cherry Heering. Spoon warm sauce over crêpes and serve immediately.

Coco Chana
(Coconut Pudding with Strawberry Jam)

Serves 6

Sheraton-Bangkok Hotel
Bangkok, Thailand

4 cups grated coconut, preferably
* freshly grated*
4 cups milk
1 tablespoon cornstarch
2 tablespoons unflavored gelatin

2 egg whites
3 tablespoons sugar
6 tablespoons strawberry jam
6 teaspoons clear Crème de Cacao

Place grated coconut, milk, cornstarch, and gelatin in a saucepan. Stir to combine, then place pan over medium heat. Stirring constantly, simmer (never boil) the mixture 8 to 10 minutes to dissolve and blend flavors. Take pan off the heat and cool down slightly.

Place a strainer lined with cheesecloth over a medium-sized bowl. Pour coconut liquid through the strainer, pressing down on the coconut to help release liquid and extract flavors. When the liquid has been pressed through, pick up the corners of the cheesecloth and twist and turn the cloth until all remaining liquid is squeezed out of the coconut. Discard the used coconut.

Place the bowl with coconut liquid in a bowl of ice water. Stir coconut liquid frequently, until it thickens to a very soft whipped-cream consistency, about 30 minutes. Take bowl out of the ice water at this point and set aside briefly.

Beat the egg whites until soft peaks form. Add the sugar, a tablespoon at a time, and beat until smooth shiny peaks form. Pour over and fold in the thickened coconut liquid.

Place 1 tablespoon strawberry jam in each of 6 goblets. Top with coconut pudding. Chill well. Just before serving, float 1 teaspoon Crème de Cacao on top of each Coco Chana.

India

Side Dishes

Cauliflower Mussalam
Maurya-Sheraton
New Delhi, India
Coconut Chutney
Chola-Sheraton
Madras, India
Naan Bread
Mughal-Sheraton
Agra, India

Entrees

Kerala Lamb Fry
Chola-Sheraton
Madras, India
Sikandari Raan
Maurya-Sheraton
New Delhi, India

Masala Chops
Maurya-Sheraton
New Delhi, India
Prawns Nisha
Mughal-Sheraton
Agra, India
Navrattan Pulau
Mughal-Sheraton
Agra, India
Murch Badam Pasanea
Maurya-Sheraton
New Delhi, India

Desserts

Carrot Halwa
Maurya-Sheraton
New Delhi, India

India

Spices from India, the flavor of the exotic subcontinent, reflect a culture of time-less mystery, subtlety and excitement. Many cooks fear attempting Indian cuisine, because they are wary of spicy foods and mistakenly think that the preparation of exotic ingredients is beyond their talents. But *The Sheraton World Cookbook* unlocks the mystery of Indian cuisine and the use of such spices as cardamom, cumin, curry, and saffron by combining their rich, unique flavors into dishes that will delight the palate and please the eye.

India brings a new dimension to vegetable dishes, rice, and breads, which are staples in that country's cuisine. The diversity of Indian cuisine is represented in its curries, from hot and spicy Madras to the rich, mild yogurt curry of Delhi. Conjur up visions of the Taj Mahal in your kitchen as you explore the temptations of India through this intriguing land's dishes.

Side Dishes

Cauliflower Mussalam

Serves 6–8

Maurya-Sheraton
New Delhi, India

1 large head cauliflower
1 tablespoon vegetable oil
8 to 10 whole cloves
¼ teaspoon crushed cardamom seeds
*   or ¼ teaspoon ground cardamom*
1½ teaspoons ground ginger

1 teaspoon anise seed
1 scant teaspoon chili powder
1 teaspoon salt
1 cup plain yogurt, lightly beaten
Garnish: Chopped fresh coriander
*   (cilantro) or chopped fresh parsley*

Preheat oven to 350 degrees. Cut off tough end of the cauliflower stem and snap off any green leaves. Steam or boil the cauliflower until tender but still slightly crisp. Remove, drain if necessary, and place cauliflower in a buttered baking dish.

Heat the oil in a small heavy pan. Add all the spices and sauté briefly, 30 seconds or so. Stir in the beaten yogurt, and simmer the sauce 1 to 2 minutes. Pour yogurt sauce over the warm cauliflower.

Place dish in preheated oven. Bake 12 to 15 minutes, until sauce is golden brown on top. Serve hot, garnished with chopped coriander or parsley. Before presenting the dish, you may remove the whole cloves if you desire.

Coconut Chutney

Makes 2 large cups

Chola-Sheraton
Madras, India

2½ cups freshly grated coconut, fairly
*   firmly packed*
½ cup chick-peas (garbanzo beans)
2 small fresh hot green chilies, seeded
*   and diced*
¾ teaspoon salt
2 tablespoons vegetable oil

2 tablespoons mustard seeds
½ teaspoon curry powder
4 teaspoons freshly minced ginger
*   root*
¼ bunch fresh coriander (cilantro),
*   minced*

Grind together, or process in a food processor, the grated coconut, chick-peas, and green chilies. Add salt. Mix until well combined.

Pour oil into a small frying pan and place over medium heat. When hot, add mustard seeds,

Continued

curry powder, and minced ginger. Stir and sauté until mustard seeds pop, about 2 minutes. Cool.

Stir together thoroughly the coconut mixture, the sautéed spices, and the fresh minced coriander. Chill well.

Before serving, stir chutney gently with a fork to lighten. Place in an attractive bowl and serve. Coconut Chutney freezes beautifully.

$\mathcal{N}$aan Bread
(Indian Flat Bread)

Makes 8 pieces   *Mughal-Sheraton*
                                                          Agra, India

Slightly chewy, tasty Naan Bread is a treat not only with Indian foods but with almost any dish that bread might accompany. Vary the toppings, if you choose to use any at all, to suit your mood or your meal.

4½ cups all-purpose flour	¾ cup milk
1 tablespoon baking powder	¼ cup plain yogurt
2 teaspoons sugar	3 or 4 tablespoons Clarified Butter
1½ teaspoons salt	(recipe, page 277)
¼ teaspoon baking soda	Optional: Poppy seeds, dried minced
2 eggs, lightly beaten	onions

Sift together the flour, baking powder, sugar, salt, and baking soda. Place in a deep bowl. Make a well in the center and pour in the eggs, mixed with the milk and yogurt. Stir until well blended. Pick up the dough and place it on a smooth surface. Knead dough 10 minutes or so, until smooth and elastic.

Grease a large bowl with clarified butter. Place the dough in the bowl, turning it once to coat with butter. Cover with a damp towel and let rest in a warm, draft-free location for 45 minutes to 1 hour.

Preheat the broiler.

When rested, divide the dough into 8 pieces. Coat your hands with clarified butter. Roll each piece of dough in your hands to coat with butter, then pat into a teardrop shape. Pat or roll the dough until it is no more than ¼ inch thick. Put 2 or 3 pieces of tear-shaped Naan Bread on baking sheets. Brush lightly with water. Sprinkle with poppy seed, dried minced onion, or other toppings if desired.

Broil the Naan Bread 3 inches below the heat source, about 2 to 3 minutes on the first side, or until golden brown. Turn and brown the other side. Watch carefully to be sure you do not burn up all your efforts. Serve hot or at room temperature.

Entrees

Kerala Lamb Fry

Serves 4

Chola-Sheraton
Madras, India

Timid eaters, beware! Even the adventurous will appreciate fire-quenching side dishes with this lamb fry.

2 tablespoons minced fresh ginger root	*½ to 1 teaspoon cayenne pepper, to taste*
2 tablespoons minced garlic	*2 tablespoons ground coriander*
2 tablespoons cashew nuts	*1 tablespoon turmeric*
¼ cup grated fresh or unsweetened dried coconut	*4 teaspoons salt*
3 tablespoons vegetable oil	*1 pound boneless lamb cut into 1-inch cubes*
1 teaspoon ground cloves	*1 small tomato, chopped*
2 sticks cinnamon, halved	*2 tablespoons fresh lime juice*
1 teaspoon ground cardamom	Garnish: *Chopped coriander leaves*
½ onion, peeled and thinly sliced	*or freshly chopped parsley*

Place ginger root and garlic in a blender or food processor and process until well combined. Add a little water if this is necessary to facilitate the process. Set aside.

Again, in a blender or food processor, chop cashew nuts and coconut together. Set aside.

Place a large heavy pan over medium-high heat. Add the oil. When the oil is hot, fry the cloves, cinnamon, and cardamom until fragrant, about 1 minute. Add the onion and the blended garlic and ginger root. Fry until onions are transparent, another 3 minutes. Stir in cayenne, coriander, turmeric and salt. Fry briefly to accentuate flavors.

Turn the heat up and add the lamb to the saucepan. Stir, scraping the bottom of the pan to dislodge the spices, until meat is browned on all sides, about 5 minutes.

Lower heat, cover pan, and simmer contents gently for 1½ hours, or until meat is tender. When the meat is tender, add the mixture of ground cashews and coconut, the tomato, and the lime juice. Simmer, covered, for 10 minutes longer. Correct seasoning.

Before serving, remove the cinnamon halves or, for a more exotic touch, leave them in. Serve garnished with ½ cup freshly chopped coriander leaves or parsley.

Sikandari Raan
(Spiced Leg of Lamb)

Serves 6

Maurya-Sheraton
New Delhi, India

Imtaz is a Sheraton chef renowned beyond his native India. He catered to the late Maharaja of Jaipur's daughter's wedding in 1947, which led to his service on many state occasions in Lucknow and New Delhi, including the state visit to India of Queen Elizabeth II in 1957. Chef Imtlaz now oversees the Mayur, Shatranj, and Bukhara restaurants at the Maurya-Sheraton. A favorite at the Bukhara is Imtaz's Spiced Leg of Lamb. It is best served with a mild yogurt sauce and a fruit chutney.

Spiced Lamb:

4½- to 5-pound leg of lamb,
  boned, rolled, and tied
1½ teaspoons salt
½ teaspoon cayenne pepper
2½ ounces fresh ginger root, peeled
  and thinly sliced

2½ ounces (25 medium-sized) fresh
  garlic cloves, peeled
2 cups red wine vinegar
1 cup dark rum
4 tablespoons unsalted butter, melted
Garam Masala (recipe follows)

Preheat oven to 475 degrees. Score entire surface of lamb evenly and deeply. Rub salt and cayenne pepper into the slashes.

In a blender or food processor, prepare a paste of the ginger root, fresh garlic, and 4 tablespoons vinegar. Spread paste evenly over lamb, working it down into the crevices.

Place treated leg of lamb in a large bowl and pour over all remaining vinegar. Let sit 20 minutes at room temperature, turning frequently. After 20 minutes, discard marinade and place lamb on a rack in a roasting pan and bake in middle of preheated oven for 15 minutes. Reduce the heat to 350 degrees and continue baking 1¾ hours longer.

Remove lamb from the oven and take out of the roasting pan. Deglaze pan with rum over low heat for 1 or 2 minutes. Untie the lamb, open and flatten it out, then place directly in the rum, dredging the lamb thoroughly on both sides. Cover and refrigerate for at least 24 hours, turning 3 or 4 times.

About an hour before serving, take lamb out of the rum, pat dry, and place in a shallow roasting pan. Pour melted butter over the meat and roast in a preheated 375-degree oven for 45 minutes to 1 hour, basting every 15 minutes.

When done and ready to serve, sprinkle lamb with 1 or 2 tablespoons of Garam Masala (recipe below). Pass remaining masala for those who wish a spicier taste.

Garam Masala:

Masalas, combinations of freshly ground spices, are used throughout India to season foods. This masala is not only excellent on lamb but will add a touch of life to other meats, poultry, fish, and vegetables as well. It will keep for months, tightly covered.

2 tablespoons ground cardamom
1 tablespoon whole cloves
1 tablespoon peppercorns

1½ three-inch cinnamon sticks
1 teaspoon cumin seeds

Grind all spices in a blender or food processor until well pulverized. A smooth, powdery consistency is the desired result. This recipe yields ⅓ cup masala.

Masala Chops
(Spiced Lamb Chops)

Serves 6

Maurya-Sheraton
New Delhi, India

This one-pan dish turns out lamb chops like you have never had before. Sautéed in a mixture of whole and ground spices, nuts, and yogurt, the final effect is of Indian flavors at their best.

8 tablespoons (¼ pound) Clarified
Butter (recipe, page 277)
1 cup finely chopped onions
2 tablespoons finely chopped garlic
1 tablespoon finely chopped fresh
ginger root
½ cup cashew nuts
2 teaspoons poppy seeds
3 whole cloves
⅛ teaspoon cardamom seeds
2 small bay leaves, crushed

6 very thick lamb chops, ⅓ to ½
pound each, well trimmed of fat
1 cup plain yogurt
¾ teaspoon ground cardamom
2 teaspoons freshly ground black
pepper
¼ teaspoon ground cinnamon
¼ teaspoon ground cloves
Salt, to taste
Garnish: Chopped fresh coriander
(cilantro) or chopped fresh parsley

Continued

Place clarified butter in a large heavy skillet over medium-high heat. Fry the onions, garlic, and ginger, stirring constantly, for about 5 minutes, or until onions are golden brown. Remove pan from heat.

Remove onions, garlic, and ginger from the hot butter and place them in a blender or food processor. Purée these ingredients, along with the cashew nuts and poppy seeds. If mixture is too dry to purée, add a few tablespoons of water.

Place frying pan back over medium-high heat. Return spice paste to the pan. Add whole cloves, cardamom seeds, and crushed bay leaves. Add the lamb chops, and fry, turning occasionally, for 10 minutes. Scrape the bottom of the pan now, and again as you continue to cook, and to keep the sauce from scorching.

Lower heat to medium and add the yogurt and ground spices. Fry approximately 10 minutes longer, continuing to turn the chops occasionally. Add ½ cup water and cook the chops 15 minutes longer, or until they are done to your satisfaction. Season with salt. Serve chops coated with yogurt sauce and garnished with chopped coriander or parsley.

Prawns Nisha
(Charcoal Grilled Prawns)

Serves 4

Mughal-Sheraton
Agra, India

Naan Bread (recipe, page 206), tender asparagus, and white rice steamed with a discreet amount of chopped green onions would be a perfect complement to these delicately delicious shrimp.

1½ cups plain yogurt	*1 teaspoon ground ginger*
8 tablespoons fresh lime juice	*1 teaspoon garlic powder*
1½ teaspoons salt	*½ teaspoon white pepper*
24 raw prawns or jumbo shrimp,	*½ teaspoon ground cardamom*
* shelled and deveined*	*½ teaspoon mace*
2 tablespoons raw cashew nuts	Optional: *Pinch of saffron*
1 tablespoon vegetable oil	

Place a muslin tea towel into a colander over a large bowl. Pour in the yogurt and allow it to drain for at least two hours.

Combine the lime juice with 1 teaspoon of the salt and add the prawns (or shrimp); stir, and let sit for about 5 minutes. Drain and discard the salted lime juice. Set prawns aside.

Fry the cashew nuts in oil to a golden brown. Remove from the oil and discard the oil.

Using a mortar and pestle or food processor, pulverize the cashews to a fine powder. Place in a bowl and mix in the ginger, garlic, ½ teaspoon salt, white pepper, cardamom, mace and, if desired, saffron.

Discard the liquid rendered by the yogurt and pour the yogurt curd into the spices, mixing well. Add the prawns, coating them thoroughly. Cover and marinate at room temperature for 2 hours, stirring occasionally.

Remove the prawns from the marinade and thread, six to a skewer, onto four skewers. Basting occasionally with the marinade, grill on a charcoal fire or under a boiler, 3 inches from the heat source, about 3 minutes on a side, or until cooked through.

Navrattan Pulau
(Rice with Cheese, Nuts and Vegetables)

Serves 10–12

Mughal-Sheraton
Agra, India

For those interested in vegetarian dishes, we recommend this fragrantly spiced rice entrée with vegetables, nuts, cheese, and fruits. It is a most satisfying dish.

8 ounces ricotta cheese
Sufficient oil for deep frying
1 tablespoon turmeric
1 cup hot water
¼ cup Clarified Butter (recipe, page 277)
¼ cup vegetable oil
½ cup blanched slivered almonds
½ onion, thinly sliced
1½ tablespoons minced garlic
3 tablespoons minced fresh ginger root

5 cardamom pods, pounded lightly
1 stick cinnamon
3 whole cloves
10 peppercorns
1 cup small cauliflower flowerettes
1 cup green peas
2 cups long-grain white rice
2 teaspoons salt
4 cups boiling water
½ cup dark raisins
½ cup sweet red cherries, pitted and quartered

Enclose the cheese in cheesecloth and form into a rectangle. Place the cheese between two small cheese or bread boards and put a light weight on top. Let sit for about 1 hour to condense the cheese and squeeze excess moisture from it. Then cut the cheese into ½-inch cubes.

Heat oil to 375 degrees. Fry cubes of cheese in small batches until they are golden brown, 45 to 60 seconds per batch. Drain the cheese. Discard the oil.

Mix the turmeric with the 1 cup hot water. Place the fried cheese into the turmeric mixture and set aside.

Place the butter and ¼ cup oil in a large skillet over medium-high heat. Fry almonds until golden, 2 to 3 minutes, and remove with a slotted spoon. Set them aside.

Add onion, garlic, ginger, cardamom, cinnamon, cloves, and peppercorns to the pan. Sauté until onions are golden, about 5 minutes. Add cauliflower and peas. Fry 2 minutes longer.

Into the same pan, put the rice. Add 2 teaspoons salt and the 4 cups boiling water. Cover, bring to a fresh boil, lower heat, and simmer 20 to 25 minutes to absorb all liquids. Remove from the heat.

Discard all whole spices, then stir in the cubed cheese, half the fried almonds, and ¼ cup of the raisins.

Continued

Place on a serving platter. Sprinkle with the remaining almonds and raisins, and with the sweet cherries.

Murch Badam Pasanea
(Cashew Chicken Curry)

Serves 6-8

Maurya-Sheraton
New Delhi, India

Entertain easily with this spicy dish. Good to look at and terrific tasting—it is even better if made ahead, allowed to sit, and reheated before serving.

4 whole chicken breasts, split,
   boned and skinned

Marinade:

¾ cup plain yogurt
1 tablespoon minced fresh ginger root
2 teaspoons white pepper
1 teaspoon ground cloves

1 tablespoon ground cardamom
¼ to ½ teaspoon cayenne pepper, to
   taste

Combine ingredients and liberally brush the thickened marinade on the chicken. Cover and refrigerate for several hours. Remove the chicken and set any remaining marinade aside for later use.

Curry:

3 tablespoons Clarified Butter (recipe,
   page 277)
½ cup chopped onion
¼ cup minced garlic
⅓ cup salted and roasted cashew
   nuts
4 whole cloves
¼ teaspoon ground cardamom

¼ to ½ cup chili powder
2 teaspoons turmeric
1¼ cups water
Garnishes: Toasted slivered almonds;
   coriander leaves, or fresh parsley
Optional: Coconut Chutney (recipe,
   page 205)

Sauté the chicken over medium heat in clarified butter until golden, about 3 to 4 minutes on a side. Remove the chicken and set aside.

Fry the onion, garlic, and cashews in the same pan until they are golden, about 2 minutes. Take the pan off the heat and scrape the contents into a food processor or blender. Add the cloves, cardamom, chili powder, turmeric, and ¼ cup water to the blender or processor. Purée into a paste.

Return the paste to the frying pan and simmer over medium heat for 5 minutes, stirring occasionally. Add 1 cup water, the sautéed chicken, and any reserved marinade and continue to cook over medium heat for 10 minutes, or until chicken is just cooked. Correct the seasoning. Serve hot, sprinkled with toasted almonds and the coriander leaves or fresh parsley. Accompany dish with white rice and Coconut Chutney.

Desserts

Carrot Halwa
(Sweet Carrot Pudding)

Serves 6

*Maurya-Sheraton
New Delhi, India*

Grated carrots, simmered and softened for hours until they reach a soft pudding stage, are a favorite sweet in India. Here, for the fast-paced American, is a carrot pudding recipe that is accomplished in a little over an hour, and with the same satisfying results.

1 pound carrots, peeled and grated
3 cups milk
1 cup heavy cream
8 tablespoons Clarified Butter (recipe, page 277)
½ cup dark brown sugar, loosely packed
¼ teaspoon cardamom seeds or ⅛ teaspoon ground cardamom

1 tablespoon dark raisins
2 tablespoons slivered, blanched almonds, toasted
2 tablespoons unsalted pistachios, toasted
2 tablespoons roasted cashew nuts, coarsely chopped
Optional: *Heavy cream*

Place grated carrots, milk, and 1 cup heavy cream in a deep saucepan and bring to a boil. Lower the heat slightly, and very gently boil (with bubbles just breaking the surface) the carrots, stirring frequently, for 1 hour, until milk and cream are substantially reduced. The mixture will equal approximately 4 cups at this point.

Stir in the clarified butter, raise the heat slightly, and cook the pudding 8 to 10 minutes, stirring constantly.

Continued

Add the brown sugar and cardamom, cooking and stirring until the pudding is sticky and masses together easily, approximately 10 to 15 minutes. Remove pan from heat.

Combine the raisins, almonds, pistachios, and cashews. Stir half of them into the Carrot Halwa. Mound the sweet on a platter, or serve in small portions in individual bowls. Garnish with the remaining nuts. Serve warm or at room temperature with a small pitcher of heavy cream, if desired.

Menu Suggestions

A Far Eastern Barbecue

Kilawing Isda
(page 186)

Ayam Paggang Ketjap
(page 196)

Fried Rice

Sari-Saring Sa Buko
(page 199)

Taj Mahal Dinner

Naan Bread
(page 206)

Murch Badam Pasanea
(page 212)

Cauliflower Mussalam
(page 205)

Coconut Chutney
(page 205)

Sliced Mangoes

Sandwiches

An International Buffet

Sandwiches

The Baja Pocket Combo
Sheraton-Harbor Island Hotel
San Diego, California

California Fancy
Miramar-Sheraton Hotel
Santa Monica, California

Danish Sandwiches
Sheraton-Copenhagen Hotel
Copenhagen, Denmark

Reuben Sandwich
Sheraton-Royal Hotel
Kansas City, Missouri

West Side Deli
New York Sheraton Hotel
New York, New York

Times Square Special
New York Sheraton Hotel
New York, New York

The Baja Pocket Combo

Serves 4

Sheraton-Harbor Island Hotel
San Diego, California

Stuffed Bread:

1 pound ground beef tenderloin
8 slices Muenster cheese, shredded
1 chili pepper, minced
2 tablespoons vegetable oil

Salt and pepper to taste
4 pieces pita bread
Tomato and Jalapeño Sauce (recipe below)

Sauté ground beef, shredded Muenster cheese, and minced chili pepper in oil until meat is browned and cheese is completely melted. Season with salt and pepper. Stuff this concoction into the bread, and spoon some of the following sauce over the stuffed bread.

Tomato and Jalapeño Sauce:

2 medium-sized tomatoes, peeled and chopped
1 jalapeño pepper, finely chopped

½ onion, finely chopped
Dash of Tabasco sauce
½ cup V-8 juice

Combine all ingredients. Chill and serve alongside stuffed bread.
This recipe makes 1 cup of sauce.

California Fancy

Single Serving

Miramar-Sheraton Hotel
Santa Monica, California

5 ounces ground beef chuck
1 kaiser roll
1 lettuce leaf
1 slice Bermuda onion

1 slice tomato
¼ avocado
2 slices cooked bacon
Garnish: *Pickle spear*

Continued

Make a hamburger patty from the ground chuck; broil the meat until done. Split and toast the roll. Place lettuce, onion, and tomato on the bottom half of the roll. Top that with the hamburger, avocado, and bacon. Cover the sandwich with the other half of the roll.

Garnish with a pickle spear.

Danish Sandwiches

Sheraton-Copenhagen Hotel
Copenhagen, Denmark

In Denmark an open-faced sandwich is a lunchtime favorite. Quick and simple to make, these sandwiches are guaranteed to be a lunch-break hit. They are meant to be eaten with a knife and fork.

Open-Faced Dana Blue Sandwich

Serves 4

Cover 4 slices of toasted sandwich bread with the following recipe:

4 ounces Danish blue cheese
2 uncooked egg yolks
Garnishes: Black pepper, chopped
  onions

Mash the cheese with a fork, then blend in the egg yolks one at a time. Garnish with black pepper and chopped onions.

Open-Faced Roast Beef Sandwich

Cover 1 slice of pumpernickel bread with a thick layer of butter so that moist topping will not soak through. Top the buttered bread with the following:

Lettuce leaf   *Chopped pickle*
3 slices roast beef   *Deep-fried onion rings*
Horseradish   *Thin slices of cucumber*

Open-Faced Smoked Eel Sandwich

Cover 1 slice of sandwich bread with a thick layer of butter. Top the buttered bread with the following:

1 ounce smoked eel
2 teaspoons chives, chopped

Open-Faced Roast Pork Sandwich

Cover 1 slice of rye bread with a thick layer of butter. Top with the following:

4 thin slices roast pork
1 tablespoon steamed, shredded red cabbage
1 tablespoon stewed prunes
2 slices apple

Reuben Sandwich

Single Serving

Sheraton-Royal Hotel
Kansas City, Missouri

2 slices rye bread
2 tablespoons Thousand Island
  dressing
2 slices Swiss cheese

2½ ounces thinly sliced corned beef
2 ounces sauerkraut
Garnish: Dill pickle

Preheat oven to 350 degrees. Place 1 tablespoon of dressing on each slice of bread. Layer each slice first with Swiss cheese, then with corned beef. Place sauerkraut on top of corned beef on one slice of bread only.

Place the slices of bread together, wrap in tin foil, and put in the preheated oven for about 10 minutes.

Unwrap the Reuben and garnish it with a dill pickle.

West Side Deli

Single Serving   *New York Sheraton Hotel*
                                                    New York, New York

3 slices pumpernickel bread
1 lettuce leaf
1 tablespoon coleslaw
2 slices tomato

2 slices turkey breast
3 slices corned beef
2 slices Swiss cheese
Garnishes: *Bermuda onion slice, dill*
    pickle, radish rose

Layer 1 slice of bread with lettuce leaf, coleslaw, and tomato. Cover with second slice of bread, and layer this slice with turkey, corned beef, and Swiss cheese. Cover with third slice of bread. Garnish with onion, pickle, and a radish rose.

Times Square Special

Single Serving   *New York Sheraton Hotel*
                                                    New York, New York

1 tablespoon diced Bermuda onions
1 tablespoon diced green bell peppers
1 tablespoon butter
1½ ounces smoked salmon, diced
3 eggs, beaten

2 slices pumpernickel bread
Garnishes: *Lettuce, tomato slices,*
    pickle, ripe olives, Bermuda onion
    slice.

Sauté onions and peppers in butter about 5 minutes, until onions are golden brown and peppers cooked. Add diced salmon and beaten eggs and fry lightly to make an omelet.

Place omelet on bread and eat as an open-faced sandwich. Decorate the plate with lettuce, tomato slices, pickle, olives, and onion, and serve.

Parties

A Festival of
Entertainment Ideas

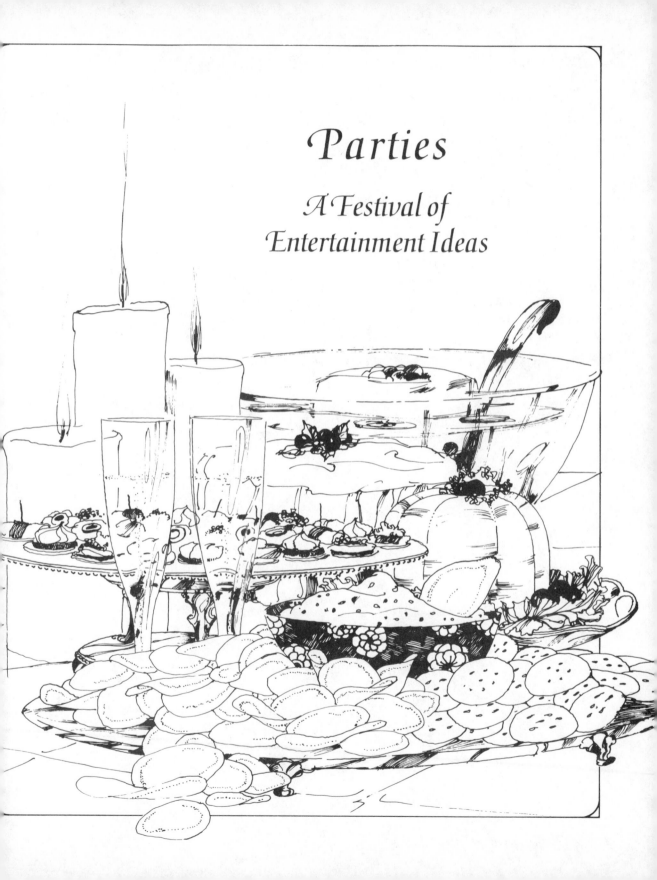

Sunday Brunch

Bloody Mary

Scrambled Eggs Bentley

Strawberry Cheese Chantilly

Sheraton Hotels in New York City

California Garden Party

California Peach Spritzer

Assorted Relish Tray with Désirée Dip,

Guasacaca Dip, San Pablo Dip, Mucho Dip

Spinach Health Salad

Avocado and Citrus Salad

California Salad

Sheraton Hotels in Southern California

New England Clambake

Outdoor Clambake

Indoor Clambake

Sheraton in Boston

Hawaii Luau

Luau Rum Punch

Lomi Lomi Salmon

Shrimp Ono Nui

Pickled Cucumber and Seaweed Salad

Kalua Roast Pig

Sukiyaki

Fried Bananas

Fried Rice

Sheraton Hotels in Hawaii

Mexican Fiesta

Margarita Cocktail

Quesadillas

Yucatan Black Bean Dip

Bola de Queso Relleno

Camerons Chan Kanab

Crema de Mango

Sheraton Hotels in Mexico

English Teaparty

Scones

Crumpets

Maids of Honor

Sheraton Hotels in London

International Holiday Party

Eggnog

Soufflé Potato Pancakes

Holiday Salad

Roast Goose

Venezuelan Hallacas

Christmas Stollen

Sheraton Hotels in the Americas and Europe

Parties

Invite your friends on a culinary journey as you re-create the party flavors of the world. It is sure to be a trip they will never forget.

Sunday Brunch

In the United States, the Sunday brunch has become a tradition that often replaces the old tradition of Sunday dinner. Served in the late morning, brunch combines breakfast and lunch, and is an informal approach to entertaining, with emphasis on minimum effort and maximum relaxation for host as well as guests. Here is a brunch that is simple and easy to prepare, and will leave you plenty of time for pleasant conversation.

Bloody Mary

Single Serving

*St. Regis-Sheraton Hotel
New York, New York*

6 ounces tomato juice
1 ounce clam juice
1/2 ounce lemon juice
Dash of salt
1/4 teaspoon celery seed
1/2 teaspoon horseradish

1/4 teaspoon Worcestershire sauce
Dash of Tabasco sauce
Dash of freshly ground pepper
2 ounces vodka
Garnishes: Fresh celery stalk with leaves,
  lemon wedge

Shake all ingredients except the vodka in a shaker or a jar with the lid on. Pour the vodka in a tall glass over ice; add the tomato juice mixture. Stir the drink with the celery stalk, decorate the glass with the lemon wedge, and serve.

Scrambled Eggs Bentley

Single Serving

1 slice white toast
3 ounces fillet of smoked trout
2 eggs, scrambled

1 teaspoon red salmon caviar
Garnishes: 2 white asparagus, 1 teaspoon
*   chopped fresh parsley*

Cover the toast with smoked trout. Top with the scrambled eggs and salmon caviar. Garnish with asparagus sprinkled with parsley.

Strawberry Cheese Chantilly

Serves 8–10

3 cups sliced strawberries
¾ cup sugar
1 tablespoon lemon juice
2 eggs, separated
1 cup plain yogurt
½ cup (4 ounces) pot or ricotta
*   cheese*

1 tablespoon grated lemon rind
Pinch of salt
1 cup heavy cream, whipped
Garnishes: Toasted chopped pecans,
*   shaved chocolate, whole*
*   strawberries*

Toss strawberries gently with ¼ cup sugar and lemon juice. Let sit at least 15 minutes, allowing strawberries time to exude their juices.

Beat egg whites in a clean, dry stainless-steel or copper bowl until stiff but not dry. Gradually add ½ cup sugar, beating until stiff, shiny peaks form.

In a large bowl, blend yogurt, cheese, egg yolks, grated lemon rind, and salt. Fold in the whipped cream, then the beaten egg whites.

Assemble in goblets or a crystal bowl, layering the cheese chantilly and strawberries, beginning and ending with chantilly. Decorate with toasted pecans, shaved chocolate, and whole strawberries. Completed dessert may be refrigerated 2 or 3 hours until served, but no longer.

California Garden Party

Sheraton Hotels in Southern California

California's climate encourages outdoor living and entertaining. Socializing is casual—friends getting together without formal invitations—and you never know how many people will drop in. In this easygoing atmosphere, you want your party food preparation to be every bit as relaxed. Here is the perfect menu for this kind of garden party: healthy vegetables, savory dips, and crisp salads enhanced with local fruits.

California Peach Spritzer

Serves 6

Spritzer:

12 ounces Peach Purée
 (recipe below)
24 ounces dry white wine

12 ounces club soda
Garnishes: Peach wedges,
 lime slices

Combine peach purée, wine, and club soda in a shaker or mixing glass. Shake or stir just enough to blend all ingredients.

Pour beverages into 6 chilled daiquiri glasses. Thread a peach wedge and a lime slice onto a cocktail pick and place across the top of each glass.

Peach Purée:

6 fresh peaches, blanched
 and sliced

2 ounces Sugar Syrup
 (recipe below)

Combine the peaches and sugar syrup in a blender; whirl until smooth. Chill until needed.

Sugar Syrup:

1 ounce water
2 ounces sugar

Combine the water and sugar in a small saucepan and boil about 5 minutes, until sugar dissolves.

Assorted Relish Tray

Serves 12

This colorful platter of vegetables, surrounded by the tempting dips given below, will be the centerpiece of your garden buffet.

Relishes:

Leaf lettuce
3 medium-sized carrots, cut
   into sticks
3 celery stalks, cut
   into sticks
2 green peppers, cut
   into rings
2 red peppers, cut
   into rings

12 radishes
12 Spanish olives
6 ripe olives
12 green onions
6 kumquats
6 small gherkins
12 cherry tomatoes

Cover platter with lettuce leaves, then arrange carrot and celery sticks, pepper rings, radishes, olives, green onions, kumquats, gherkins, and cherry tomatoes in an attractive display.

Désirée Dip:

Makes 3 cups

8 ounces cauliflower
2 avocados, cut in pieces
1 banana

3 ounces Pernod
Salt and pepper, to taste
Garnish: 3 strawberries

Place cauliflower, avocados, and banana, Pernod, salt, and pepper through a blender. Blend to a coarse consistency.

Guasacaca Dip:

Makes 3 cups

5 avocados, finely chopped
1 red pepper, finely chopped

Salt and pepper, to taste
4 tablespoons mayonnaise

1 green pepper, finely chopped	Dash of Tabasco sauce
1 red onion, finely chopped	½ teaspoon cayenne pepper
2 cloves garlic, finely chopped	½ teaspoon cumin powder

Combine all ingredients in a blender. Blend thoroughly until smooth.

San Pablo Dip:

Makes 1 cup

6 ounces shrimp	1 clove garlic
3 ounces gherkins	4 ounces brandy
1 herring	2 ounces lemon juice

Put all ingredients through a blender; do not grind too fine. Salt and pepper to taste.

Mucho Dip:

Makes 2 cups

⅛ teaspoon saffron	8 ounces Port Salut cheese
6 ounces brandy	4 ounces yogurt
8 ounces Morbier cheese	1 tablespoon chopped mint

Cook saffron in brandy and reduce liquid to half. Put cheeses and yogurt and the saffron-brandy mixture through a blender. When mixed well, add chopped mint.

Spinach Health Salad

Serves 6-8

1 pound leaf spinach, cleaned and stemmed	4 ounces sliced fresh mushrooms
	3 ounces sunflower seeds
5 ounces raw cauliflower bits	1 hard-cooked egg, grated

Toss the spinach with the cauliflower, mushrooms, and sunflower seeds. Top with the grated egg. Serve with your favorite dressing.

Avocado and Citrus Salad

Serves 20-24

Salad:

2 heads romaine lettuce, cleaned
   and cut
4 grapefruit, sectioned
5 oranges, sectioned

4 avocados, sliced
Garnish: 2 roasted sweet peppers,
   julienned

Dressing:

1 quart Italian dressing
3 ounces honey
4 ounces half and half

1 ounce poppy seeds
Salt and pepper, to taste

Place romaine lettuce in an attractive bowl. Arrange grapefruit, oranges, and avocados on top neatly.

Mix Italian dressing, honey, half and half, poppy seeds, salt, and pepper and pour over the salad.

Garnish with julienned roasted sweet peppers and serve.

California Salad

Serves 4

Salad:

2 heads romaine lettuce, cut into
   1-inch strips
2 tomatoes, peeled and cut into
   wedges
1 ripe avocado, peeled and diced

½ cup minced Bermuda onions
2 large mushrooms, sliced
½ cup fresh grated Parmesan
   cheese
4 ounces bacon, crisp and hot

Dressing:

7 tablespoons olive oil	2 tablespoons fresh lemon juice
½ teaspoon salt	1 teaspoon ground black pepper
1 clove garlic	2 drops Worcestershire sauce
3 tablespoons red wine vinegar	1 coddled egg (1½ minutes)

Prepare large wooden salad bowl with 1 tablespoon olive oil; add salt, rub with garlic, then remove garlic.

Add romaine lettuce, tomatoes, avocado, onions, and mushrooms, and sprinkle with cheese.

Mix remaining olive oil, vinegar, lemon juice, and seasonings thoroughly. Add egg and whip vigorously. When ready to serve, pour dressing over salad, toss with bacon, and present.

New England Clambake

New Englanders often celebrate summer holidays with a traditional clambake. Be sure to allow plenty of time for this steamed feast. The entire event—from gathering the stones to enjoying the final meal—will take about six hours. While the food steams safely under seaweed and canvas, all you have to do before the feast is savor the sunset and salt air. Then it is just a matter of eating fragrant lobsters, clams, corn, and chicken. Let your clambake be accompanied by crusty French bread, fresh green salad, and lots of beer. The traditional dessert is watermelon. The portions given here are generous, which is in keeping with clambake philosophy—serve more than you can eat, and you will eat more than you think.

You do not need to have sand and sea to have a clambake. At home you can use a large pot. The cooking method is basically the same as for the outdoor clambake—steam everything thoroughly. Clambakes traditionally use fresh seaweed, but at home the salt-sea flavor can be gotten by substituting *nori*, a common Japanese dried seaweed. *Nori* is packaged and sold in gourmet sections of stores or in Japanese markets. Unlike fresh seaweed which remains relatively whole, dried seaweed disintegrates as it boils, but the effect is not unpleasant. In the indoor clambake we specify ingredients for six hungry people, but the recipe is easily scaled up or down.

Outdoor Clambake

Serves 10

Sheraton-Boston Hotel
Boston, Massachussetts

Large rocks
Wood for fire
2 bushels seaweed
20 potatoes
6 onions, unpeeled
5 broiler chickens, split

10 large live lobsters
12 dozen clams
20 ears corn
Large tarpaulin
Garnishes: Melted butter,
lemon wedges

Dig a hole in the sand about 5 feet in diameter and 1 foot deep. Line the hole with large rocks. Place hardwood on the rocks and ignite a fire. This fire should burn for several hours.

Lay more large rocks on the burning wood and continue burning until the rocks are very hot. Cover them with a layer of seaweed that has been rinsed in fresh water.

Add potatoes in their skins and unpeeled onions onto the seaweed. Then add another layer of rinsed seaweed to cover.

Over this seaweed, place split broiler chickens wrapped in tinfoil and seasoned. Then add another layer of rinsed seaweed to cover.

Place the live lobsters on the seaweed. Then add another layer of rinsed seaweed to cover.

Add scrubbed cherry stone clams or soft-shelled steamer clams. These should be wrapped in cheesecloth. Then add another layer of rinsed seaweed to cover.

Remove the silk from 20 ears of corn, but do *not* remove the husks. Place this corn onto the seaweed.

Cover with a wet tarpaulin. Weight the covering on all ends and bake for 2 to 3 hours, or until the clams begin to open. Serve with melted butter and lemon wedges and lots of cold beer!

Indoor Clambake

Sheraton-Boston Hotel
Boston, Massachussetts

Serves 6

3 chickens, split in half
Salt and freshly ground black
   pepper, to taste
4 to 6 dozen clams, well scrubbed
6 ears corn
Fresh seaweed, rinsed well; or 10
   to 12 large sheets nori (Japanese
   dried seaweed)

6 large live lobsters
Garnishes: *Melted butter, lemon*
   wedges

Season the chicken halves with salt and pepper and wrap them in cheesecloth, one bundle per person. Also wrap the scrubbed clams in loose bundles of cheesecloth. Take corn and pull back husks without tearing them off. Remove the silk threads surrounding the corn and replace the husks.

Line the bottom of 2 12-quart pots with a generous layer of seaweed or 2 sheets of nori in each pot. Add enough cold water to come up to a depth of ¼ to ½ inch. Cover the pots and bring contents to a boil.

Place wrapped chicken in each pot. Lay fresh seaweed or a sheet of nori over chicken. Cover and continue gently boiling approximately 20 minutes. Add the lobsters (3 per pot) and more seaweed. Cover and gently boil 5 minutes. Divide the corn between the pots. Boil, covered, 10 minutes longer. Finally, add the wrapped clams, again dividing equally between the pots, and cook approximately 10 to 15 minutes, covered, until the clams open. (Discard any clams that fail to open when the rest are cooked.)

Remove all ingredients from the pot and serve, steaming hot, with melted butter and lemon wedges.

Hawaiian Luau

The original name for this feast was *Pā'ina* or *Aha'aina*. *Pā'ina* literally means any kind of party with food. Today's *Pā'inas,* or luaus, feature Kalua Roast Pig, Lomi Lomi Salmon, Luau Rum Punch, and other delicious island favorites featured here.

The Hawaiians have luaus to celebrate many occasions, such as weddings and anniversaries. Today's "baby luau," celebrated in honor of the first birthday of a child, is loosely connected to the ancient ritual *Aha'aina Mawaewae.* This celebration was to guarantee the child safe passage through life. The "baby luau" is also reminiscent of the *Aha'aina Pala,* a feast meant simply to express *Aloha* (goodwill) to the firstborn. It is as meaningful today as the *Aha'aina Pala* was to the Hawaiians of old.

Whatever the occasion, there are no hosts in the world like the Hawaiians, and the profusion of food and *Aloha* at any luau is overwhelming. A luau is the perfect way to make your guests feel especially honored!

Luau Rum Punch

Makes 2 gallons

*Princess Kaiulani Hotel
Honolulu, Hawaii*

14 ounces dark rum
10 ounces grenadine
28 ounces pineapple juice

28 ounces orange juice
28 ounces grapefruit juice
20 ounces 7-Up

Blend all ingredients together in a large punch bowl, add lots of ice cubes, and let your guests serve themselves.

Lomi Lomi Salmon

Princess Kaiulani Hotel
Honolulu, Hawaii

Serves 4-6

1 cup fresh salted salmon, cut into
small dice
1 cup green onions, chopped

1 cup white onions, chopped
3 cups fresh tomatoes, diced

Mix all ingredients and serve chilled in individual bowls or in a buffet bowl.

Shrimp Ono Nui
(Coconut Shrimp)

Princess Kaiulani Hotel
Honolulu, Hawaii

Serves 6

24 large raw shrimp, peeled
$\frac{1}{2}$ cup all-purpose flour

2 eggs
3 cups shredded coconut

Dredge shrimp in flour, then in eggs. Roll the shrimp through shredded coconut, covering them thoroughly.
 Deep-fry shrimp at about 375 degrees, until they are brown.
 Serve with cocktail sauce to which crushed pineapple is added according to taste.

Pickled Cucumber and Seaweed Salad

Sheraton-Kauai Hotel
Kauai, Hawaii

Serves 6

$3\frac{1}{2}$ ounces wakame seaweed
1 cucumber, thinly sliced
$\frac{1}{2}$ teaspoon salt
$\frac{1}{2}$ cup white vinegar

2 tablespoons soy sauce
1 tablespoon shredded fresh ginger
1 tablespoon sugar
2 ounces minced clams

Continued

Soak the seaweed in cold water until it becomes tender. (Depending on the quality of the wakame, this will take 10 to 30 minutes.)

Slice the cucumber, salt lightly, and let stand 30 minutes. Drain liquid.

Cut the seaweed into 1½-inch strips. Mix together the vinegar, soy sauce, shredded ginger, and sugar.

Combine wakame, cucumber, and minced clams in a salad bowl. Pour the vinegar-soy dressing over it, mix gently, and serve.

Kalua Roast Pig

Serves 8-10

Princess Kaiulani Hotel
Honolulu, Hawaii

If digging a pit in your back yard is out of the question, but you want to go Hawaiian anyway, consider this Kalua Roast Pig. In fact, if you don't confess to the liquid smoke, your guests will start looking for the pit the minute they see the platter of shredded pork.

Ti leaves, long, slender, dark green leaves of the ti tree, are used to encase many foods in Hawaii, much as corn husks are used in Latin America and banana leaves are used in other parts of the world. Leaves not only enclose and protect their contents, but they trap valuable moisture and impart flavor as well.

If ti leaves are not grown in your area, they often can be found in florists' shops. If not, consider substituting dried palm leaves, which are frequently sold in oriental markets.

10 to 15 ti leaves or dried palm
leaves, soaked to soften,
then shaken dry
4½- to 5-pound pork picnic shoulder
roast or a Boston shoulder roast

2 teaspoons coarse salt
1½ tablespoons liquid smoke
¼ cup water

Preheat oven to 300 degrees. Line a deep roasting pan with ti leaves.

Season the pork roast with salt. Cover the meat with ti leaves and tie up with string. Place wrapped meat in pan on top of leaves, then cover meat with more leaves. Pour a mixture made of the liquid smoke and water over the meat and leaves. Seal the pan tightly with tinfoil to prevent moisture from escaping.

Roast the pork at least 3 hours, until very well done and to the point of overdone. The meat is taken off the bones and shredded by hand, never cut with a knife.

Sukiyaki

Princess Kaiulani Hotel
Honolulu, Hawaii

Serves 4

This easy-to-manage way of cooking at the table is the perfect answer for the chef who likes to enjoy his friends while cooking a meal they will rave about. Your guests should be encouraged to serve themselves from the common pot. A wok is best; an electric frying pan works but is much less elegant. Serve Sukiyaki with warmed sake, and you may never want to leave the table.

The recipe calls for shirataki, which are long, thin yam noodles that are called "cellophane noodles" in some shops.

Sukiyaki:

1¼ pounds boneless top sirloin of
   beef, very thinly sliced
1 ounce beef suet
2 large onions, peeled, halved, and
   cut into ½-inch slices
1 pound cooked shirataki

½ pound tofu, drained and cut into
   ¼-inch dice
½ pound mushrooms, cleaned and
   with stems trimmed
2 bunches watercress, washed, with
   stems trimmed
Optional: 4 eggs

Sauce:

½ cup water
½ cup mirin (Japanese cooking
   wine)

½ cup shoyu (Japanese soy sauce)
2 tablespoons sugar

To facilitate slicing the beef, first freeze it until it is firm, then take it out of the freezer and place it in the refrigerator for about 7 or 8 hours before you plan to slice it. When ready for slicing, cut the beef into paper-thin slices 1 inch wide by 2 inches long. If you are going to use the beef soon, set it aside at room temperature until it is completely thawed. Otherwise, cover and refrigerate for later use.

To serve, arrange all Sukiyaki ingredients decoratively in a large shallow bowl.

Blend sauce ingredients in a separate bowl. Place the bowl with the Sukiyaki ingredients, the bowl of sauce, and an electric frying pan or electric wok on the dinner table.

Bring the electric frying pan or wok to medium or medium-high heat. Rub with suet. Remove suet and put in ⅓ of the onions and ⅓ of the shirataki and cook about 1 minute. Push these ingredients to one side. Into the electric pan put ⅓ of the sauce and ⅓ of the beef. Cook meat approximately 1 minute, then push to the side also. Add ⅓ each of the tofu, mushrooms, and watercress. Continue to cook the contents of the pot, turning them occasionally until the meat and vegetables are cooked to taste.

If you wish, serve each diner with a small bowl containing a beaten, raw egg. The diner is to dip the hot food into the egg to coat it before eating. As your guests eat, continue to cook the rest of the meat and vegetables in the pan, adding more sauce as deemed necessary.

Fried Bananas

Serves 6

Princess Kaiulani Hotel
Honolulu, Hawaii

6 bananas
2 cups all-purpose flour
2 eggs, beaten

1 1/2 cups bread crumbs
1 1/2 cups shredded coconut

Peel the bananas and cut them in half laterally (across). Roll the bananas in flour and then in the beaten eggs. Finally, roll the bananas in an equal mixture of bread crumbs and shredded coconut.

Deep fry bananas to a golden brown color and serve with Fried Rice (recipe follows).

Fried Rice

Serves 10-12

Princess Kaiulani Hotel
Honolulu, Hawaii

1/2 cup vegetable oil
5 cups cooked white rice
5 ounces ham, chopped

1 cup chopped green onions
5 eggs, beaten
1/4 cup soy sauce

Heat the oil in a frying pan, or even better, in a wok. Place rice, ham, and green onions in the pan and stir-fry over moderate heat about 3 minutes. Add scrambled eggs and mix everything well. Then add the soy sauce, mix again, and serve.

Mexican Fiesta

This fiesta is inspired by the *posada,* a religious and folkloric party celebrated in Mexico for a period of nine days prior to Christmas. Mariachi music and strolling guitarists add to the gay atmosphere. *Piñatas,* papier-mâché animal figures filled with fruit and candy, are hung from the ceiling; blindfolded guests must then break them with poles, releasing the goodies for everyone to gather up.

You can create a joyous fiesta of your own any time during the year. Decorate your table lavishly with flowers and brightly colored chinaware full of the Mexican treats that follow.

Margarita Cocktail

Single Serving

Maria Isabel-Sheraton Hotel
Mexico City, Mexico

To make a Mexico fiesta a double feast, celebrate with this popular cocktail.

1 ½ ounces tequila
½ ounce Triple Sec

1 tablespoon lemon juice

Mix all ingredients together with crushed ice. Serve in a champagne glass that has been salted around the rim.

Quesadillas

Makes 12 Quesadillas

Cancun Sheraton Hotel
Cancun, Mexico

Crisp, golden packages encase flavorful cheese. Enhance them with any of a variety of complementary fillings, such as shredded green onions, diced tomatoes, diced mild chili peppers, a sprinkling of precooked chorizo, or shredded chicken.

Continued

Quesadillas (continued)

12 corn or flour tortillas, 6 to 8
   inches in diameter
¾ pound Monterey Jack cheese,
   thinly sliced
2 or more tablespoons minced hot
   chili peppers, such as jalapeño,
   yellow wax chilis

¼ cup (approximately) vegetable
   oil
Garnishes: Watercress, 1 cup Chili
   Salsa (recipe, page 276)

Lay out the tortillas. Arrange equal portions of cheese on the bottom half of each. On the cheese, spread ½ teaspoon or more of the hot chili peppers. If you wish, add any of the fillings mentioned above or use one of your choice. Fold the empty half of the tortilla over the filling. (If the tortilla will not fold easily, try again after it has been warmed slightly in the frying procedure.)

Heat a large comal or heavy frying pan. Film the bottom of the pan with some of the oil, replenishing as necessary. Fry the tortillas, turning occasionally, until the outside is golden brown and crispy and the cheese has melted.

Remove the Quesadillas from the heat and garnish with watercress. Serve immediately. Pass the Chili Salsa.

Yucatan Black Bean Dip

Serves 10-12

Cancun Sheraton Hotel
Cancun, Mexico

1 pound dried black beans
1 tablespoon salt
1 pound lean ground pork
2 teaspoons oregano
2 tablespoons butter
1 cup chopped onions
5 medium-sized radishes, sliced
1 to 4 teaspoons seeded, minced
   hot green chili peppers

6 tablespoons fresh lemon juice
1 cup canned green chili salsa
½ pound grated Monterey Jack
   cheese
¼ cup chopped fresh coriander
   leaves (cilantro) or fresh parsley
Taco chips

Soak the beans overnight in water. Drain. To the beans add 6 cups fresh water and 1 teaspoon salt. Bring to a boil, cover, and simmer for 2 hours, or until beans are tender. Remove the beans with a slotted spoon and set aside.

Bring bean stock to a boil; add ground pork and oregano. Bring to second boil. Drain stock. Reserve the parboiled pork.

Melt butter in a large heavy saucepan over medium heat. Sauté the onions, radishes, and peppers until limp. Add beans, boiled pork, lemon juice, and remaining salt. Lower heat, cover, and simmer 10 to 15 minutes, or until tender. Pour in the salsa, add almost all the cheese, and continue simmering until cheese melts.

Pour bean dip into a serving dish, sprinkle with reserved cheese and chopped coriander, and surround with taco chips. Serve warm.

Bola de Queso Relleno
(Stuffed Cheese)

Serves 6-8

Cancun Sheraton Hotel
Cancun, Mexico

5 pound wheel of Edam cheese
2 whole chicken breasts
4 cups Chicken Stock (recipe, page 279)
2 teaspoons dried granulated chicken bouillon (or 2 cubes dried chicken bouillon
⅓ cup chopped onions
1 clove garlic, peeled and minced
1 tablespoon vegetable oil
1 pound ground beef

¼ cup raisins
2 ounces pimentos
1 teaspoon salt
¼ teaspoon pepper
1 tablespoon dried granulated beef bouillon or 3 cubes dried beef bouillon dissolved in ¼ cup hot water
2 eggs, lightly beaten
¾ cup masa harina (dehydrated, treated corn flour)
Chili Salsa (recipe, page 276)

Cut a lid off the top of the cheese. Using a sharp knife, remove and hollow out the cheese wheel until you have a shell of cheese approximately ¾ inch thick. Reserve the interior cheese for other uses. Wrap the cheese shell and refrigerate until needed.

Place chicken breasts and the chicken stock in a saucepan, cover, and poach them for about 15 minutes to cook through. Remove pan from heat and allow breasts to cool down in the stock.

When breasts are cool, remove the chicken, saving the stock. Skin and bone the chicken, then shred the chicken meat. Discard the skin and bones. Place shredded meat in a serving bowl and set aside until ready to serve.

Put chicken stock back on the heat and reduce liquid, at a gentle boil, to 3 cups. Stir the chicken bouillon into the hot stock. When dissolved, set stock aside.

Preheat oven to 400 degrees.

In a large skillet over medium heat, fry the onions and garlic in 1 tablespoon oil until golden

Continued

brown. Raise the heat slightly, add the beef, and fry until beef is well browned. Add the raisins, pimentos, salt, pepper, and beef bouillon, stirring well. Pour in the eggs, stirring to scramble them into the meat mixture. When eggs are cooked, take pan off the heat.

Take cheese out of refrigerator, unwrap, and peel off the waxy coating protecting the outside of the cheese. Fill cheese with the warm meat mixture. Place in a shallow baking dish and bake for about 10 minutes, until cheese is warm but not completely melted.

While cheese is baking, bring reduced chicken stock to a boil. Stir in the masa harina. Cover and let simmer 10 minutes.

Serve the Queso Relleno as soon as it is soft and warm, accompanied by bowls of warm masa sauce, fresh Chili Salsa, and shredded chicken. Slice the stuffed cheese shell into wedges, allowing dinner guests to help themselves to the toppings.

Camerones Chan Kanab

(Deep-Fried Marinated Shrimp)

Serves 2-3

Cancun Sheraton Hotel
Cancun, Mexico

The annatto (achiote) seeds in this recipe can be found in Latin American stores. They give a delicate golden color to the shrimp.

12 raw jumbo shrimp 1½ to 2 ounces each, shelled but with tails left on, deveined and butterflied (cut almost in half lengthwise, opened and flattened out)
¼ cup fresh orange juice
⅓ cup fresh lemon juice

1 tablespoon annatto (achiote) seeds, crushed
1 tablespoon mashed garlic
1 teaspoon oregano
½ teaspoon cumin
Sufficient oil for deep frying

Place butterflied shrimp in a shallow dish. Combine all the remaining ingredients except the oil and pour over the shrimp. Cover and refrigerate 1 to 2 hours, turning shrimp occasionally.

Take shrimp out of the marinade and deep-fry at 365 degrees on a deep-fry thermometer for about 1 minute, or until shrimp are just cooked through. Serve with Spanish rice while hot.

Crema de Mango

Maria Isabel-Sheraton Hotel
Mexico City, Mexico

Serves 12

Mango trees, originally from East India, now flourish in Latin America. The mango's orange-colored flesh can be eaten as is, sprinkled with lime juice, or puréed and made into desserts such as this one.

4 pounds (about 5) ripe mangoes
3 tablespoons fresh lime juice
1½ cups heavy cream, whipped
1 cup diced pecans
2 large oranges, peeled, seeded,
*   diced, and drained*

4 (or more) tablespoons sugar
Garnishes: *Maraschino cherries,*
*   fresh mint leaves*

Peel, seed, and purée mangoes with lime juice in a food processor or blender. Transfer mango purée to a large bowl, fold in the whipped cream, pecans, and drained orange pieces. Sweeten to taste with sugar. Spoon into dessert bowls or glasses. Chill thoroughly. Serve decorated with maraschino cherries and fresh mint.

English Tea Party

Afternoon tea is more than a simple drink in England. It is a ceremony and an occasion to entertain friends with pleasant and light conversation. The brightly polished tea silver and traditional cakes and sandwiches are displayed on a table before the hostess begins to serve.

The English pride themselves on being the only people in the world who know how to make a good cup of tea. Here is the way they do it: fill a kettle with fresh cold water and bring it to a boil. Just before the water boils, warm the teapot by filling it with hot water that is discarded when the pot feels warm. Then put one heaping teaspoon of tea per cup into the pot. By this time the water should be boiling (never let it boil too long). Pour the boiling water onto the tea leaves in the pot and allow the tea to brew for five minutes. Stir and pour. Guests add their own milk, which should be cold, and then sugar.

The afternoon tea would not be complete without finger sandwiches. To make them, top a buttered slice of white bread with any of the following toppings: thinly sliced, seasoned cucumbers; chopped egg with mayonnaise and watercress; or thinly sliced cheese and tomato. Cover with another buttered slice of white bread, trim crust and cut into four finger-sized squares. Also serve a variety of fresh cakes, such as Maids of Honor, Crumpets, or Scones, the recipes for which follow.

Scones

Makes 1½-2 dozen

Sheraton Park Tower Hotel
London, England

Scones are delicately sweet, finely textured biscuits. They are good with just butter, but some would argue that they are better with butter and a pot of strawberry jam.

2 cups all-purpose flour
2 teaspoons baking powder
3 tablespoons sugar
⅛ teaspoon salt

6 tablespoons butter, cut in ¼-inch
*   pieces and thoroughly chilled*
2 eggs
6 tablespoons plain yogurt

Preheat oven to 400 degrees.

Sift flour, baking powder, sugar, and salt together. Using a pastry blender or your fingertips, work the butter into the flour mixture until it resembles coarse meal.

Separate one of the eggs. Reserve the white. Beat the egg yolk with a second egg until frothy. Stir in the yogurt, then add to the flour mixture. Work dough as little as possible to prevent toughening. Stir until dough can be gathered into a compact ball.

Roll dough out to approximately ½-inch thickness. Cut with a floured 2-inch biscuit or cookie cutter. Beat the reserved egg white with a fork till frothy. Brush the egg white on the top of each scone.

Bake the scones for 10 to 15 minutes, or until lightly browned. Serve while still hot.

Crumpets

Makes approximately 8 crumpets

*Sheraton Park Tower Hotel
London, England*

English muffins are none other than crumpets. They are so easy to make that there is no excuse for eating store-bought ones. Make several batches, eat some, freeze some, and give some to friends to help brighten their mornings.

*¼ ounce active dried yeast
5 tablespoons lukewarm water
½ teaspoon sugar
1½ cups sifted all-purpose flour
¼ teaspoon salt*

*7 tablespoons lukewarm milk
1 egg, lightly beaten
2 tablespoons softened butter
2 tablespoons Clarified Butter
    (recipe, page 277)*

Mix yeast, water, and sugar together in a small bowl. Set bowl aside in a warm, draft-free location, 10 to 15 minutes, until contents bubble, as proof the yeast is active. If it does not bubble, discard the mixture and start again with fresh yeast.

Sift flour and salt into a medium-sized bowl. Create a well in the center. Pour in the yeast mixture, milk, and egg. Add the softened butter; whip or beat all until well combined. (Mixture will be loose at this point.) Cover the bowl with a tea towel and let rise in a warm, draft-free location until double in bulk, about 1 hour.

When mixture has risen, brush the bottom of a heavy skillet with some of the clarified butter. Place pan over medium heat. Arrange buttered crumpet rings in the pan, filling each ring ⅓ of the way up with batter. (If you have no crumpet rings, you can use cans 1½ inches high by 3 inches wide, cutting off the tops and bottoms of the cans before using. A 7-ounce tuna fish can works perfectly.)

Continued

Cook until open bubbles form on the surface and the bottoms are brown, 1 to 2 minutes. Remove the rings, turn, and brown the other side. Continue making crumpets until all batter is used. Regrease the rings as necessary. Serve warm, with butter and jam.

Maids of Honor
(Miniature Almond Pastries)

Makes 3 dozen pastries

Sheraton Park Tower Hotel
London, England

These small, golden almond pastries are perfect for teas, afternoon gatherings, and, naturally, weddings.

Rich Pastry Shell (recipe, page 281)
2 egg yolks
½ cup sugar
6 tablespoons ground almonds
1 tablespoon all-purpose flour
2½ teaspoons finely grated
*   lemon rind*

3 tablespoons heavy cream
⅓ cup raspberry jam
1 ounce (¼ cup) sliced almonds
1 tablespoon sugar

Preheat oven to 375 degrees.

Lightly grease miniature muffin tins (ones with cups about 1¾ inches in diameter). Set aside.

Make one recipe Rich Pastry Shell. Chill the pastry well, preferably overnight. When it is well chilled, roll out the pastry, one-half at a time, preferably on a cold surface, until no more than ⅛ inch thick. (Lightly flour the work surface and rolling pin if necessary, but avoid overflouring or pastry may toughen.)

Using a 2½-inch round cookie or biscuit cutter, cut out pastry rounds. Gently press the soft pastry rounds into the greased muffin tins.

Beat together the egg yolks, sugar, ground almonds, flour, and grated lemon rind. Add the cream, and beat until smooth.

Drop a very small amount of raspberry jam, about ¼ teaspoon, into the bottom of each miniature pastry. Spoon on top approximately 1 teaspoon of almond filling, filling each pastry cup almost to the top. Place 1 or 2 sliced almonds on top of each one. Finally, lightly sprinkle 1 tablespoon sugar over all.

Bake Maids of Honor for about 20 minutes, or until golden brown. Let pastries cool slightly before taking them out of the tins.

International Holiday Party

Each part of the world celebrates the holiday season with its own unique festive menus. Here is a collection of authentic recipes from different countries so that you can bring an international flavor to your holiday table.

Eggnog

Serves 10-12

The Sheraton Centre
New York, New York

12 egg yolks
1 quart vanilla ice cream, softened
1½ to 2 cups brandy

1 teaspoon vanilla extract
2 cups heavy cream
Freshly grated nutmeg

Beat egg yolks until they are thick and light. Add softened ice cream. Slowly pour in brandy (to taste) and vanilla extract, stirring until a smooth eggnog base results. For best results, let this base rest for several hours or overnight, refrigerated.

Stir in chilled heavy cream. Serve sprinkled with freshly grated nutmeg.

Soufflé Potato Pancakes

Makes 3 dozen pancakes

Sheraton Bal Harbour
Bal Harbour, Florida

2½ pounds potatoes
4 eggs, separated
½ cup finely chopped onions
½ cup sifted all-purpose flour

2 teaspoons salt
¼ teaspoon white pepper
6 to 8 tablespoons margarine

Continued

Peel potatoes and place them in ice water to prevent their browning until ready to grate.

Place egg yolks in a large bowl. Lightly beat the yolks, stir in onions and flour mixed with salt and pepper.

Pat the potatoes dry. Coarsely grate them onto a tea towel. Squeeze potatoes in the towel to release unwanted moisture.

Add potatoes to egg-onion mixture and blend well. Whip egg whites until stiff but not dry and fold into batter.

Melt 1 tablespoon margarine in a large heavy skillet over medium heat. For each pancake, drop 1 heaping tablespoon of batter into the pan. Flatten into thin, 3-inch wide pancakes. Sauté 2 to 3 minutes on a side, until golden brown and cooked through. Add more margarine to the pan as necessary to complete cooking all the batter.

As they are done, place pancakes in a 200-degree oven to keep warm. Serve immediately.

Holiday Salad

Sheraton Lancaster Resort
Lancaster, Pennsylvania

Serves 10-12

Salad:

2 cups finely chopped cranberries
1 cup sugar
20 ounces canned crushed pineapple
6 ounces lemon-flavored gelatin

1½ cups orange juice
1½ cups chopped celery
½ cup chopped pecans
2 tablespoons freshly grated orange
   rind

Marinate chopped cranberries in sugar for 1 hour at room temperature. Drain pineapple and pour juice into a measuring cup. Add water to juice if necessary to make 1 cup.

Bring juice to a boil, add gelatin, and stir until dissolved. Add sugar-coated cranberries and orange juice. Let mixture cool down until it begins to thicken slightly.

When the mixture has thickened, fold in pineapple, celery, pecans, and orange rind. Pour into a 6-cup mold. Chill several hours or overnight, until firm. Serve with the following dressing.

(continued page 257)

Sikandari Raan & Naan Bread *(India)*

Crêpes Surprises au Chartreuse *(Far East)*

English Tea Party. Left to right: Scones, Crumpets, Maids of Honor, Finger Sandwiches *(Parties)*

Marak Perot Kar *(Middle East)*

Brazilian Feijoada *(Latin America)*

oster Play Pan *(Far East)*

Holiday Salad Dressing:

½ cup heavy cream
½ cup mayonnaise
3 tablespoons sour cream

1½ teaspoons freshly grated
lime rind

Whip cream until soft peaks form. Stir in the mayonnaise, sour cream, and grated lime. Chill well.

Roast Goose

Sheraton-Copenhagen Hotel
Copenhagen, Denmark

Serves 8-10

Goose:

8- to 10-pound goose
Salt and pepper
1½ cups dried pitted prunes

3 cups cored, coarsely chopped
apples

Preheat oven to 400 degrees. Rinse the goose well and pat dry. Salt and pepper interior and exterior of bird. Mix prunes and chopped apples; fill goose with them. Truss goose well so that its shape holds while roasting.

Place goose on a rack in a shallow pan and roast in the preheated oven 30 minutes. Remove goose from oven. Lightly prick the goose all over to help release the fat, then return to the oven for 30 minutes longer. Draw off melted fat from the pan throughout the roasting process as necessary.

After the first 1 hour of roasting, prick the goose again, reduce oven temperature to 350 degrees, and continue cooking about 2 to 2½ hours longer, until done. Signs of a well-done goose are clear juices when the leg meat is pierced and an internal temperature of 185 degrees registered on a meat thermometer.

Let the goose rest 10 to 15 minutes before carving. Discard fatty stuffing; if desired, a separate Apple-Prune Stuffing can be prepared to serve with the goose.

Continued

Apple-Prune Stuffing:

5 cups dried, pitted prunes
6 cups coarsely chopped apples
7 cups water
¼ cup fresh lemon juice

½ cup sugar
3 sticks cinnamon
4 tablespoons butter
1 teaspoon fresh grated lemon rind

Place prunes and chopped apples in a large pan. Pour in water and lemon juice; add sugar and broken cinnamon sticks. Stir well, bring to a boil, cover, reduce heat to low, and simmer 5 minutes, until apples soften slightly and prunes plump up.

Drain and place stuffing in a covered casserole dish. Dot with butter, sprinkle on grated lemon rind, and toss lightly. Reheat in a warm oven before serving.

Venezuelan Hallacas

Makes 24 hallacas

Macuto-Sheraton Hotel
Caracas, Venezuela

Hallacas, more than any other food, symbolize Christmas for Venezuelans. Delicious meaty morsels are surrounded by a tender corn dough, then steamed to perfection in colorful banana leaves.

We have substituted more readily available wrappings than banana leaves for use in making the hallacas. But if you are fortunate to have access to these large, beautiful leaves, plan on using them for truly authentic results.

Meat Filling:

1 pound top round, cut into ¼-
    ½-inch dice
1 pound lean pork, cut into ¼- to
    ½-inch dice
¼ pound bacon strips, cut into
    ½-inch lengths
3 medium-sized tomatoes, peeled
    and seeded

1 onion, peeled
3 cloves garlic, peeled
1 tablespoon salt
2 teaspoons marjoram
1 medium-sized leek, diced
¼ cup capers
1 tablespoon mustard relish pickles

¼ *cup red wine vinegar*
1 *bell pepper, cut into* ¼- *to* ½-*inch*
  dice
1 *teaspoon Worcestershire sauce*

1½ *tablespoons dark brown sugar*
Salt and pepper, to taste
½ *cup raisins*

Put beef, pork, and bacon in a large pan. Purée the tomatoes with the peeled onion and garlic. Add mixture to the meat pan along with the salt, marjoram, and leek. Cover and bring to a boil. Lower heat and continue cooking until all meat is tender, about 2 hours.

When meat is tender, add to the meat mixture the capers, mustard pickles, vinegar, bell pepper, Worcestershire sauce, and sugar. Salt and pepper to taste.

Raise the heat to high and cook the filling, stirring, until almost all liquid in the pan has evaporated, about 10 minutes. Add the raisins and set filling aside.

Masa Dough:

⅔ *cup lard or vegetable*
  shortening
1 *teaspoon annatto (achiote) seeds*
2 *cups masa harina flour (de-*
  hydrated, treated corn flour)

1 *teaspoon salt*
1 *teaspoon cayenne pepper*
1⅓ *cups warm water*

Over a low heat, melt ⅓ cup lard with the annatto seeds. Simmer 2 to 3 minutes.

Whip remaining lard until fluffy. Beat in masa harina, salt, cayenne pepper, and water. Finally, beat in melted, strained lard, discarding annatto seeds.

Form dough into 24 balls.

Final Preparations:

24 *dried corn husks (or 24 nine-*
  inch squares parchment paper or
  tinfoil)
1 *pound cooked, shredded chicken*
  meat
4 *hard-cooked eggs, sliced*

½ *cup blanched almonds*
2 *ounces pimentos, sliced*
5 *ounces pimento-stuffed olives,*
  cut in half
Tabasco sauce

Put a ball of Masa Dough in the center of each corn husk. Flatten dough out to ⅛-inch thickness. Top each masa-coated husk with an equal distribution of the meat mixture, chicken, hard-cooked eggs, almonds, pimentos, and olives. Sprinkle on Tabasco sauce to taste.

Fold corn husks to completely encase the filling. Tie each hallaca with thin strips of corn husk or kitchen string. When tightly assembled, steam hallacas for 1 hour. Serve piping hot.

Note: Hallacas are easily refrigerated or frozen. Reheat by steaming again until hot.

Christmas Stollen

Royal Hawaiian Hotel
Honolulu, Hawaii

Makes 2 large loaves

2 cups milk, scalded and cooled to
  85 degrees
3 packages active dry yeast
1½ cups sifted confectioners' sugar
7 to 8 cups sifted all-purpose flour
1½ mixed candied fruits, diced
1½ cups raisins
1 cup butter, softened

2 teaspoons cinnamon
1½ teaspoons salt
2 eggs
¼ cup rum
1 teaspoon freshly grated lemon
  rind
Optional: *Confectioners' sugar or*
  vanilla sugar

Pour warm, scalded milk into a medium-sized bowl. Sprinkle on and gently stir in the yeast and 2 tablespoons sugar. To proof the yeast, allow mixture to sit undisturbed in a warm, draft-free location 10 to 15 minutes, until bubbles form. Stir in 1 cup flour. Set aside again in a warm, draft-free spot for about 30 minutes, until mixture rises and becomes quite spongy.

Place candied fruits and raisins in a large bowl. Sprinkle on them 3 or 4 tablespoons flour and toss fruits to coat well.

Whip butter in a large bowl until smooth. Add remaining sugar, cinnamon, and salt, and continue beating several minutes until light and fluffy. Add the eggs, one at a time, the rum, and the lemon rind, making sure ingredients are well combined.

When the sponge mixture is ready, gently stir it into the above batter. Begin beating in 7 cups or more sifted flour until a soft dough results. Knead the dough on a lightly floured surface 10 or 15 minutes, until smooth and elastic. Gently knead in the flour-coated fruits.

Place stollen dough in a large, well-buttered bowl. Turn over once. Cover with a towel and let rise in a warm, draft-free location until doubled in size, about 1½ to 2 hours.

When dough has risen, punch down the dough and divide it in half. Roll each half into a tapered oval, about 8 inches by 11 inches. Fold stollen dough over lengthwise ¾ of the way toward the opposite side.

Put stollen on greased baking sheets, cover, and let rise until doubled in bulk, 45 minutes to 1 hour. Bake in a preheated oven at 400 degrees for 35 minutes, or until golden brown. Cool.

If desired, cooled loaves may be sprinkled liberally with confectioners' sugar or vanilla sugar. (Vanilla sugar is made by placing 1 or 2 vanilla beans in 2 cups sugar. Let sugar sit, covered, for 2 or 3 days, until it takes on the flavor of the bean.)

Beverages

A Toast to the World

Beverages

Apple cider à la Maxwell's Bar
Frankfurt-Sheraton Hotel
Frankfurt, West Germany

Bicentennial
Sheraton-Schiphol Inn
Amsterdam, The Netherlands

The Blizzard
Sheraton-Hartford
Hartford, Connecticut

The Captain Cook
Sheraton-Villa Inn
Burnaby, British Columbia

Chi Chi
Sheraton-Molokai Hotel
Molokai, Hawaii

Glögg
Sheraton-Copenhagen Hotel
Copenhagen, Denmark

Margreet
Sheraton-Schiphol Inn
Amsterdam, The Netherlands

Marielle
Sheraton-Schiphol Inn
Amsterdam, The Netherlands

Molokai Mule
Sheraton-Molokai Hotel
Molokai, Hawaii

Peach Colada Frappé
Sheraton-Atlanta Hotel
Atlanta, Georgia

Pied Piper Sour in the Rough
Sheraton-Palace Hotel
San Francisco, California

Pink Palace
Royal Hawaiian Hotel
Honolulu, Hawaii

Seabreeze
Sheraton at St. Johns Place
Jacksonville, Florida

Sundowner
Sheraton-Maui Hotel
Maui, Hawaii

Vanda Daiquiri
Sheraton-Molokai Hotel
Molokai, Hawaii

Pharisaer Grog
Frankfurt-Sheraton Hotel
Frankfurt, West Germany

Café Brûlot
Sheraton-New Orleans Hotel
New Orleans, Louisiana

Waikoloa Coffee
Sheraton Royal Waikoloa
Hawaii, Hawaii

Apotheker
Frankfurt-Sheraton Hotel
Frankfurt, West Germany

Apple Cider à la Maxwell's Bar

Single Serving   *Frankfurt-Sheraton Hotel*
                                                    Frankfurt, West Germany

½ *ounce crème cassis*
6 *ounces apple cider*
3 *ounces soda*

Pour the crême cassis over ice in a tall glass. Add the cider and soda, stir, and serve.

Bicentennial

Single Serving   *Sheraton-Schiphol Inn*
                                                    Amsterdam, The Netherlands

3 *ounces Bourbon*   1 *ounce dry orange Curaçao*
2 *ounces sweet vermouth*   Garnish: *Maraschino cherry*

Stir all ingredients together. Serve over ice in an 8-ounce glass. Decorate with a maraschino cherry.

The Blizzard

Serves 2   *Sheraton-Hartford*
                                                    Hartford, Connecticut

The Blizzard is perfect for those who like their drinks not too sweet, not too strong. Its mild fruit flavor makes it appropriate for afternoons or evenings.

8 *ounces apple juice*   2 *ounces grapefruit juice*
4 *ounces pineapple juice*   2 *ounces vodka*
4 *ounces orange juice*   Optional: *Grenadine*
2 *ounces cranberry juice*

Stir all ingredients together. Color with grenadine if desired. Serve over ice in tall, frosted glasses.

The Captain Cook

Serves 2

Sheraton-Villa Inn
Burnaby, British Columbia

2 strips lemon peel
4 ounces pineapple juice
1½ ounces Lemon Hart rum
½ ounce Bacardi light rum

1 ounce Grand Marnier
Garnish: Fresh pineapple or orange
wedges

Fill two 8-ounce glasses ¾ full with crushed ice. Twist lemon peel over each glass to release lemon oils. Discard peel. Mix remaining ingredients and pour over ice. Garnish with fresh fruit. This recipe may be increased proportionately for larger quantities.

Chi Chi

Single Serving

Sheraton-Molokai
Molokai, Hawaii

This is a popular Hawaiian drink similar to Piña Colada, but it is made with vodka.

1¼ ounces vodka
3 ounces pineapple juice

1 ounce coconut syrup
Garnish: Pineapple slice

Place all ingredients in a blender with crushed ice; blend. Serve in a tall, frosted glass. Garnish with a pineapple slice.

Glögg
(Hot Christmas Punch)

Serves 4

Sheraton-Copenhagen Hotel
Copenhagen, Denmark

14 ounces red wine
8 ounces Port wine
1 orange peel
2 whole cloves
1 stick cinnamon

3 tablespoons raisins
3 tablespoons sugar
1 tablespoon peeled blanched
almonds, chopped
2 ounces aquavit

Combine all ingredients except the aquavit in a saucepan. Heat mixture just to the boiling point. Pour drink into punch glasses. Add to every glass ½ ounce of aquavit and serve.

Margreet

Single Serving

Sheraton-Schiphol Inn
Amsterdam, The Netherlands

1½ *ounces cherry brandy*
1½ *ounces Amaretto*
1½ *ounces Coco Ribe*
2 *ounces orange juice*

Dash of lemon juice
Garnishes: *Orange slice, maraschino cherry*

Shake all ingredients in a shaker or a jar with the lid on. Serve over ice in a tall glass, decorated with an orange slice and a maraschino cherry.

Marielle

Single Serving

Sheraton-Schiphol Inn
Amsterdam, The Netherlands

2 *ounces Sambuca*
2 *ounces Cointreau*
1½ *ounces heavy cream*

Garnish: *Pinch of ground coffee or coffee bean*

Shake all ingredients. Serve in a champagne coupe without ice. Decorate with a coffee bean or a pinch of ground coffee.

Molokai Mule

Serves 6

Sheraton-Molokai Hotel
Molokai, Hawaii

12 *ounces orange juice*
6 *ounces fresh lime juice*
6 *ounces Orgeat syrup*
6 *ounces brandy*
6 *ounces light rum*

6 *ounces Lemon Hart 86-proof rum*
½ *teaspoon Angostura bitters*
Garnish: *Pineapple wedges, sprig of fresh mint, orchids*

Continued

Mix and pour the ingredients over crushed ice in 14-ounce mugs or glasses.
Decorate with pineapple wedges, fresh mint, and orchids.

Peach Colada Frappé

Serves 2–3

Sheraton-Atlanta
Atlanta, Georgia

Peach Colada Frappés taste as good as they look. Deliciously light, fruity, and refreshing, serve them on a hot afternoon for dessert, or any time you want a treat.

3 cups packed crushed ice
1 ounce rum
1 ounce peach brandy
1 ounce Piña Colada Mix
1 ounce heavy cream

1 large ripe peach, skinned, halved,
*   and pitted; or 2 large canned halves*
Garnish: *Sprig of fresh mint*

Place large, bowl-shaped glasses in the freezer to frost.
Fill a blender with the crushed ice. Pour in the liquids and add peach halves. Purée drink thoroughly. Serve in frosted glasses, garnished with a fresh sprig of mint.

Pied Piper Sour in the Rough

Single Serving

Sheraton-Palace Hotel
San Francisco, California

Once you have made whiskey sours based on this successful Sheraton recipe, you will never buy packaged sour mixes again.

4 ounces fresh orange juice
2 ounces Rye whiskey
1½ ounces fresh lemon juice

1 teaspoon superfine sugar
Garnish: *Lemon or orange slices*

Pour all ingredients into a cocktail shaker or pitcher over ice. Shake or stir well. Pour into a tall glass. Garnish with lemon or orange slices.

Pink Palace

Single Serving

Royal Hawaiian Hotel
Honolulu, Hawaii

A sweet but typical tropical drink for those lazy warm afternoons on the beach.

1 ounce Grand Marnier
1 ounce light rum
1 ounce pineapple juice
1 ounce lemon juice
½ ounce coconut syrup

¾ ounce grenadine
1 ounce half and half
Garnishes: *Pineapple wedge,*
maraschino cherry, sprig of fresh
mint

Place all ingredients in a blender with crushed ice; blend. Serve in a chilled tall glass. Decorate with pineapple wedge on the rim. Top the drink with the maraschino cherry and a sprig of mint.

Seabreeze

Single Serving

Sheraton at St. Johns Place
Jacksonville, Florida

1¼ ounces white rum
2 ounces orange juice
2 ounces pineapple juice
¼ ounce coconut syrup

¼ ounce lime juice
Garnish: *Crème de Menthe, sprig of*
fresh mint

Place crushed ice in a blender. Add rum, juices, coconut syrup, and lime juice; blend. Pour in an 8½-ounce goblet. Lace with Crème de Menthe and garnish with a sprig of mint.

Sundowner

Single Serving

Sheraton-Maui Hotel
Maui, Hawaii

This drink was created for those romantics who like to enjoy the sunset in a special way.

¾ ounce Cointreau
¾ ounce Galliano

1 ounce lemon juice
1½ ounces cognac or brandy

Combine all ingredients and serve over ice in a 10-ounce balloon glass.

Vanda Daiquiri

Single Serving

Sheraton-Molokai
Molokai, Hawaii

1½ ounces light rum
½ ounce dark rum
1 ounce pineapple juice

½ ounce lemon juice
Dash of corn syrup

Place all ingredients in a blender with crushed ice; blend. Serve in a chilled cocktail glass.

Pharisaer Grog

Single Serving

Frankfurt-Sheraton Hotel
Frankfurt, West Germany

6 ounces black coffee
2 teaspoons sugar
2 ounces dark rum

1 tablespoon loosely whipped heavy
cream

Boil the coffee, sugar, and rum together in a small copper pot for about 1 minute. Pour liquid in an Irish Coffee glass, then crown the drink with the cream.

Café Brûlot

Serves 4

Sheraton-New Orleans Hotel
New Orleans, Louisiana

2 sticks cinnamon
¼ cup orange rind
¼ cup lemon rind
4 whole cloves

5 sugar cubes
½ cup brandy
4 tablespoons Grand Marnier
3 cups black coffee

Combine cinnamon, fruit rinds, cloves, and sugar in flambé pot. Add the brandy and Grand Marnier and blend. Ignite the mixture as it begins to boil and stir until sugar dissolves. Add the coffee slowly and attempt to keep the flambé going. Pour through a small strainer into demitasse cups, then serve.

Waikoloa Coffee

Single Serving

Sheraton Royal Waikoloa
Hawaii, Hawaii

1 ounce Kahlua liqueur
6 ounces black coffee
3 tablespoons whipped cream

Pour Kahlua liqueur into a mug of black coffee. Top with whipped cream.

Apotheker

Single Serving

Frankfurt-Sheraton Hotel
Frankfurt, West Germany

The ultimate cure in any language for the universal hangover is the following concoction.

1 ounce Fernet Branca
1 ounce Amer Picon

½ ounce Crème de Menthe
Dash of Angostura bitters

Stir all ingredients well in a cocktail glass. Serve without ice.

Basics

Hollandaise Sauce

Makes 1¼ cups

3 egg yolks
2 tablespoons fresh lemon juice
2 tablespoons boiling water

⅛ teaspoon salt
Pinch of white pepper
12 tablespoons (6 ounces) hot melted butter

Using a wire whisk, beat egg yolks in the top of a double boiler for about 1 minute, until pale. Whisking the yolks constantly, slowly drizzle in the lemon juice, then the hot water. Season with salt and pepper.

Place the pan over hot water. Whisk until yolks begin to thicken. Still whisking rapidly, drizzle in hot melted butter very slowly. If at this point (or at any other time), egg yolks seem to be getting too hot and are in danger of curdling, lift pan off the heat and place in a bowl of ice water to cool down. Then return pan to the heat and continue cooking.

When all the butter is added, and the sauce is thick and smooth, remove pan from heat. Sauce is best used immediately.

Béchamel Sauce
(White Sauce)

Makes 2 cups

It is traditional to season a béchamel with minced onions (they are later strained out), salt, pepper, and perhaps cloves or nutmeg. Our béchamel has absolutely no seasoning because it is used as a base in the recipes.

4 tablespoons butter
4 tablespoons all-purpose flour
2 cups milk

Melt butter in a heavy saucepan over moderate heat. Add flour and stir with a wire whisk 3 to 4 minutes to help cook out the flour taste. Gradually add the milk, stirring constantly. Simmer the sauce an additional 15 to 20 minutes, stirring occasionally.

Sauce may be cooled, covered, and refrigerated. Reheat it over low heat.

Brown Sauce

Makes 1 cup

Brown sauce is a wonderfully rich concoction, deep in flavor, that can be added to an infinite variety of dishes. A traditional sauce can take a while to prepare, then must simmer for several hours to achieve perfection. Because this long time is not always available, we present a simplified, modified version that works well for the small amount of brown sauce called for in the recipes.

2 tablespoons butter
1 tablespoon minced shallots
2 tablespoons all-purpose flour

1 cup Beef Stock (recipe, page 278)
¼ teaspoon Worcestershire sauce

Melt the butter in a heavy saucepan over medium heat. Add the shallots and sauté them until they are tender. Stir in the flour and cook 3 to 4 minutes. Gradually add the stock, stirring constantly. Season with Worcestershire sauce. Simmer 10 to 15 minutes longer, stirring occasionally. Strain the sauce.

Use sauce immediately or cool, cover, and refrigerate. Reheat sauce over low heat.

Chili Salsa

Makes 3 cups

2 pounds firm but ripe tomatoes
4 teaspoons minced onion
2 garlic cloves, minced
1 teaspoon salt
¼ teaspoon pepper

2 or more hot chili peppers, seeded
  and diced
Optional: *2 teaspoons chopped fresh*
  coriander (cilantro)

Place tomatoes in a saucepan and cover with water. Bring to a gentle boil and simmer tomatoes 8 to 10 minutes. Drain, cool slightly, then peel and seed the tomatoes. Put them in a blender with all other ingredients and purée. Pour into small bowls. Serve at room temperature.

Clarified Butter

Makes 1 cup

Clarified butter is a real boon when you are frying or sautéeing. The milk solids in unclarified butter, which are removed when butter is clarified, are responsible for the burned, bitter particles that ruin the flavor of very hot butter.

Melt ½ pound of butter in a small heavy saucepan over low heat. Do not stir it or disturb it in any way.
 When butter has melted, gently take the pan off the heat. Skim off any surface foam. Let butter sit for 1 to 2 minutes to allow milk solids to settle. Pour off the clear yellow butter. Discard the sediment.
 Clarified butter may be used immediately or cooled, covered, and refrigerated.

Coconut Milk

Makes 1 cup

Naturally, the best coconut milk is made using fresh coconut, as specified in our first recipe. If you lack the time to prepare it from scratch, however, use dried unsweetened coconut, which is available in health food stores, as specified in our second recipe. And frozen coconut milk can be found in some food specialty stores.

In any case, coconut milk is made by combining equal amounts of coconut with hot water. You can adapt the recipe to suit your quantity needs.

Fresh Coconut Milk:

  1 cup grated fresh coconut meat
  1 cup boiling water

To ensure the freshness of the coconut, shake it and listen for the gurgle of liquid inside.
 To open a coconut, pierce the three dark dots that form a triangle on one end of the shell. Pour out the liquid. (Discard liquid or use in other ways.) Using a hammer, or the dull side of a cleaver, tap the shell all over until it cracks and breaks. Pry out the meat of the coconut.

Continued

Grate the white coconut meat or, using a strong, sharp knife, chop the meat finely, leaving the brown skin on the meat. Place the coconut and water in a blender or food processor and blend 1 or 2 minutes to achieve a crudely puréed mixture.

Line a strainer with a double thickness of cheesecloth and place it over a bowl. Pour coconut mixture into the strainer, allowing the hot liquid to drain through. When it is cool enough to handle, pick up the cheesecloth, twist, and squeeze out as much remaining liquid as possible. Discard the cheesecloth and depleted coconut.

Use coconut milk immediately, or refrigerate briefly. Freeze any coconut milk that you do not plan to use in 1 or 2 days.

Dried Coconut Milk:

1¼ cups (2 ounces) shredded unsweetened
   dried coconut
1¼ cups boiling water

Make Dried Coconut Milk just as you would the fresh variety.

Beef Stock

Makes about 3 quarts

2 pounds cracked veal shanks or
   knuckles
2 pounds marrow bones
2 pounds cracked beef bones
3 pounds beef chuck, cut into chunks
4 quarts cold water
2 carrots, peeled and cut into 1-inch
   slices
3 medium-sized onions, peeled and
   quartered

4 ribs celery
1 whole bulb garlic, unpeeled
2 bay leaves
4 whole cloves
10 peppercorns
6 fresh parsley sprigs
½ teaspoon thyme
½ teaspoon marjoram
2 teaspoons salt

Broil the meat and bones about 3½ inches from the heat source until they are brown all over. Place them in a large soup or stock pot. Add the cold water and bring to a boil over high heat, then lower heat and simmer for 5 minutes, skimming off foam as it collects. Add all the other ingredients, cover, and simmer—never boil—for about 5 hours at which time all the flavorful juices in the meat and vegetables will have been exuded.

After the stock has been cooked, strain it carefully through several layers of cheesecloth, reserving only the stock. Skim off fat. Cool, cover, and refrigerate.

Stock may be kept in the refrigerator for 1 or 2 days; for longer storage, it should be frozen.

Reduced Beef Stock:

If the recipe you are using requires an intensified beef flavor, boil 2 cups of beef stock, uncovered, over high heat until it is reduced to ½ cup.

Chicken Stock

Makes about 4 quarts

2 2½-3-pound chickens, cut into
  pieces
4 quarts cold water
2 medium-sized unpeeled onions,
  washed and coarsely chopped
3 stalks celery, cut into chunks
10 fresh parsley sprigs
3 carrots, trimmed, scrubbed, and cut
  into chunks

1 large clove garlic, peeled and
  minced
2 bay leaves
1 tablespoon salt
10 peppercorns
3 cloves

Wash and drain chickens. Save livers for another use. Place the cut-up chicken and the water in a large soup or stock pot and bring to a boil, uncovered, over high heat. Skim off any foam as it rises.

Add the other ingredients, lower heat, partially cover, and simmer—never boil—for about 2½ hours.

After the stock has been cooked, strain it carefully through several layers of cheesecloth, reserving only the stock. Skim off all the fat. Cool, cover, and refrigerate.

Stock may be kept in the refrigerator for 1 or 2 days; for longer storage, it should be frozen.

Reduced or Condensed Chicken Stock:

If the recipe you are using requires an intensified chicken flavor, boil 2 cups of chicken stock, uncovered, over high heat until it is reduced to ¼ cup.

Fish Stock

Makes about 4 quarts

A fish store will usually sell the heads, tails, and carcasses of fish very reasonably. Be sure to freeze fish stock if you plan to keep it for more than a day or two.

8 pounds fish trimmings
3 medium-sized onions, peeled and
    chopped
1 carrot, trimmed, scrubbed, and
    sliced
10 fresh parsley sprigs

1 bay leaf
1 teaspoon thyme
2 teaspoons salt
2 tablespoons fresh lemon juice
3 cups dry white wine
4 quarts cold water

Place fish trimmings in a large soup or stock pot. Add the remaining ingredients. Over high heat bring stock almost to a boil, skimming any foam. Lower heat to medium and simmer, uncovered, for 30 minutes, continuing to remove foam as it forms.

After 30 minutes, strain the stock through several layers of cheesecloth, reserving only the stock. Cool, cover, and refrigerate.

Basic Pastry Shell

Makes one 9-inch shell

1¾ cups sifted all-purpose flour
½ teaspoon salt
6 tablespoons solid vegetable
    shortening

2 tablespoons cold butter
2 to 4 tablespoons ice water

Sift the flour and salt into a mixing bowl. Cut in the shortening and butter with a pastry cutter or two knives until mixture resembles coarse meal. Sprinkle 2 tablespoons ice water over mixture and mix lightly until dough can be gathered together. If dough is too dry and it crumbles, add a little more water until it comes together. Form dough into a ball, wrap, and refrigerate at least 1 hour.

When dough is chilled, roll it out on a lightly floured surface until slightly larger than the pie pan. Place pastry in the pan, fold over, and flute the edges. Chill the pie shell for 30 minutes to 1 hour before baking blind, or filling and baking.

Rich Pastry Shell

Makes one 9-inch pie shell

2 cups all-purpose flour
Dash of salt
¾ cup butter, softened

2 egg yolks, lightly beaten
2 tablespoons water

Place flour and salt in a large bowl. Make a well in the center and put into it the butter, yolks, and water. Using your fingertips, gradually pull in the flour. Mix until all ingredients are well combined and dough forms a ball. Cover. Chill several hours before using.

Preheat oven to 450 degrees. Roll out the dough and place in a 9-inch pie pan. Prick the bottom several times with a fork. Bake 12 to 15 minutes, or until crust is crisp but not brown.

Sponge Cake

Makes one 9-inch cake

Sponge cake is delicious plain or sprinkled with liqueurs or a little powdered sugar. Or it car become the body of a delicious dessert. The recipe given here is for a 9-inch sponge cake, which is suitable for English Sherry Trifle (page 145), but the recipe is easily doubled and baked for a Strawberry Short Cake (page 70).   For the latter, see the Strawberry Short Cake variation (page 282) for slight changes in ingredients and procedures

1 cup sifted cake-flour
½ teaspoon baking powder
¼ teaspoon salt
3 eggs, at room temperature,
   separated

⅔ cup sugar
1 tablespoon grated orange rind or 1
   teaspoon grated lemon rind
¼ cup fresh orange juice; or ¼ cup
   water, plus 1 teaspoon vanilla

Preheat the oven to 350 degrees. Lightly grease the bottom (not the sides) of a 9-inch cake pan. Cut out and place a circle of waxed paper in the bottom of the pan. Set pan aside.

Sift together the flour, baking powder, and salt. Set aside briefly.

Beat the yolks with an electric mixer 2 to 3 minutes, until they are pale yellow. Sprinkle on the sugar and continue beating 5 minutes longer, until yolks are thick in texture and quite pale.

Using a spoon, stir the orange rind and orange juice into the thickened egg yolks. Gradually stir in the sifted flour mixture.

Beat egg whites until peaks that are stiff but not dry form. Stir ¼ of the beaten egg whites into the sponge cake batter to lighten it. Then, very gently, fold in the remainder of the egg whites. Pour into the prepared pan, and bake, in the lower third of the oven, about 35 minutes, or until done. The cake should spring back when center is gently pressed with a fingertip.

Let cake cool down in the pan for about 10 minutes. Turn out, remove waxed paper, and let cake cool on a wire rack.

Strawberry Short Cake:

To prepare a sponge cake for the Strawberry Short Cake on page 70, simply substitute ¼ cup purée strawberries for the ¼ cup orange juice and use 1 teaspoon lemon rind in place of the orange rind. All other ingredients remain the same. Note that *two* 9-inch sponge cakes are needed for the Strawberry Short Cake.

Graham Cracker Crust

Makes one 9-inch crust

> 1½ cups graham cracker crumbs
> ¼ cup sugar
> 5 tablespoons melted butter

Lightly butter a 9-inch pie pan. Mix together the crumbs, sugar, and melted butter until well combined. Press into buttered pan.

Bake graham cracker crust in a preheated 350-degree oven 8 to 10 minutes, until crust is very lightly browned and crisp. Take out of the oven and cool down. If time permits, chill well before filling.

Weights, Measures, and Metric Conversions

WEIGHTS AND MEASURES:

1 teaspoon = ⅓ tablespoon
1 tablespoon = 3 teaspoons
2 tablespoons = ⅛ cup or 1 fluid ounce
4 tablespoons = ¼ cup or 2 fluid ounces
5⅓ = ⅓ cup or 2⅔ fluid ounces
8 tablespoons = ½ cup or 4 fluid ounces
16 tablespoons = 1 cup or 8 fluid ounces
¼ cup = 4 tablespoons
⅜ cup = 5 tablespoons or ¼ cup plus 2 tablespoons
⅝ cup = 10 tablespoons or ½ cup plus 2 tablespoons
⅞ cup = ¾ cup plus 2 tablespoons
1 cup = ½ pint or 8 fluid ounces
2 cups = 1 pint or 16 fluid ounces
2 pints = 1 quart, liquid, or 4 cups
4 quarts = 1 gallon, liquid
8 dry quarts = 1 peck
4 pecks = 1 bushel
1 pound = 16 ounces

METRIC CONVERSION TABLE:

Dry Ingredients

Ounces to Grams:

Ounces	Grams	Ounces	Grams
1	28.35	9	255.15
2	56.70	10	283.50
3	85.05	11	311.85
4	113.40	12	340.20
5	141.75	13	368.55
6	170.10	14	396.90
7	198.45	15	425.25
8	226.80	16	453.60

Grams to Ounces:

Grams	Ounces	Grams	Ounces
1	0.03	9	0.32
2	0.07	10	0.35
3	0.11	11	0.39
4	0.14	12	0.42
5	0.18	13	0.46
6	0.21	14	0.49
7	0.25	15	0.53
8	0.28	16	0.57

Pounds to Kilograms

Pounds	Kilograms
1	0.45
2	0.91
3	1.36
4	1.81
5	2.27

Kilograms to Pounds

Pounds	Kilograms
1	2.205
2	4.41
3	6.61
4	8.82
5	11.02

Liquid Ingredients

Liquid Ounces to Milliliters:

Liquid Ounces	Milliliters	Liquid Ounces	Milliliters
1	29.57	6	177.44
2	59.15	7	207.02
3	88.72	8	236.59
4	118.30	9	266.16
5	147.87	10	295.73

Milliliters to Liquid Ounces:

Milliliters	Liquid Ounces	Milliliters	Liquid Ounces
1	0.03	6	0.20
2	0.07	7	0.24
3	0.10	8	0.27
4	0.14	9	0.30
5	0.17	10	0.33

Quarts to Liters:

Liters to Quarts:

Quarts	Liters	Liters	Quarts
1	0.95	1	1.06
2	1.89	2	2.11
3	2.84	3	3.17
4	3.79	4	4.23
5	4.73	5	5.28

Gallons to Liters:

Liters to Gallons:

Gallons	Liters	Liters	Gallons
1	3.78	1	0.26
2	7.57	2	0.53
3	11.36	3	0.79
4	15.14	4	1.06
5	18.93	5	1.32

Index

D

E

F

G

H

I

K

J

L

S

X

Y

Z